Picturing the Human

PICTURING THE HUMAN

The Moral Thought of Iris Murdoch

Maria Antonaccio

OXFORD
UNIVERSITY PRESS

2000

OXFORD
UNIVERSITY PRESS

Oxford New York

Athens Auckland Bangkok Bogotá Buenos Aires Calcutta
Cape Town Chennai Dar es Salaam Delhi Florence Hong Kong Istanbul
Karachi Kuala Lumpur Madrid Melbourne Mexico City Mumbai
Nairobi Paris São Paulo Singapore Taipei Tokyo Toronto Warsaw

and associated companies in
Berlin Ibadan

Copyright © 2000 by Maria Antonaccio

Published by Oxford University Press, Inc.
198 Madison Avenue, New York, New York 10016

Oxford is a registered trademark of Oxford University Press

Library of Congress Cataloging-in-Publication Data
Antonaccio, Maria.
Picturing the human : the moral thought of
Iris Murdoch / Maria Antonaccio.
p. cm.
Includes bibliographical references and index.
ISBN 0-19-513171-1
1. Murdoch, Iris—Ethics. I. Title.
BF604.M873A57 2000   99-41886
170'.92—dc21

1 3 5 7 9 8 6 4 2

Printed in the United States of America
on acid-free paper

PREFACE

This is not a book about Iris Murdoch's life; it is a book about her ideas. The distinction, though not absolute, is important to make in this case, since Murdoch was such a beloved figure to so many. To her reading public, she was above all the author of twenty-six complex and hugely entertaining novels. To others, she was a brilliant philosophical mind whose criticisms of both analytic philosophy and existentialism were decisive for many later thinkers. Even those unfamiliar with her writings may recognize her as one half of the remarkable couple she formed with her husband John Bayley, a marriage of more than forty years that was often documented with both reverence and wit in literary magazines. Moreover, she was known throughout her life as an extraordinarily kind and self-effacing person who answered every piece of fan mail with a personal letter, was widely sought after for advice by friends and strangers alike, and was even described as a "saint"—a living exemplar (though she would never have thought so) of the idea of goodness that was central both to her philosophy and her fiction. More recently, her life became poignantly familiar to many people through the publication of her husband's memoirs, written as he watched her descend inexorably into the Alzheimer's that finally claimed her life in 1999.

It is difficult to write about Murdoch without being drawn into her life and personality, rather than concentrating on the substance of her thought. Nevertheless, readers will not find here a book about Murdoch's life (though one hopes that a biography will soon be written). They will find, rather, a systematic effort to present her main ideas in a coherent argument that will be of interest to scholars and students of ethics, as well as others seeking to understand her philosophical contributions to contemporary thought. By focusing exclusively on her ideas, my aim is to emphasize something that might be in danger of fading from view; namely, that Murdoch was, to put it bluntly, more than simply a kindly novelist urging us to be good. She was, rather, an exceptionally creative and morally passionate thinker who witnessed some of the devastating horrors of the twentieth century and was trained in some of its dominant philosophies—and yet never ceased defending the always unfashionable notion of goodness.

Murdoch pursued her philosophical inquiry without the kind of consoling sentimentality that might render a philosophy of the good merely facile, or an affront to the real. She would not have been surprised by those who would ask her, "With all this talk of goodness, what about evil?" In fact, she asked that question repeatedly herself. At the end of *Metaphysics as a Guide to Morals*, she wrote: "The average inhabitant of the planet is probably without hope and starving . . . Can one go on talking about a spiritual source and an absolute good if a majority of human kind is debarred from it?" Such a question is never far beneath the surface of Murdoch's philosophical prose, and her full answer to it is only given in the sum total of her writings. But a clue may be found in the epigram she chose (by way of Paul Valéry and Simone Weil) for her final philosophical work: "*Un difficulté est une lumière. Une difficulté insurmontable est un soleil.*" (A difficulty is a light. An insurmountable difficulty is a sun.) The images of sun and light, so prominent in Plato, recur throughout her philosophy and signal the ambiguous power, as she understood it, of the good—its ability to illuminate the dark void of suffering, misery, or despair that attends every human life to some degree; but equally, its tendency to burn away the false consolations one reaches for in such circumstances.

Murdoch's philosophy of the good does not console us in our suffering, or save us from the pain of loss or shattered hope. Rather, it burns and singes with the knowledge that "almost everything that consoles us is a fake"—including, sometimes, the idea of goodness itself. If it is not to collapse into illusion, Murdoch believed, the idea of goodness must remain open even to the reality of its own *absence* in any particular human life. And yet, seeing this, she still dared to speak of the possibility of "making a spiritual use of one's desolation"—not, she insisted, by filling the void with lies and fantasy, but by living close to the painful reality and trying to relate it to something good. Even then, "one's thoughts return (hopelessly) to the imprisoned and the starving and to experiences of loss, ignominy, or extreme guilt." But an insuperable difficulty is a sun, she wrote. "Try again. *Wait.*"

A book that takes ideas such as these for its subject matter cannot fail, almost in spite of itself, to pay tribute to the life of the thinker that produced them, even if its central focus is on the ideas themselves more than that life. I hope that this book will encourage readers to a deeper engagement with a philosopher who was above all, a friend of the good.

This book would not have been possible without the help of my family, teachers, colleagues, and friends. I am especially indebted to William

Schweiker, whose critical guidance aided my thinking about this project from its beginnings at the University of Chicago to its final revisions. I also thank David Tracy for his scholarly insight, James M. Gustafson for first introducing me to Murdoch's thought, and Lee Yearley for his encouragement at a very early stage of my research. I also wish to thank two former teachers, H. Ganse Little, Jr. and Mark C. Taylor, whose influence remains strong even when it may be least apparent.

This work also benefited from a conference on Murdoch's thought held at the University of Chicago in May 1994, later published as *Iris Murdoch and the Search for Human Goodness* (Chicago: University of Chicago Press, 1996). The contributors clarified important aspects of Murdoch's thought for me and enriched my understanding of her significance. The presence of Dame Iris at that conference made an indelible impression on all those fortunate enough to spend time with her. I express special thanks to W. Clark Gilpin, Dean of the University of Chicago Divinity School, and William Schweiker for making the conference and Murdoch's visit possible.

I gratefully acknowledge the friends who gave generously of their time, intellect, and invaluable support to help me think about Murdoch and related matters over several years, especially Diane Perpich, David Rehm, and Daniel W. Smith. Other friends deserve special mention for providing intellectual companionship and steadfast encouragement while this book was in its final stages, especially Carol Wayne White, Richard B. Miller, Kelton Cobb, Heidi Gehman, Jeffrey S. Turner, Sarah Farrant, and Laura Jack. I also wish to thank my colleagues, both past and present, associated with the Religion Department at Bucknell University for their support and interest, including William Becker, Joseph LaBarge, Douglas Sturm, John Grim, Mary Evelyn Tucker, Eric Mazur, Carol Wayne White, and Stephanie Snyder.

Finally, I owe an incalculable debt of gratitude to my parents, Charles and Therese, and my sister Carla for their life-giving support, patience, and endless faith in me, which never cease to astonish. Their sustaining presence in my life has been the best proof I know of the reality of the good.

CONTENTS

Picturing the Human

1

IRIS MURDOCH AND CONTEMPORARY
MORAL INQUIRY

How are we to think about morality in an age in which the very notion of the self has been challenged and every claim about the good is disputed? This book examines one of the most compelling contemporary responses to this question. The moral philosophy of Iris Murdoch presents an important challenge to current ethical inquiry: the effort to reclaim a notion of the self as individual and to reconceive its relation to an idea of moral value or the good. Specifically, Murdoch seeks to retrieve the notion of consciousness as morally central to an account of human being and, further, to conceive consciousness as inescapably related to an idea of the good. Such an argument is bound to be controversial in an intellectual climate characterized by an unrelenting critique of the idea of subjectivity, as well as a suspicion of any attempt to make substantive claims about humanity or the human good.

At the basis of these current assumptions lies a profound shift in sensibility the implications of which for ethical inquiry have not yet been fully appreciated. As Seyla Benhabib has insightfully remarked, the significance of postmodernism for contemporary thought is that it demonstrates that *"the paradigm of language has replaced the paradigm of consciousness"*[1] in contemporary philosophical reflection. This shift from consciousness to language alters the very character of ethical inquiry in our period, since at a fundamental level it calls into question the human origin and end of thinking in favor of linguistic and other systems that seem to reduce human subjects to a mere "discursive effect" of the system. In this respect, postmodern thought has sometimes been characterized as "antihumanist" in its affirmation of the primacy of impersonal systems over individual subjects and users of language.[2]

It is precisely here that Murdoch offers a compelling alternative to current thought. Against the displacement of the notion of consciousness in favor of the authority and primacy of language, Murdoch retrieves consciousness as the fundamental mode of human moral being. In doing so, she seeks to defend the reality and value of the human individual as irreducible, and thus to resist its absorption into linguistic and other impersonal systems. What makes this attempt so distinctive is that Murdoch does not simply ignore the contemporary turn to language; rather, she takes language with the utmost seriousness. The force of her position, I hope to show, is that beyond the turn to language, Murdoch finds once again the uniqueness and density of individual consciousness. In her judgment, the individual remains an autonomous speaker and user of language, as well as a being with inward depths and experiences that cannot be reduced to a system of public or collective meanings.

Yet it would be misleading to suggest that Murdoch was only or even primarily engaged in a debate with postmodernism. In fact, her defense of the notion of consciousness and its integral relation to an idea of the good contributes even more centrally to the contemporary debate over the nature of moral subjectivity in moral theory, political philosophy, and religious ethics. In contrast to the critiques of subjectivity advanced by many contemporary thinkers, many others have continued to refer meaningfully to the self as moral agent by calling attention to the evaluative dimensions of human subjectivity. One of the crucial insights to emerge from this line of thought is the extent to which discourse about the self entails claims about value or the good. To take a notable example, Charles Taylor has argued in *Sources of the Self* that under the sway of certain scientific assumptions, modern moral theory has concealed the extent to which our identity as selves is inseparable from an account of our activity as evaluators and the diverse goods to which we are committed. Human identity is constituted by a framework of questions about value—by distinctions, commitments, and attachments which delimit a moral world and which challenge any strictly nonnormative account of human subjectivity. "Selfhood and the good, or in another way selfhood and morality," Taylor writes, "turn out to be inextricably intertwined themes."[3]

Murdoch's thought has played a significant role in the critical assessment of modern ethical thought advanced by Taylor and others. Throughout her diverse philosophical, political, and literary writings over a half-century, she protested against reductionistic accounts of the human individual bequeathed by modern philosophy and modern science. In a famous essay written in the 1950s, she wrote:

> We live in a scientific and anti-metaphysical age, in which the dogmas, images, and precepts of religion have lost much of their power. We have not recovered from two wars and the experience of Hitler. We are also the heirs of the Enlightenment, Romanticism, and the Liberal tradition. These are the elements of our dilemma: whose chief feature, in my view, is that we have been left with far too shallow and flimsy an idea of human personality.[4]

This diagnosis of our situation, though dated in certain respects, continues to describe fundamental features of life in western democracies, and it signals the basic context and challenge addressed by Murdoch's ethics. Murdoch had witnessed firsthand, while working in refugee camps after World War II, the devastating effects of the totalitarian political forces of the twentieth century on human lives. She had studied, as a philosopher at Oxford and Cambridge, the thought of neo-Hegelian philosophers such as F. H. Bradley, which seemed to diminish the reality of the individual person. She had observed, as a novelist and critic, the rise of Symbolist trends in modern poetry and literature, which seemed to question the importance of the portrayal of character in literature. In the face of such powerful cultural expressions of the idea that "only the whole is real," Murdoch insisted—in language which resonates intentionally at times with Kierkegaard's protest against Hegel—that the particular and individual are paradigmatic of the real. That conviction, I will argue strenuously in the conclusion, gains renewed and perhaps surprising relevance in cultural circumstances in which the idea of "systems" (e.g., information, global, economic, ecological, and so forth) has become the primary trope for thinking about reality. Despite the dramatic changes in philosophical trends in the half-century since Murdoch began writing, her thought revivifies—in striking and often unexpected ways—an idea that has often been either demonized as an outdated and destructive legacy of "Enlightenment rationality" or else disturbingly resurrected in triumphalist philosophies of the will.

These remarks indicate some of the reasons for undertaking a study of Murdoch's ethics today, but there are others to be noted as well. Murdoch was best known as one of the most gifted and prolific novelists of the twentieth century, yet the enormous influence of her moral philosophy has been less widely recognized.[5] Indeed, Murdoch's classic volume *The Sovereignty of Good*, a collection of three seminal essays, is arguably one of the most influential and widely read works in moral philosophy to appear in the last fifty years.[6] In spite of this widespread influence, however, and acknowledging the numerous literary critical studies of her novels that have appeared over the years, a systematic and coherent exposition of Murdoch's thought has yet to be written. This book is the first treatment of Murdoch's thought in the context of current religious and philosophical ethics, based on a comprehensive reading of her philosophical works.

The present inquiry is warranted for several reasons. First and most important, Murdoch's writings on ethics, art, literature, and politics anticipate much of the current agenda in ethical inquiry. This agenda includes renewed interest in Platonic ethics and virtue theory, a reopening of the debate over the relation between philosophy and literature, the retrieval of moral realism in ethics, the contemporary critique of liberalism, and the relation between ethics and religious discourse. A sustained account of the central ideas and arguments in Murdoch's work that helped to initiate this agenda is overdue. Second, the publication of two new volumes of Murdoch's work now offer the most extended and readily available statement of her philosophy to date: her Gifford Lectures, *Metaphysics as a Guide to Morals*, and a collection of her writings, *Existentialists and Mystics: Writings on Philosophy and Literature*, edited by Peter Conradi.[7] Both of these recent works make a more comprehensive overview of Murdoch's philosophy accessible to a wider audience. Finally, the need for a systematic account of Murdoch's thought has gained a measure of urgency and indeed poignancy in light of her recent death from Alzheimer's disease (in February 1999 at the age of 79) and the awareness that her remarkable philosophical career has not yet been fully appreciated or documented.[8]

The aim of the book is threefold. First, I attempt to present systematically and coherently the central themes of Murdoch's moral thought. Second, I demonstrate her contribution to ethical inquiry by placing her work in the context of current debates in moral theory, religious ethics, and political philosophy regarding the nature of human subjectivity and its relation to discourse about the human good. And third, I outline the constructive implications of Murdoch's thought for contemporary ethical inquiry based on a critical assessment and elaboration of her position. In order to clarify these aims, I want to begin by outlining the context and argument of the book as a whole.

Section I. Moral Subjectivity and the Problem of Freedom in Contemporary Ethics

The modern period since the Enlightenment has often been characterized by an affirmation of human autonomy and a concomitant demise of appeals to authority as the ground for normative claims. As Jeffrey Stout has written, "[M]odern thought was born in a crisis of authority, took shape in flight from authority, and aspired from the start to autonomy from all traditional influence whatsoever."[9] As a result, human reason and experience, rather than the authority of religious claims or divine commands, became the final court of appeal for the validation of human beliefs and practices. Such validation derives its legitimacy from the fact that the rational human agent is free—that is, unconstrained by external influence.

Kantian ethics in particular affirms the rational autonomy of the human agent and the rejection of religious and metaphysical beliefs as heteronomous constraints on human reason. While ancient theories of morality defined the virtuous life as right relation or conformity to a divine or cosmic order independent of the human will, modern moral thought has insisted with Kant that the rational will alone should be determinative of our normative purposes.[10] Freedom defined in this way is what Isaiah

Berlin famously termed "negative" freedom, a freedom won by breaking free from external obstacles or constraints such as the natural order, the will of others, or forms of external authority.[11] Morality in the modern period was thus severed both from the normative claims of a stable cosmic or natural order, on the one hand, and from the contingencies of history and tradition, on the other. Taken radically, this conception of freedom aspires to transcend the given altogether and results in a "situationless" freedom: once we overcome every external obstacle or constraint on the rational will, there is no longer anything to be free *from*.[12] Complete freedom in this sense is therefore empty, devoid of content and abstracted from any situation that would provide it with a defining purpose. Charles Taylor addresses the dilemma posed by this understanding of freedom in his study of Hegel: "[M]uch philosophical thought in the last century has been engaged with this problem," he writes; "how to go beyond a notion of the self as the subject of a self-dependent will and bring to light its insertion in nature, our own and that which surrounds us, or in other terms, how to situate freedom?"[13]

The problem of freedom that has dominated post-Kantian ethics remains at the heart of the question of the self in our period. Murdoch is no exception to this, since she herself poses the problem of the self in terms of freedom at crucial points in her philosophy. Freedom is important to notions of subjectivity because the way we conceive human freedom is directly connected to how we conceive various human capacities (such as reason, will, or language) as well as the self's relation to an idea of moral value. The question that must be asked is, "Freedom from, or in relation to, what?" Is freedom to be understood as a transcendental feature of human selfhood that guarantees autonomy from any particular or determinate conception of the good, as many Kantians would argue? Or is freedom achieved only gradually, as the self recognizes its relation to normative purposes that arise from its situation, as many moral particularists would hold? What is the scope of human freedom in relation to social, material, and linguistic realities?

In keeping with Taylor's claim, current narrativist and communitarian forms of ethical thought can be seen as attempts to provide a notion of freedom that is grounded in the acceptance of a defining situation. The modern insistence on the radical autonomy of the rational will has been replaced by a recognition of the ways in which individual identity is never "unencumbered," but is conditioned by natural and social environments, formed within particular human communities and traditions of thought. The situation that defines our freedom is affirmed as part of us and constitutive of our very agency, rather than viewed "as a set of limits to be overcome, or a mere occasion to carry out some freely chosen project."[14] This acknowledgment that human freedom must be situated in relation to the given features of natural, social, and historical existence is directly connected to the insight that selfhood and the good are integrally related.

To say that the self and the self's freedom cannot be abstracted from a situation that defines its purposes and ends is just to say that the self is integrally related to some account of the good. Yet in spite of this general shift in the modern conception of freedom, contemporary moral theory still faces the problem of how to define in substantive terms the nature of the good in relation to which moral identity is constituted, and of delimiting the scope and content of freedom with respect to that situation. If the good can no longer be understood as a purely formal notion, a function of the freely choosing will, neither can it derive its content simply from conformity to a pattern of nature or pre-existent state of affairs. We need a conception of the self that both acknowledges our freedom *and* allows that freedom to be conditioned by the contingent facts of our situation.

Murdoch's thought is best understood in the context of contemporary attempts to articulate an adequate account of moral subjectivity and, specifically, a subjectivity situated in relation to an adequate account of the good. Her work is significant in this regard, I contend, because it represents a mediating position between two broad alternative lines of thought in contemporary ethics: between those thinkers in the Kantian tradition who believe that the self constitutes its own world through its acts and choices apart from determination by the givens of its situation, and those thinkers descending from Hegel who believe that the aims and purposes of the self are in fact constituted by the givens of its natural, social, and historical existence in particular communities. Murdoch's position may be interpreted as an attempt to articulate a conception of the self and the self's freedom that avoids the problems of both Kant, on the one hand, and Hegel, on the other. The Kantian view—which she chiefly associates with Sartrean existentialism and traditional liberal theory—is solipsistic, in her judgment, because it defines the self's freedom over against the givens of its situation; while the Hegelian view—which she characterizes as "romantic"—threatens the separateness and particularity of the agent with absorption into the totality of its relations. In this fashion, Kant and Hegel function largely as "types" in relation to which Murdoch works out her constructive view.

This basic division of positions is evident in the current debate between liberals and communitarians over the description of the self as either "unencumbered" or "radically situated." An analogous debate exists in religious ethics between those who believe that the self has some capacity to transcend the commitments given by its situation, and those who appeal primarily to a narrative or tradition-based grounding for the self and its norms. These debates provide a contemporary context for my analysis of Murdoch's thought in this book. My account of these positions below will necessarily be schematic for the sake of clarity.

On one side of the debate are those who argue that the self grounds its identity and its moral claims through some existential decision or transcendental act that escapes the contingencies of the self's situation. For example, liberal theorists such as John Rawls[15] argue that the articulation of principles of justice for a liberal society depends upon a procedure that brackets all particular substantive accounts of the self and the self's good in order to ensure that the principles arrived at are nonpartisan. The subject of the procedure, roughly a variant of the Kantian noumenal self, chooses principles of justice in an initial situation that is abstracted from any particular or existing historical context. Alternatively, existentialists such as Sartre argued that the self constitutes itself and its values through its choices, and that the human task is to strive for an authentic freedom that is unconditioned and uncompromised by social custom, the will of others, or the contingencies of nature. This type of position is taken up and transformed in religious ethics by thinkers such as Paul Tillich who hold an "agential" theory of the constitution of moral identity.[16] On Tillich's view, moral identity is grounded with respect to the actions taken by the agent in relation to himself or herself according to a conception of law rooted in the divine being which actualizes the agent's freedom.

On the other side of the debate I am tracing are those who argue that human subjectivity is not self-constituting but is itself constituted with respect to some antecedent order of value. So-called communitarian critics of liberalism such as Michael Sandel argue that selfhood does not exist prior to and independent of its relations and commitments, but is constituted in and through them. We are not "unencumbered" selves who originate our own moral claims, but members of a community bound by moral ties antecedent to our choices.[17] In a similar vein, Alasdair MacIntyre, arguing explicitly against existentialism in *After Virtue*, insists that there is no way of founding personal identity apart from the social and historical features of human existence. The self is always the bearer of a particular social identity that is embedded in the story of the community of which it is a part.[18] In religious ethics, this position is represented by narrative ethicists such as Stanley Hauerwas who hold a "social" theory of the constitution of moral identity.[19] For Hauerwas, Christian existence is a distinctive form of moral identity that is formed in relation to the specific narratives and practices of the Christian community, rather than in relation to a general account of human existence.

A third group in the contemporary debate occupies a mediating position between the two alternatives. Proponents of this view, among whom I would include Charles Taylor and Seyla Benhabib, share the concern of liberal and existentialist ethics to preserve the self-transcending capacity of human beings and believe that liberalism has articulated some of our most significant moral and political values.[20] But at the same time, they recognize that autonomy is always mediated by social, linguistic, historical, and other forces that shape and inform moral identity. These thinkers would criticize the legacy of modern individualism implicit in both exis-

and liberal theory because it defines the self apart from and over any antecedent order of value and recognizes as valid only the claims originated by the self.

Murdoch is among those who occupy this third mediating position. Against contemporary liberals and others who argue that moral identity is constituted by the self's choices apart from any substantive conception of the good, she held that moral identity is constituted by a prior framework of value. Indeed her moral psychology rests on a fundamental correlation between the notions of self and good. Yet on Murdoch's view, the appeal to a narrativist or communitarian conception of identity runs the risk of denying the self's capacity to transcend its social roles, and thus may fall prey to the distortions of the social totality, or may cede too great a measure of its responsibility to the authority of existing arrangements. Murdoch's conception of the self attempts to preserve the self's integrity without isolating it from a world of others that defines its normative claims and purposes. In effect, she charts a middle course between what she sees as the dangers of a model of autonomy by which the self wholly transcends contingency (its relations to nature, history, and others), and a model that dissolves or assimilates the self into these contingent relations.

In addition to engaging the contemporary debate over the nature and constitution of moral subjectivity, Murdoch's position also engages current forms of thought that call the very idea of the self into question, notably poststructuralism. In contrast to the positions noted above, which presuppose some notion of selfhood and agency and differ mainly on how these are to be understood, poststructuralism attempts to "unsettle" the notion of the self as agent. As Mette Hjort writes:

> Taking issue with philosophers such as Kant, Hegel and Sartre, poststructuralists proposed a decentred conception of subjectivity in which the alleged fiction of autonomous agency was replaced by a series of discursive effects. On the poststructuralist account, the discrete entities that we in everyday interaction refer to as 'individuals' do not in any meaningful way shape the course of their lives. Instead, their characteristic modes of behaviour are entirely determined by a cluster of irreducibly social entities, of which language is the most important.[21]

In her last philosophical work, *Metaphysics as a Guide to Morals*, Murdoch challenges at least two crucial features of this description that are important for purposes of the present discussion. First, she challenges poststructuralism's attack on the notion of the individual, which she believes is part and parcel of the general attack on the notion of self-consciousness in post-Cartesian philosophy. The second and related point is that Murdoch believes poststructuralism amounts to a form of "linguistic determinism" that understands the self as a "discursive effect" of language rather than a user and speaker of language. By denying the idea of the individual as agent, in other words, poststructuralism cedes human freedom over to the system of language. As Hjort puts it, "Poststructuralists . . . would have us believe that the beings we commonly call 'agents' in fact are merely patients passively registering the effects of discursive events."[22] Murdoch's constructive position directly challenges these claims by insisting on a defense of consciousness and the individual against absorption into linguistic and other systems. This is one of the central contributions of her work to contemporary thought.

My placement of Murdoch's position among contemporary options regarding the self and its freedom is obviously not innocent, and it has implications for my characterization of her general philosophical method. The corollary to Murdoch's insistence that moral subjectivity escapes complete determination by social and other forces is her conviction that moral philosophy is properly a form of metaphysics. Although Murdoch shared to some extent the contemporary suspicion of general truths and universal judgments characteristic of the current so-called antitheorist trend in ethics[23] and although she was cognizant of the historical nature of moral claims and concepts, she did not take the historicist turn represented by thinkers such as Alasdair MacIntyre. She was concerned to admit historical and social particularity into her account of the self (to the point of criticizing two of her heroes, Kant and Plato, for their fear of the particular and the contingent), but this concern did not compel her to undertake a narrative history of the self and its goods.[24] Rather, Murdoch's thought gives renewed respectability to a neglected option in modern moral theory, the attempt to construct a metaphysical ethic.

This appeal to metaphysics means, in part, that the defining "situation" Murdoch envisioned as the framework for morality and moral agency is neither the one occupied by the solitary rational will (as in Kantian thought), nor that of the historical community (as in Hegelian thought), but rather "reality"—the setting of human existence that is always "both more and other than our descriptions of it."[25] Any grounding for moral claims that falls short of this runs the risk of too easily identifying a provisional, contingent, or distorted state of affairs as normative. In short, Murdoch insisted that morality must endeavor to be a form of metaphysical realism,[26] and she was wary of appeals to consensus or community as an easily corruptible standard for moral claims.

Murdoch's metaphysical realism represents a constructive alternative both to liberal ethics in the Kantian tradition and to contemporary narrativist or communitarian accounts of the moral self. Liberal ethics, as I noted earlier, rules out substantive accounts of the self and the good in order to safeguard the freedom of the rational agent from any defining "situation." The task of ethics is limited to the articulation of fair procedures for deliberation about justice rather than constructing a more extended and substantive picture of the self and the world that might be provided by metaphysical or religious beliefs. Further, liberal theory's emphasis on a particular conception of freedom results in an overly behaviorist or act-centered view of the moral self that ignores the inner life of consciousness and the cognitive and affective dimensions of human personality. Murdoch challenged what she judged to be liberal theory's constricted view of morality and moral agency in two ways: first, by challenging the autonomy of morality from substantive beliefs about self and world; and second, by criticizing liberal theory's will-centered or voluntarist anthropology. These two themes are closely related, since Murdoch's effort to retrieve a metaphysical framework of value for moral life and thought entails a correlative shift in our view of the self as a being constituted not only by its public choices but also by its inner beliefs, desires, and perceptions. This provides an opening for the expansion of the moral domain to include the full range of human cognitive activity—from the fluid and momentary movements of consciousness associated with a person's reactions and perceptions of the world and others, to the more fixed or stable thought patterns associated with a person's political convictions or religious beliefs.

As these remarks suggest, Murdoch's thought shares much of the contemporary criticism of the liberal theory of the self represented by the appeal to a tradition- or narrative-constituted account of moral subjectivity. Like these critics, she argues for a more "situated" account of the self than that of liberal theory, an account that makes the concept of the particular individual rather than the rational agent or citizen central to moral theory. Further, and correlatively, Murdoch would likely have supported the efforts of these critics to articulate a substantive rather than a procedural conception of the human good. Yet Murdoch's conception of morality as a form of metaphysical realism betrays an important divergence from many contemporary narrativist and communitarian accounts of ethics. For Murdoch, morality and moral agency must be situated in relation to an authoritative good, one which she sometimes associates with traditional theological attributes such as transcendence, unity, perfection, necessity, and ineffability.[27] Murdoch conceives the good not primarily in relation to diverse human practices (as in MacIntyre's account), nor in relation to a particular religious tradition (as in a narrativist position such as Hauerwas's), but rather in relation to a realistic standard that is both internal to consciousness and also surpasses it.

This brings me to the major substantive argument of the book. Murdoch's attempt to frame a metaphysical ethic in an age that she believed is characterized above all by "the elimination of metaphysics from ethics" touches each of the central themes of her moral thought. Given the intimate relation between morality, the self, and the good, these chapters must be seen as necessarily interrelated.

Section II. The Argument of the Book

I begin in Chapter 2 by presenting Murdoch's retrieval of metaphysics as providing a framework for moral subjectivity and as situating ethics within a general view of human existence. Murdoch understands metaphysics as a form of critical reflection on reality and on the nature of human beings through the building of complex images, metaphors, and conceptual frameworks.[28] Taking Plato as a preeminent example of this method, she contends that the great moral philosophers of the past presented "a total metaphysical picture of which ethics forms a part. The universe, including our own nature, is like this, they say."[29] The forms of modern ethics with which Murdoch's thought is chiefly concerned, Anglo-American linguistic analysis and the existentialism of Jean-Paul Sartre, have forsaken this sort of analysis by severing the connection between metaphysics and ethics. The consequence, in her view, has been the impoverishment of a richly creative area of human thought, as well as a "denuding" of our view of the human self.

Murdoch emphasizes the constructive and "figurative" dimension of metaphysical theorizing in order to challenge the claims of analytical philosophers such as R. M Hare to ethical neutrality. Her understanding of metaphysics is thus part of a more general argument for a particular understanding and use of moral language as a form of "imaginative construction." Renouncing the scientific pretensions of the method of linguistic analysis in which she was trained at Oxford and Cambridge, Murdoch was one of the first to undertake a critique of the so-called naturalistic fallacy underlying the analytic claim of ethical neutrality. One of the many effects of her argument in subsequent ethics has been the realignment of morality with art and aesthetic perception rather than with science. This insight has since been refined and developed in diverse and influential ways by thinkers such as Hilary Putnam, Martha Nussbaum, Nelson Goodman, and others. Moral philosophy as Murdoch conceived it involves "the making of models and pictures of what different kinds of men [sic] are like," in order "to analyse and describe our own morality and that of others."[30] It is a process of clarifying our existing concepts, and developing new ones, in the course of offering an evaluative description of human moral being. Thus, it can never be a purely logical or neutral undertaking with universal results; rather, "moral theory is an activity whose purpose and justification is *moral*."[31]

With respect to the substantive aspect of her metaphysics, the fundamental problem that Murdoch's position seeks to address is the following: "Is morality to be seen as essentially and by its nature centred on the individual, or as part of a general framework of reality which includes the individual?"[32] The first alternative, Murdoch believed, is exemplified by Kantian moral philosophy and its variants (such as existentialism), which assume that the moral will is autonomous and "that morality must be self-contained."[33] The second alternative is represented by Hegel and other "natural law" types of morality (such as Thomism and Marxism), in which "the individual is seen as held in a framework which transcends him."[34] Although a fuller exposition of this distinction must await later chapters, Murdoch seems on the whole to favor the second option: the retrieval of "a general framework of reality which includes the individual" is the task of a metaphysical ethic as she conceives it. However, Murdoch retained a concern for the reality and value of the individual that I believe makes it impossible to classify her unambiguously as a Natural Law type of moralist. The implications of this tension in Murdoch's thought will be explored at several points throughout the book.

This second major theme of Murdoch's moral philosophy, her understanding of the self as a unique individual, is already implicit in her understanding of the form and content of metaphysical theorizing. In contrast to liberal forms of ethics, Murdoch believed that moral philosophy must reflect upon and analyze not only the agent's public actions and the decisions and choices that lead to action but also the internal phenomena of moral struggle and moral fault, the effort to become morally better, and the failure to become so. This inclusion of an analysis of the inner life in moral reflection requires a more complex moral psychology than modern existentialism and analytic philosophy have provided. Specifically, it requires a shift from a predominantly voluntarist view of the self to a more cognitivist one. This shift signals a major contribution of Murdoch's moral psychology to contemporary ethics, the retrieval of the notion of consciousness rather than the will as the "mode" of human moral being. My treatment of this theme is divided between two chapters.

In Chapter 3, I present Murdoch's critique of Sartrean existentialism and linguistic analysis as philosophies that deny the significance of consciousness in morality and hold an unrealistic conception of moral freedom. Sartre's account of consciousness negates its relation to a realm of value, including that of nature, institutions, and other persons; while linguistic analysis denies the very notion of consciousness altogether, seeing the "inner life" as epiphenomenal in relation to outward behavior and public meanings. Both philosophies hold a voluntarist conception of freedom, according to which freedom is a value-creating activity of the human will rather than a cognitive response to a moral world that precedes the agent's act of choice. I analyze Murdoch's constructive response to these philosophies in Chapter 4, where I present her moral psychology and her defense of the concept of the individual. These rest on a retrieval of the notion of consciousness as the fundamental mode of human moral being, and on the claim that consciousness is internally structured according to an implicit notion of moral value or the good. I attempt to show that this understanding of consciousness and its relation to moral value answers the deficiencies in the existentialist and linguistic analyst positions analyzed in Chapter 3.

Chapter 5 specifies Murdoch's understanding of the idea of the good and relates it to her normative account of moral existence. This chapter is synthetic in its attempt to show that Murdoch's notion of consciousness is formally structured by a twofold notion of the good. This consists of a formal component with both transcendental and perfectionist aspects, and a substantive component specifying the content of the ideal of perfection. I show that despite its starting point in consciousness, this account of the good avoids subjectivism because it defines the good as a *reflexive* principle that both presupposes consciousness (as transcendental condition) and surpasses it (as an ideal of perfected moral knowledge which transcends egoism). To this end, I characterize Murdoch as a "reflexive" or "hermeneutical realist"[35] and show that her account of the good is validated by a version of the ontological proof.

Murdoch distinguishes two kinds of arguments in her proof for the good correlative to two dimensions of consciousness: first, a formal argument with transcendental and perfectionist components; and second, a substantive argument that articulates the normative meaning of the ideal of perfection. The formal sense of the good can be understood in relation to what Charles Taylor calls the "inescapable framework" of qualitative distinctions and strong evaluations within which human beings exist. Murdoch makes the same point using the Platonic imagery of the good as the light of the sun by which we see all other things.[36] The self and the good are correlative notions at this level by virtue of the fact that selves are valuing agents who live their lives "under the aspect" of the good. The good is a transcendental notion that provides the condition for the possibility of moral identity without itself specifying any substantive conception of value or identity.[37] Further, the transcendental idea of the good includes the notion of perfection even at this formal level. This is because the idea of value itself presupposes qualitative distinctions of worth that depend on the notions of good and bad, better and worse, truth and falsity in relation to some ideal of "the best" or most perfect.[38]

The second, substantive meaning of the idea of the good sp[...] specifically moral content of this idea of perfection as a standa[...] critical evaluation of egoistic consciousness. Because human beings in Murdoch's view are by nature selfish and sunk in a reality deformed by their own fantasies, the good requires a transformation of the self through the purification of psychic eros, which is the motive force of human moral being. On this account, the idea of the good represents an ideal of perfected (i.e., realistic or illusionless) knowledge that is paradigmatically expressed in the apprehension of the reality of other persons. Because human beings are riddled by distorted loves and consoling fantasies, the good in this sense is a "reality principle" that corrects selfish illusion by right vision.

The chapter on the good marks the end of my exposition of the central themes of Murdoch's moral theory. In the final chapter, I complete the aims of the book by assessing the validity of the argument in terms of its internal consistency and in relation to the current debates in ethics out-lined earlier. In addition, I develop the constructive implications of my interpretation of Murdoch, especially her defense of the notion of con-sciousness and the individual in the face of current cultural and philo-sophical challenges to this notion.

Having outlined the main argument of the book, it remains for me to raise several important interpretive issues that must be addressed before any attempt can be made to take the measure of Murdoch's philosophical work in the current academic and cultural context. Since these issues arise largely from particular features of Murdoch's life and thought, a brief biographical sketch of her career may help to provide a context for the discussion that follows.

Section III. Preliminary Interpretive Considerations

The basic outlines of Murdoch's life are well known.[39] Born in 1919 in Dublin, an only child of Anglo-Irish parents, Murdoch knew from an early age that she would be a writer (she began writing stories at the age of nine or ten); but she always knew that she would do something else as well.[40] Her desire for philosophy came much later, after studying classics at Somerville College, Oxford, taking a "first" in Greats (ancient history, Greek, Latin, and philosophy) in 1942. In fact, her ambition was to become an art historian or archaeologist,[41] but World War II intervened and she spent two of the war years as a civil servant, working as an Assistant Principal at the Treasury (1942–44) and two years working with refugees as an Administrative Officer with the United National Relief and Rehabil-itation Administration (1944–46) in London, Belgium, and Austria. Her experiences in Belgium and also Paris after World War II and her intro-duction to Sartre and to existentialism in 1945 were influential in her decision to pursue the study of philosophy.[42] She held the Sarah Smithson Studentship in philosophy at Cambridge during 1947–48 and narrowly missed being taught by Ludwig Wittgenstein, whose thought dominated the intellectual atmosphere there at the time.[43] She returned to Oxford in 1948 and was for fifteen years a Fellow of St. Anne's College and University lecturer in Philosophy, where she subsequently became an Honorary Fel-low. From 1963–67 she was Lecturer at the Royal College of Art in London, but never again held a regular teaching post.

Murdoch published her first major philosophical work, *Sartre, Romantic Rationalist*, in 1953 while teaching at Oxford, and her first novel, *Under the Net*, just one year later, having already destroyed five completed manu-scripts of earlier novels. Six more novels as well as numerous treatises on philosophical, political, religious, and literary topics were published before her retirement from teaching at Oxford in 1963. She subsequently published an additional nineteen novels, as well as five major philosophical works and several essays. Her Gifford Lectures, delivered in 1982 and published as *Metaphysics as a Guide to Morals* in 1992, represent the most comprehensive and mature statement of her philosophical position.[44] Throughout her career she gave numerous public lectures and attended international conferences on topics in both philosophy and literature.

Such an impressively hybrid résumé of literary-philosophical activity raises a host of interpretive questions for any study of Murdoch's thought, and specifically for the three previously stated aims of this book. The first aim poses the problem of finding an interpretive method adequate to the task of giving systematic shape to the philosophical arguments embedded in Murdoch's highly original, disparate, and unsystematic essays. The lack of any overt philosophical system in Murdoch's scholarly works may be partly intentional: she was always suspicious of "false unities" and totalizing forms of thought.[45] But the breadth of Murdoch's intellectual and artistic commitments, as well as the fertile nature of her intelligence, might have made the development of such a system unlikely in any case. The point that needs emphasis is that the neglect or suspicion of "system" in Murdoch's philosophy does not mean that her thought is incoherent or lacking in intellectual rigor or focus. It is in fact a major task of this study to show otherwise. But it does mean that a comprehensive reading of Murdoch's thought requires an interpretive method that can clarify her implicit systematic concerns without forcing them into forms and categories alien to her own thought. I have tried to address this interpretive problem by articulating what I call a "conceptual hermeneutic" that takes seriously Murdoch's insistence that the task of philosophy is to provide compelling "pictures" of the human through the careful and creative use of concepts and conceptual schema. That is, I use Murdoch's own philosophical concepts and metaphors as the key to her systematic concerns and as a clue to the organizing principles of her ethics. Given the importance of this interpretive method to this study as a whole, I have reserved a fuller discussion of it for the last section (IV) of this chapter.

The second aim of the book raises a different sort of interpretive problem that can be addressed more immediately: the problem of interpreting Murdoch's work, some of it written more than forty years ago, as contributing to the current debates in ethics outlined earlier in this chapter. The majority of Murdoch's philosophical treatises were written as a critical response to the philosophies dominant in the 1950s at the beginning of her career—namely, Anglo-American linguistic philosophy and philosophy of mind (represented in the work of R. M. Hare, Stuart Hampshire, Ludwig Wittgenstein, and others),[46] and the existentialism of Jean-Paul Sartre. Since then, of course, there have been significant shifts in the western intellectual and cultural landscape, during which the views of some of her early interlocutors have changed significantly (Hampshire is a notable example), while others have undergone an intense period of critical scrutiny and reassessment (as in the case of Sartre).⁴⁷ Further, although Murdoch kept up with more recent intellectual developments, her decision to pursue a full-time literary career meant that she was not compelled to respond to many of the specific debates in contemporary religious and philosophical ethics with which I seek to engage her.

These contextual considerations have prompted the following interpretive decisions. First, given the central importance of analytic linguistic philosophy and Sartrean existentialism in the early formation of Murdoch's constructive thought, these will figure prominently in my exposition of her work in the following chapters. In presenting these positions, I have made no attempt to account for subsequent developments in the thought of such figures as Hampshire, Hare, or others, nor to imagine how they might have responded to Murdoch's criticisms. Rather, my primary concern throughout has been to clarify what was at stake *for Murdoch* in these arguments, recognizing that my treatment of her position in relation to her interlocutors may appear somewhat one-sided as a result. Second, given that Murdoch never directly addressed some of the contemporary debates that are central to this study, my attempt to place her thought in the current intellectual landscape must rely on arguments she made in other contexts. While the success of this effort must await the argument of the book as a whole, my claim is that Murdoch's ideas resonate in the current context with a force that testifies to their continuing value in fulfilling what she believes is a central task of ethical inquiry: "The provision of rich and fertile conceptual schemes which help us . . . to connect, to illuminate, to explain, and to make new and fruitful places for reflection."⁴⁸

The final interpretive problem that must be addressed arises from Murdoch's dual career as novelist and philosopher. Since my aim in this book is to offer a systematic treatment of Murdoch's philosophy, the question of how (and whether) to relate her philosophical and her literary corpus is unavoidable. Practically speaking, since Murdoch's novels have already been the subject of excellent literary critical work, I have refrained in this study from an analysis of the novels.⁴⁹ Nor have I speculated on the supposed "implied philosophy" of the novels in comparison with the explicit philosophical positions advanced in Murdoch's non-fictional works. Instead, my guiding assumption has been that Murdoch's philosophical thought has an integrity and importance of its own that deserves a systematic and book-length treatment on its own terms. The book's intention is to offer something that the existing literary critical studies of Murdoch's novels do not—a general philosophical framework for an assessment of her thought as a whole. Accordingly, my use of the secondary literature on Murdoch's fiction is limited by my systematic and conceptual focus.⁵⁰

Murdoch's production of both literary and philosophical works also raises a more general issue concerning the relation between philosophy and literature. Murdoch is often cited as an advocate of the recent turn to literature in moral philosophy, which has produced some of the most influential work in ethics to appear in the past decade or so.[51] Yet there is evidence to suggest that Murdoch wanted to maintain a firm boundary between philosophy and literature, with respect to both her own work and in general. Questioned repeatedly in interviews about the relation of her philosophical and literary works, she always resisted the notion that she was a so-called philosophical novelist in the manner of Sartre, Beauvoir, and others.[52] She insisted that her philosophy did not intrude on her fiction, and that her characters should not be considered "mouthpieces" for her own philosophical views.[53] Moreover, Murdoch consistently defended the autonomy of art and the artist from the obligation to serve any explicit social, moral, or political cause. She especially abhorred the attempt by totalitarian political regimes to manipulate art for propagandistic purposes.[54] These considerations suggest that there is ample warrant in Murdoch's own position for treating her moral philosophy separately from her fiction.

Aside from her own work, Murdoch defended the distinction between literature and philosophy on principle. In an interview with Bryan Magee, she argued that literature and philosophy are two radically different kinds of writing and endeavor: "Philosophy aims to clarify and to explain, it states and attempts to solve very difficult highly technical problems and the writing must be subservient to this aim." In contrast, "art is fun and for fun, it has innumerable intentions and charms. . . . It is full of tricks and magic and deliberate mystification. Literature entertains, it does many things, and philosophy does one thing."[55] Such comments once prompted Martha Nussbaum, a prominent theorist and practitioner of the literary turn in philosophy, to cite Murdoch as exemplifying modern philosophy's hostility toward the use of literary works and methods in its own modes of inquiry.[56] Commenting in *The Fragility of Goodness* on the Magee interview, Nussbaum writes,

> Even Iris Murdoch, one of the few contemporary Anglo-American philosophers who is also a distinguished literary writer, claims that the philosophical style, the style that seeks truth and understanding rather than mere entertainment, will be pure of non-intellectual appeals. . . . Murdoch seems to assume that there is a philosophical style that is content-neutral, suitable for the fair investigation of all alternative conceptions. She assumes as well that this style is the style of plain hard reason, pure of appeals to emotion and sense.[57]

Although Murdoch's comments in the Magee interview lend support to Nussbaum's characterization, this does not yet tell the full story of Murdoch's views on the matter.[58] In the same interview, Murdoch finds an important point of connection between philosophy and literature in her assertion that although philosophy and literature operate by different rules and appeal to different aspects of human intellect, neither activity is value-neutral. Since both are cognitive activities of the human mind, they are inevitably "saturated" in the moral: "[T]hough they are so different, philosophy and literature are both truth-seeking and truth-revealing activities. They are cognitive activities, explanations . . . literature is like philosophy in this respect."[59] For this and other reasons, Murdoch has often (despite Nussbaum) been claimed as a proponent rather than a detractor of the literary turn in philosophy. Exemplary in this respect is her comment in *The Sovereignty of Good* that "literature is an education in how to picture and understand human situations,"[60] suggesting that literature may share some of the aims of moral philosophy. There are also numerous places in her essays where she suggests that moral rationality and moral perception are more like the activities of the artist or the sensitive novelist than the supposed objectivity or value-neutrality of the scientist.

This rather complex set of considerations suggests that one can find good arguments in Murdoch's work to support the view that literature and philosophy are sharply distinct—as well as the view that they are importantly alike. The more compelling issue regarding Murdoch's views on philosophy and literature, therefore, may lie elsewhere. In my judgment, Murdoch's contribution to the debate over philosophy and literature has less to do with their proper status and relations as forms of human discourse, and more to do with a deeper question concerning the status of language itself. Whatever differences one may properly wish to draw between them, philosophy and literature share the medium of language, and it is a major claim of Murdoch's thought that language is an inescapably moral medium. Her persistent attention to the evaluative nature of all language represents the real value of her thought for a possible rapprochement between literature and philosophy. In this respect, her position cuts deeper than the usual lines of the philosophy-literature debate. However one might assess the relationship between her own literary and philosophical works, Murdoch provides essential conceptual resources for bringing philosophy and literature together as forms of "metaphysical" (in her sense) theorizing that rely on the reflexive and imaginative capacities of human consciousness.[61] From this perspective, Murdoch's views on metaphysics, consciousness, and language are crucial to any discussion of the relation of philosophy and literature in her thought. These can be explored on the basis of her philosophical works alone, and will be significant themes in the chapters that follow.

In the final section of this introduction, I return to the question of the hermeneutical method of this study by giving a fuller account of the interpretive principles guiding my reading of Murdoch's philosophical works.

Section IV. Reading Murdoch: The Hermeneutical Method of the Book

A clarification of interpretive method is especially important in the case of a thinker like Murdoch. Given the range and diversity of her writings on ethics, philosophy, art, religion, and politics over a span of forty or fifty years—not to mention a substantial literary corpus of novels as well as drama and poetry—Murdoch's thought does not lend itself to any obvious or single approach. This difficulty is only exacerbated by the fact that of her philosophical writings, only three can be considered "monographs" in the usual sense: *Sartre, Romantic Rationalist, The Fire and the Sun: Why Plato Banished the Artists*, and *Metaphysics as a Guide to Morals*. Her best known work, *The Sovereignty of Good*, while unified in its basic theme, is a collection of three essays written for different occasions; and the rest of her philosophical writings are mostly essays written in response to diverse problems and debates in philosophy, politics, and literary criticism.[62]

Furthermore, even the monographs noted above are not standard approaches to their subject matter. The Sartre book is a synthetic analysis of his novels, philosophy, and politics against the background of modern European thought. The book on Plato is a seamless text of ninety pages that treats Plato's famous hostility to art synthetically in relation to other aspects of his thought, as well as to the thought of Kant, Freud, Tolstoy, Wittgenstein, Derrida, and others. Finally, if one turns to *Metaphysics as a Guide to Morals* expecting a metaphysical "system," one finds instead that Murdoch has made the *avoidance* of system a guiding principle of both the form and the content of her metaphysics.[63]

In the face of such a disparate, unsystematic, yet substantial and significant body of work, how does one proceed to order and interpret Murdoch's thought? To answer this question, one can distinguish two possible approaches that one might adopt as interpretive methods. These approaches are not mutually exclusive, but may be distinguished for purposes of clarification. First, one might propose to construct a genetic argument that traces the development of Murdoch's philosophy from her earliest to her most recent writings, noting the major phases and transitions of her thought over the course of her career. Alternatively, one might approach Murdoch's work exegetically by providing careful expository readings of individual texts. Either approach might be useful in rendering a difficult body of work more systematic.

My own approach incorporates elements of both of these strategies, but is also importantly different. Although I note certain developments in Murdoch's thought from her earlier essays to the mature statement of her position represented by *Metaphysics as a Guide to Morals*, and though I do engage in close expository readings of portions of the major texts, my approach is best classified as "conceptual" rather than either genetic or exegetical. That is, I identify what I take to be the basic concepts, metaphors, and structural principles of Murdoch's thought and use these as an interpretive key to read and order her texts. This involves developing a "vocabulary" of conceptual terms drawn from specific texts, and using them to illuminate the structure of her thought as a whole.

The conceptual hermeneutic that I employ in the following chapters has affinities with Murdoch's own philosophical method. Moral philosophy, she believed, needs a method appropriate to the nature of human beings as imaginative, self-interpreting creatures. As I noted earlier in this introduction, Murdoch understands metaphysical reflection as a form of imaginative construction that makes use of concepts, images, explanatory schema, and metaphors to describe reality and human existence. In her view, metaphysics is not (as some analytic philosophers would hold) a logically neutral attempt to explain the nature of reality, but a "figurative" activity of creating myths, concepts, and images to describe and illuminate human moral existence. In short, metaphysics is a moral activity with a realistic intention. Thus Plato's allegory of the cave or his image of the Good as the sun are intended to describe the nature of reality and also to suggest a method for attaining knowledge of that reality. These Platonic images recur repeatedly in Murdoch's thought as primary examples of metaphysical theorizing.

Murdoch uses precisely this kind of conceptual analysis in the form of "pictures" and images of human existence in order to analyze moral identity in relation to the good. A prominent example of such a picture is the well-known anecdote from *The Sovereignty of Good* concerning a mother's (M) changing impressions of her daughter-in-law (D). Murdoch uses this ordinary example of concrete moral deliberation to illuminate the way in which the private activities of consciousness and perception are inherently evaluative in nature. Like Plato's allegory of the prisoners in the cave who learn to distinguish between appearance and reality, Murdoch describes M as engaged in a pilgrimage toward clear vision.[64] Through a disciplined effort of moral attention, she progresses from a perception of D distorted by jealousy and egoism to a more just and compassionate appreciation of D's personality. The M and D example will function in the book in numerous contexts to help illuminate several aspects of Murdoch's thought, including her understanding of the moral status of consciousness, the role of moral language in the progress of moral vision, and the centrality of the individual as the primary object of moral attention.

In addition to the M and D example, Murdoch formulates other explanatory pictures of the moral life in the form of conceptual dyads or oppositional pairs. The "binary" or dualistic aspect of Murdoch's imagination has been noted by at least one literary critic in connection with the plotting, characterization, and titles of her novels. Peter Conradi has observed that "Murdoch's is essentially a dualist imagination"[65] and notes several examples of this fact from both her fiction and her philosophy:

> Her imagination has always worked by such embattled pairings and through dialectic—'The Sublime and the Good', *The Nice and the Good*, existentialist and mystic, neurotic and conventional, *The Fire and the Sun*, *Nuns and Soldiers*: many of the novels turn on the paradox of two worlds,

one ordinary, one spiritual, and two heroes, one contemplative, one active.[66]

Given this pattern of dualistic pairings in Murdoch's thought, I want to distinguish three types of conceptual dyads in her philosophical writings in order to clarify the importance of these oppositions as an interpretive tool for understanding her thought.

First, Murdoch constructs what might be called conceptual "persona," which represent abstract theoretical positions in the form of identifiable human types. These include Totalitarian Man and Ordinary Language Man, the Liberal moralist and the Natural Law moralist, the existentialist and the mystic, the saint and the artist, the citizen and the moral-spiritual individual, to note several.[67] These types are primary illustrations of Murdoch's conviction that moral philosophy involves "the making of models and pictures of what different types of men are like" in order to describe our own morality and that of others.[68] By creating such models as the Liberal view and the Natural Law view, for example, Murdoch illustrates two entirely different conceptions of human agency and freedom.

Second, Murdoch constructs several "descriptive contrasts" that are intended to present alternatives which are in need of some sort of mediation. These include the contrast between neurosis and convention, the crystalline novel and the journalistic novel, liberalism and romanticism, intuitions and rules, and others. However, it is important not to expect some sort of "Hegelian synthesis" in Murdoch's treatment of these pairs. Rather, she proposes different kinds of mediation depending on the case. For example, in the case of neurosis and convention, the terms of the contrast represent "twin dangers" that Murdoch believes an adequate account of art and morality should avoid. At other times, as in the case of the contrast between intuitions and rules, the opposition represents two necessary aspects of morality, each of which is incomplete without the other and must be held in tension.

Third and finally, Murdoch uses oppositions between major philosophical figures in a similar fashion: to describe alternative viewpoints that help to define a normative position by way of contrast. Interestingly, these often include Kant as one pole of the opposition (e.g., Kant and Hegel, Kant and Plato, Kant and Mill); but they include other contrasting figures as well (e.g., Hobbesian empiricists and Kierkegaardian existentialists as two distinct heirs to Hegel, as well as Hegel and Kierkegaard). This treatment of contrasting pairs of philosophical positions is important given the claim of this book that Murdoch articulates a *mediating* position between various alternatives in current moral inquiry, especially between options influenced by Kant and Hegel. It suggests that my placement of Murdoch's position among contemporary options is not merely fortuitous, but is related to a structural principle basic to her thought as a whole. It also indicates that Murdoch's approach to the mediation of opposites is complex and rarely yields a straightforward synthesis. She often holds contrasts in unsystematic tension, or oscillates between them as convincing but irreconcilable perspectives. A detailed assessment of how Murdoch's thought mediates between contemporary alternatives in moral inquiry must await the conclusion of the book.

By using this conceptual approach to Murdoch's thought rather than the more familiar genetic and exegetical approaches noted above, certain implications follow for the presentation of the chapters to come. It means, first, that rather than simply treating these elements once in an exposition of the text from which they are drawn, I return to them in different chapters, deepening the analysis with each new context of discussion. This is especially the case with the example of M and D from *The Sovereignty of Good*, which is a particularly rich illustration of many of Murdoch's complex theoretical points. Second, it means that I use some concepts to show that Murdoch's overall position is even more complex than she sometimes suggests. For example, although Murdoch seems to sympathize with Natural Law morality over Liberal morality in the text in which she introduces these types, I contend that her thought *as a whole* does not support this characterization of her position. Therefore, I use the contrast between the Liberal and Natural Law views at several points to bring out an aspect of Murdoch's thought that can only be appreciated in a larger context. The consequence of this conceptual approach is that the book may sometimes appear repetitive. But my intention is to demonstrate the richness of Murdoch's conceptual schemes for ethical reflection, as well as to show the internal coherence of her thought as a means of "picturing the human."

2

METAPHYSICS AND ETHICS

Murdoch's effort to retrieve a metaphysical conception of ethics in a century that has been, in Franklin Gamwell's phrase, "so decidedly unfriendly to metaphysics"[1] is one of her most significant contributions to contemporary ethical inquiry. Challenging what has been called the "dominant consensus" against metaphysics in modern moral theory, Murdoch criticizes the attempt to sever morality from any normative framework that might determine the agent's purposes and threaten the agent's autonomy. Equally, however, she resists the alternative attempt to define the agent's purposes within a framework narrowly delimited by the conventions and institutions of a historical community or tradition. Against both options, Murdoch appeals to a metaphysical notion of ethics in order to ground moral claims with respect to a normative conception of "the real." For this reason, understanding the relation between metaphysics and ethics in Murdoch's thought is essential to understanding her moral realism.

An account of Murdoch's metaphysics also provides the crucial background for her attempt to correlate an account of the self with an idea of the good. That is, her retrieval of metaphysics represents the formal condition for her attempt to shift the locus of value from the solitary agent toward a more inclusive moral ontology. Murdoch charges her two primary opponents, analytic ethics and existentialist ethics, with isolating the agent from any normative framework. This chapter will focus especially on analytic ethics, since Murdoch's critique of existentialism is concerned more directly with its conception of selfhood and human freedom and will be treated in Chapters 3 and 4. But in both cases (and despite the substantial differences between them), she argues that linguistic analysis and Sartrean existentialism share "a terror of anything which encloses the agent or threatens his supremacy as a center of significance. In this sense both philosophies tend toward solipsism. Neither pictures virtue as concerned with anything real outside ourselves."[2] Murdoch relates the absence of an encompassing framework for moral agency in these philosophies to the subjectivism of their approach to ethics. The individual agent is presented as essentially alone, not surrounded "by any structure larger than himself, such as might be represented by a metaphysical belief or by an institution,"[3] and as completely free, choosing and acting on his own responsibility. Consequently, neither of these philosophies succeeds in articulating a criterion for morality that resists collapse into the human will.

In order to establish the relations among Murdoch's retrieval of metaphysics, her correlative reconception of the moral agent, and her defense of moral realism, my argument will move through several related steps. In Section I, I explicate Murdoch's account of the "elimination of metaphysics" from modern moral theory, focusing especially on her early essays. Tracing this development to the influence of Hume and Kant, Murdoch challenges the legacy of these two thinkers in modern British empiricism by directly contesting the anti-metaphysical and anti-naturalistic assumptions of Anglo-American moral philosophy. In Section II, I show that Murdoch's defense of a metaphysical and naturalistic conception of ethics allows her to conceive the moral agent as part of a larger framework of value, rather than as a solitary agent who creates values by his or her choices. Finally, in Section III, I introduce important topics in Murdoch's metaethics in order to clarify the formal norm of her realist conception of ethics, including a preliminary discussion of her ontological argument for the reality of the good.

Section I. A. The Elimination of Metaphysics from Ethics in Modern Moral Philosophy

Though a defense of metaphysical thinking was a consistent feature of Murdoch's thought from the early essays of the 1950s to her last major study *Metaphysics as a Guide to Morals*, the context of her argument shifted considerably over the years. Initially, at least, her retrieval of metaphysics must be understood in the context of the demise of metaphysical thinking in modern moral philosophy, particularly in Anglo-American moral inquiry during the middle years of the twentieth century.[4] The fundamental issue at stake in the debate with her analytic contemporaries was whether ethics can or should be conceived as a discipline separable from a larger normative account of reality and human existence. Murdoch insisted (with Plato and other ancient moral thinkers) that ethics cannot proceed independently of such an account. Yet she was not simply retrieving or recurring to a premodern conception of metaphysics, as the pervasively Platonic cast of her thought might suggest; she also acknowledged the Kantian critique of metaphysics as an established part of the western philosophical inheritance. In this respect, Murdoch's conception of metaphysics revises and reconstructs important aspects of both Plato and Kant's thought.

In order to see how this is the case, we need to understand how the so-called elimination of metaphysics from moral philosophy came about in the first place. Murdoch once told an interviewer that "my main interest is in moral philosophy and in explaining morality in a philosophical sense which I feel can't be done without the reintroduction of certain concepts which in the recent past have been regarded as metaphysical in some sense which made them impossible."[5] In an early essay, "A House of Theory," she traces this sense of the "impossibility" of metaphysics—which many regard as the most characteristic feature of philosophical reflection in the modern period—to the influence of Hume and Kant on modern British empiricism. Modern analytic philosophy, she asserts, "follows Hume and Kant in regarding sense experience as the only basis for knowledge, and it follows Kant in attempting more specifically to show that concepts not so based are 'empty.' "[6] Murdoch treats these historical figures as representing broad currents of thought in modern moral theory (noncognitivism and prescriptivism, respectively) rather than giving a highly nuanced account of their arguments.

Speaking first of Hume and of British moral philosophy generally, Murdoch writes, "We have always been empiricist, anti-metaphysical in philosophy, mistrustful of theoretical systems."[7] Murdoch takes Hume to be the source of the conservative tradition of what she calls "Tory scepticism" against metaphysical theorizing in British moral and political philosophy, which can be summed up in the dictum: "Don't theorize: let habit and tradition solve your problems."[8] For Hume, any sense of moral order that a civilized society possesses rests on the cultivation of certain moral instincts and habits of mind, rather than on values that are conceived to be inherent in the nature of things. Moral beliefs are all "equally irrational," but some are "inevitable and convenient" for the functioning of life in society.[9] "Hume, who wished to maintain as rigorously as possible that we know only what our senses tell us, denied the existence of moral 'facts' or 'realities,' analyzed moral concepts into non-rational feelings and imaginative habits, and was prepared to let basic empirical concepts suffer the same fate."[10]

Murdoch sees in Hume the root of what we now call "noncognitivism" in ethics—that is, the argument that ethical statements or propositions are not like other types of propositions, such as those of natural science.[11] Ethical propositions do not have any truth-value that can be verified in terms of the observation of sensible events. Precisely because they are ethical, in other words, such propositions are not fact-stating and thus can be neither true nor false. Hume's view is in this respect a direct predecessor of the influential view propounded by Wittgenstein in the *Tractatus*, and quoted frequently by Murdoch: "In the world everything is as it is and happens as it does happen. In it there is no value—and if there were it would be of no value. If there is a value which is of value, it must lie outside all happening and being-so. For all happening and being-so is accidental."[12] This view expresses what Murdoch regards as "the whole spirit of modern ethics," namely, the argument that "you cannot attach morality to the substance of the world."[13] If value cannot reside in the world of things, it must originate in the human will. Human beings alone are responsible for the values they hold. Since morality is something we create, it is always possible for us to question or revise our values, and to safeguard our autonomy from dogmatic forms of belief.[14]

Kant's elimination of metaphysics from the sphere of morality took on a somewhat different form than Hume's. If Hume's position on metaphysical theorizing falls into the category of "Tory scepticism," Kant's view exemplifies what Murdoch calls "scientific scepticism," which can be summarized in the dictum: "Don't theorize: empirical truths are unsystematic and moral truths can't be demonstrated; so be an undogmatic but rational respecter of persons."[15] Kant attempted more systematically than Hume "to show why our knowledge was limited to certain kinds of object, and in doing so pictured the mind as solely concerned with the objects of empirical observation and science."[16] While Kant accorded to certain beliefs the important status of "regulative ideals," he generally regarded all other metaphysical or religious beliefs as superstitions—that is, as unable to be defended save by the illegitimate trespass of reason beyond its bounds. Murdoch sees in Kant the source of later forms of "prescriptivism" in ethics, by which Kant's belief in Reason was converted into a formula "which purported to give the defining characteristics of any moral judgment as such,"[17] such as rationality, universality, and consistency. Thus philosophical method in ethics came to distinguish the *form* of morality from the actual *content* of moral beliefs, which was considered "a matter of personal decision and not a proper subject for analysis."[18]

The empiricist reduction of knowledge to what could be based on and tested by experience had devastating effects, in Murdoch's view, on that "variegated area of moral belief or ideology"[19] that had been the purview of traditional metaphysical ethics. This area was constituted by "the special religious and social concepts"[20] that previous moral philosophers took to be important guides to moral choice. Surprisingly, given her general discomfort with Hegel as a "romantic" thinker, Murdoch finds Hegel's critique of metaphysics more congenial to her own views than that of either Hume or Kant. Hegel, she believes, revised the Kantian critique in a fundamental way "when he conceived the categories as the forms not only of our knowledge of empirical objects, but also of our apprehension of social, psychological and spiritual realities, and subjected them to historical treatment."[21] Hegel affirmed that we may have real knowledge of "non-empirical" realities and, unlike both Hume and Kant, he "did not regard the fact that a belief or theory had rested upon a discredited type of philosophical argument as automatically denuding the theory of philosophical interest or even of truth."[22] On the contrary, Murdoch notes approvingly that Hegel "did not class theories as either whole truths or total errors, but allowed to all the influential beliefs that men have held the status of interpretation and discovery of the world."[23] This high philosophical regard for the knowledge-bearing aspect of human beliefs is what Murdoch particularly admires in Hegel, and is the feature of his position that most resembles her own. It is unfortunate, then, in her view, that modern British moral philosophy has taken its inspiration on this point not from Hegel, but from Hume and Kant. It is precisely this area of belief that is regarded by the later empiricist tradition as not subject to empirical test or observation, and thus as having no cognitive content.

This empiricist view finds its most radical expression in the verification principle of the logical positivists, which holds, as A. J. Ayer states it, that "the meaning of a statement is determined by the way in which it can be verified, where its being verified consists in its being tested by empirical observation. Consequently, statements like those of metaphysics to the truth or falsehood of which no empirical observation could possibly be relevant, are ruled out as factually meaningless."[24] Since metaphysical language has no factual content, the only use it can have is to express something nonfactual, such as the "attitudes" of the speaker.[25] Metaphysical beliefs thus come to be seen in analytic ethics as "personal evaluations and social recommendations disguised as truths about the nature of man."[26] Since such beliefs were not demonstrable by philosophical argument—and "it was the mistake of the old philosophers to think that they were"[27]—they came to be regarded "as the idiosyncratic 'color' of a moral attitude, something nebulous and hazy, which for purposes of exposition and example was best analyzed away into actual choices at the empirical level."[28] Moral beliefs are not regarded as genuine facts or discoveries of the world, on this analytic view, but can be reduced to emotivist "attitudes" that are ancillary to the essential subject matter of philosophy.[29] Therefore, it is the "logical and morally neutral" task of the modern analytic philosopher "to pierce this disguise, and to separate the solid recommendation from the conceptual mask which comes away, as it were, empty."[30]

The anti-metaphysical temper of modern analytic ethics can clearly be seen in the remarks of the Oxford philosopher Anthony Quinton, during a symposium on the subject of "Philosophy and Beliefs" with his Oxford colleagues Stuart Hampshire, Iris Murdoch, and Isaiah Berlin, published in 1955. I quote Quinton at some length as representative of the viewpoint that Murdoch is challenging:

> It appears to me that most of the strong feelings that have been generated about contemporary analytic philosophy—what its opponents delight in calling 'Logical Positivism'—arise from a confusion which is

common to both parties in the dispute. . . . What has taken place, it seems universally to be agreed, is the elimination of metaphysics. . . . And there is good reason for people to think this is the central point at issue. . . . The fact is that what analytic philosophers want to extrude from philosophy, and what their critics want to see put back into it, is *Weltanschauung*: recommendations of a moral, political and religious order. But both sides are labouring under a misapprehension. For *Weltanschauung* has never been the principal concern of those who would generally be agreed to be the greatest philosophers . . . [M]any philosophers securely in the great tradition—Plato, Spinoza, Kant—held attitudes to life, and gave public expression to them as appendages to or even parts of their philosophy. But these attitudes to life are not what gives these men their importance in the history of philosophy. . . . In the philosophy of the great tradition . . . the presentation of attitudes to life is either secondary or absent. But what they did discuss is still discussed by contemporary analytic philosophers—substance, universals, truth, the nature of logical and mathematical truths, our knowledge of the external world, the nature of mind, and the logical character of moral thinking.[31]

Quinton asserts that both the critics of analytic philosophy and its proponents are mistaken if they believe that modern analytic philosophy represents a fundamental departure from the traditional practice of philosophy. That is, he denies that there was ever a time in the history of philosophy when substantive religious, political, or moral conceptions of the world (what he calls "attitudes to life" and what Murdoch would consider metaphysical beliefs) were the central subject matter of philosophy. On Quinton's view, the idea of a "metaphysical ethic" is both historically inaccurate and conceptually confused. There has never, in his view, been a necessary connection between the so-called technical questions of philosophy—which he believes constitute the primary subject matter of "the great tradition"—and those vaguer and more subjective "attitudes to life" that are a purely contingent feature of a philosopher's work. The mistake of the metaphysical philosophers was precisely to believe that there was such a connection. He quotes with approval Ayer's view that " 'much of what appears as metaphysics involves the discussion of important points of logic,' "[32] and contends that what cannot be reduced to logic is therefore dispensable as a set of attitudes with no philosophical relevance. The elimination of metaphysics is to be welcomed, on this view, if it means the elimination of positive content from the domain of "logical" inquiry.

Murdoch's response to Quinton's views, which exemplify much of what she opposes in analytic philosophy generally, focuses on two central points of contention that will be elaborated more fully in the next section of this chapter. The first point is partly historical. Contrary to Quinton, she argues that linguistic philosophy does in fact represent a radical and unwelcome departure from previous philosophy, in which moral beliefs were not considered merely "attitudes," but fundamental cognitive discoveries of the world. This way of doing philosophy proceeded by means of the imaginative theorizing and creation of moral concepts that Quinton and others regard as illegitimate. The second point concerns what Murdoch regards as "the most important argument in modern moral philosophy—indeed it is almost the whole of modern moral philosophy," the argument against naturalism or the separation of facts and value. Quinton's belief in the logical independence of "philosophical doctrines" from "moral and political attitudes" exemplifies this idea. Murdoch rightly sees the rejection of metaphysics and the rejection of naturalism as two related arguments in the more general philosophical outlook of the linguistic analysts that she seeks to challenge. Therefore her defense of a metaphysical ethic must also contend with the so-called naturalistic fallacy.

I. B. The Retrieval of Metaphysics and the Debate over Naturalism

In defending metaphysics against the arguments of Quinton and others, Murdoch believed that she was simply following the lead of the great moral philosophers of the past. Thinkers such as Plato, for example, presented "a total metaphysical picture of which ethics forms a part. The universe, including our own nature, is like *this*, they say."[33] Such philosophers "invented concepts expressive of moral belief and presented them as if they were facts concerning the nature of the mind or of the world."[34] On this traditional or premodern view of metaphysics, no strict separation was made between the descriptive account of the nature of reality and human existence, and the evaluation of that reality. Moral beliefs, and the concepts used to express them, were regarded precisely as *facts about the world*, rather than separable judgments added on to a neutral description. Ethics, on this account, was not separable from a larger account of the real, but a constitutive part of it. Nor was metaphysics a purely "technical" philosophical description of the components of reality, as Quinton describes it, but a presentation of moral beliefs. As Paul Johnston remarks, "[W]e can see why ethics should have been such an intimate part of much past philosophy, for in expounding a conception of the universe (a picture of the world) one is also delineating an ethic."[35]

Stuart Hampshire makes essentially the same point about the coincidence of descriptive and evaluative aims in traditional metaphysics in an early essay on "Metaphysical Systems." He argues that metaphysics was traditionally motivated by a moral aspiration, such that the knowledge it yielded had the character of moral insight: "[T]o show the nature of reality was to show the place of man in nature, and therefore his proper duties and purposes; it was to show the way to his salvation, to the kind of knowledge that would set him free from his ordinary interests and preoccupations."[36] In other words, metaphysics was perceived to be a fundamentally *moral* inquiry into the nature of reality and human existence, and one whose aim was to transform or liberate the human agent by revealing the knowledge of his or her proper place in the scheme of things. Murdoch was in substantial agreement with this view. Both metaphysics and ethics share a common task: to produce a descriptive account of reality that will at the same time reveal the best life for human beings to be a life lived in conformity with that reality. With the loss of a total metaphysical picture of the world as the conceptual background to the study of ethics, she argues, "We have suffered a general loss of concepts, the loss of a moral and political vocabulary. We no longer use a spread-out substantial picture of the manifold virtues of man and society. We no longer see man against a background of values, of realities, which transcend him."[37]

At the heart of Murdoch's concern about the demise of metaphysical thinking is a deeper anthropological worry about the effect of this loss on our ability to theorize adequately about the reality of human beings. In other words, beneath the seemingly technical philosophical debate over the status of metaphysical thinking lies a more substantive debate over how we picture the human. The analytic rejection of metaphysics signals an attempt to produce a purely descriptive or ethically neutral study of morality that highlights certain features of the human such as choice, rationality, and freedom. Murdoch's attempt to defend a metaphysical ethic, in contrast, signals her intention to provide an explicitly normative account of the human agent against a background of values that transcend human choice.

The biggest obstacle to providing such an account is the argument against naturalism, which is already implicit in the analytical philosophers' attempt to separate description from evaluation in philosophical inquiry. In this respect, the anti-naturalistic argument poses a formidable challenge to the central presupposition of metaphysical ethics: that moral claims relate ineluctably to descriptive claims about reality. Consequently, Murdoch spends a great deal of energy in her early essays combating it, and her arguments have had far-reaching effects. The contemporary philosopher Cora Diamond notes that Murdoch was among the first to criticize two "virtually unquestionable" and closely related ideas held by analytic philosophers in the 1950s: "that it is a logical error to attempt to infer any evaluative conclusion from factual premises, and that there is a fundamental distinction between fact and value."[38] Diamond goes on to claim that "If analytical philosophy [today] no longer accepts as unquestionable the idea of a gap between fact and value, this has much to do with Iris Murdoch's earlier writings."[39] Given the philosophical impact of Murdoch's critique of the fact-value distinction as well as its centrality to her defense of metaphysics, her arguments deserve careful exposition.

Murdoch asserts that the argument against naturalism as it appears in modern analytic ethics is actually "a very finely knit complex of mutual supporting arguments"[40] that can be divided into several component parts.[41] As presented in her landmark essay "Vision and Choice in Morality," these components include the following: (1) an argument against the existence of metaphysical entities, in both a "strong" and a "weak" form; (2) a closely related argument about the meaning of moral terms in relation to nonmoral terms; (3) the use of these arguments to make the more narrowly logical point that "any argument which professes to move directly from fact to value contains a concealed evaluative major premiss" [sic]; [42] and (4) a moral argument of an essentially "liberal" type, which recommends: "don't be dogmatic, always reflect and argue, respect the attitudes of others."[43] By breaking the argument down into its constituent elements, Murdoch hopes to expose its flaws and diminish some of its force. "The total argument," she writes, "has sometimes been presented as if it were the exposure of a quasi-logical mistake; if we dismember it, however, we can see that only (3) has a strictly logical air. We can also more coolly decide which parts are acceptable and what it is able to prove."[44] In what follows I will examine each of these arguments in turn.

Murdoch distinguishes between a strong form of the anti-metaphysical argument, derived from the logical positivists, "which claims that all concepts of metaphysical entities are empty";[45] and a weak form, closer to Kant, which holds only that "the existence of such entities cannot be philosophically established."[46] She accepts the weak form of the anti-metaphysical argument to the effect that, for example, "there are no philosophical proofs of the existence of God, but it is not senseless to believe in God."[47] Some of the key moral conceptions of previous metaphysical ethics (such as God, or the rational will, or Plato's idea of the Good) are neither senseless nor useless, but simply "cannot be established by certain familiar types of philosophical argument."[48] Thus Murdoch supports the anti-metaphysical argument to the extent that it may legitimately be used to show that "moral beliefs were often supported by erroneous arguments."[49] In some cases, she concedes, "the philosopher in question is not able to establish, by the argument he uses, the structure that he describes."[50]

However, Murdoch rejects the stronger version of this argument, which holds that the critique of certain erroneous metaphysical arguments is enough *wholly* to discredit the use of metaphysical concepts in moral philosophy. The attempt by the linguistic analysts to eliminate metaphysics from ethics, she argues, "does not *ipso facto* 'discredit' the area of moral belief, properly understood as an area of conceptual moral exploration."[51] The linguistic analysts advance the strong thesis that metaphysical concepts are not only "nonverifiable" but also "empty," and therefore useless, by connecting their argument against metaphysics to an argument against deriving moral values from facts. In other words, they argue that even if there *were* philosophically established metaphysical entities, "we could not base an analysis of morality upon them since it is impossible to argue from *is* to *ought*, from facts to values."[52]

By embracing a weaker form of the argument against metaphysics, Murdoch was attempting to reserve an important use for metaphysical beliefs from the analytic critique as an "area of conceptual moral exploration," and to separate the argument about metaphysics from any subsequent argument about facts and values. The fate of metaphysical entities and beliefs should not in her view be determined, as the linguistic analysts would have it, by unexamined assumptions about the relation between facts and values. The arguments against metaphysics "only prove that we cannot picture morality as issuing directly from a *philosophically established* transcendent background, or from a factual background. But this is not yet to say that the notion of *belief* in the transcendent can have no place in a philosophical account of morality."[53] In sum, it does not follow that just because "we cannot establish transcendent metaphysical structures by philosophical argument then such structures cannot be the basis of ethics."[54]

Murdoch's defense of the "weak" form of the critique of metaphysics raises several questions that she leaves unaddressed. An obvious one, to my mind, is whether she is arguing for something like "the will to believe" or even a type of "philosophy of 'as if,'" where one persists in holding certain "unproven" beliefs because there is some compelling reason or benefit (existential, psychological, and so forth) to be derived from so doing. If Murdoch were making such an argument, however, it would seem directly to contradict her standing as a moral realist, since realism presumably requires a more robust defense of the "objective reality" (however construed) of metaphysical ideas and concepts than this apparently weak appeal to subjective "belief." A fuller consideration of this issue must be deferred until my discussion of Murdoch's realism later in this chapter and in Chapter 5. But some initial light on the problem might be shed by considering briefly where Murdoch's argument on metaphysics positions her in relation to Kant and the question of the moral use of metaphysical beliefs.

Murdoch sees her critique of metaphysics as essentially Kantian in its contention that the existence of entities such as God cannot be philosophically established, and thus cannot strictly speaking be objects of empirical knowledge. She insists, with Kant, that this critique neither wholly discredits the *belief* in metaphysical entities nor prevents the use of metaphysical ideas in moral philosophy. However, Kant conceived both a theoretical use for such concepts (i.e., as ideas which "regulate" our knowledge of empirical reality) and a practical use (i.e., as postulates which support the operation of moral reason). Murdoch, eschewing the theoretical-practical distinction, describes such beliefs as "ideal end-points" of moral knowledge. For example, she describes the idea of perfection in these terms throughout her philosophy, as well the idea of the good and the notion of reality itself. Such ideas are not postulated, in Kant's sense, nor are they ideals that regulate our experience of empirical reality; rather, they are concepts that guide moral perception on its pilgrimage toward the real. Murdoch's difference from Kant on this point reflects a deeper contrast in their views of the fundamental moral dilemma of human life: for Kant, the problem resides in the evil will; for Murdoch, it resides in the tendency of the ego to efface the reality of others. Accordingly, Murdoch follows Plato rather than Kant in her contention that the moral life represents a pilgrimage from appearance to reality, and that moral perception presupposes a fundamental *relation* between knowledge and morality that cuts across the theoretical-practical distinction. From this perspective, Murdoch's appeal to "belief" is less a form of intuitionism or a philosophy of "as if," as it is an attempt to save the epistemic and cognitive value of metaphysical beliefs by reaffirming the connection between morality and knowledge, or value and cognition.[55] Such a connection is at the very center of Murdoch's moral thought, and will emerge more clearly as we proceed.

We must turn now to the second and third components of the analytic argument against naturalism, which might be called the argument from meaning (2) and the logical argument (3), respectively. Murdoch's argument becomes particularly dense and concentrated concerning these points because she sees them as closely related but also as importantly different. Arguments about the relation of fact and value, she writes, "can be faulty either because they involve a definition of moral terms in non-moral terms (the case dealt with by (2)) or because they are elliptical (the case dealt with by (3)). These alleged mistakes are closely related but not identical."[56] Taking the latter case first, Murdoch states that the logical argument in its most familiar form is "designed merely to point out that a statement of value cannot be derived directly, and with no further help, from an ordinary statement of fact."[57] Or to put it more summarily: "To reach an imperative conclusion we need at least one imperative premise."[58] In other words, the naturalistic fallacy is targeted at arguments that depend on a suppressed evaluative premise to draw their conclusion. Murdoch's task in "Vision and Choice" is to see whether such arguments are indeed fallacious.[59]

Murdoch states outright that she accepts the logical argument against naturalism for certain limited purposes. She gives the following example to show why she thinks there is something valuable in the critique of suppressed premises:

Someone who says "Statistics show that people constantly do this, so it must be all right" . . . should have it pointed out that he is concealing the premiss [sic] "What is customary is right." He must also realise (it would be argued) that "What is customary is right" is a moral judgment freely endorsed by himself and not a definition of "right." The notion that "customary" defines "right" may be the psychological cause of, or the would-be reason for, the curtailing of the argument, but it is not the same thing as the curtailing of the argument. The man may publicise his premiss [sic], still insisting on the definition. In many cases, of course, the exposure of the premiss [sic] destroys the appeal of the argument, which may depend (as in the example above), on the hearer's imagining that he has got to accept the conclusion or deny the plain facts; and I would certainly want to endorse many arguments of [this] type whose purpose is solely to achieve such an exposure.[60]

In an illuminating discussion of this passage, Diamond argues that this example suggests important points of both agreement and disagreement between Murdoch and the analytic critics of naturalism. First, Murdoch agrees with the linguistic analysts "that an important kind of flaw in some arguments that proceed from fact to value is the suppression of premises."[61] In the above example, the premise "what is customary is right" is exposed as a concealed assumption that may invalidate a moral argument made on its basis. But where Murdoch and the analytic philosophers differ is in the *reasons* such an exposure is important. Murdoch agrees that once the premise "what is customary is right" has been exposed to view, the fallacious nature of the argument can be avoided only by supplying a further premise that justifies the evaluative conclusion. However, whereas "for the analytical philosophers, the need for the further premise is tied to the supposed existence of a logical gap between fact and value; for Murdoch, the need for the further premise and the point of exposing it are tied to a quite different conception of moral rationality."[62]

The model of moral rationality implicit in Murdoch's interpretation of this example is one that presses the question of concealed premises (i.e., "Are you not assuming that such-and-such?") not for reasons of abstract logic, but rather for reasons related to moral responsibility. As Diamond explains, "In Murdoch's account, what is the matter with suppressing a premise in a moral argument may be that the hearer of the argument will not grasp the possibilities open to him, will think that he is forced to the conclusion by undeniable facts."[63] As Murdoch puts it above, the compelling appeal of an argument based on suppressed evaluative premises may derive from the idea that one "has got to accept the conclusion or deny the plain facts." Many of us, Diamond notes, are tempted to use arguments of precisely this type "when we justify to ourselves things which we want to do but which we cannot clearly square with conscience."[64] We may, for example, rationalize a course of action by telling ourselves that "the thing we are tempted to do is all right because generally done" (i.e., "what is customary is right"). "What is going on in such cases may be a kind of evasion, a kind of refusal to take responsibility."[65] Diamond's point is that, while Murdoch does not dispute that naturalism is indeed a fallacy in cases where a premise is being suppressed, and that the exposure of such a premise is philosophically useful and legitimate, her reasons for valuing such an exposure are moral rather than strictly logical. This suggests a radically different conception of moral rationality than that of the analytical philosophers.

The issue of moral rationality emerges more clearly when we turn to the argument from meaning (component (2) above), which Murdoch considers "closely related but not identical" to the suppression of premises component. The argument from meaning holds that moral terms cannot be derived from nonmoral (i.e., empirical) terms. This reproduces the logical prohibition against deriving values from facts at the level of moral language. Empirical terms are considered "factual" in a sense that is open to all observers, while moral terms are understood to express an agent's *evaluation* of the facts, which is a function of the agent's own choice of criteria for what is valuable. As Diamond explains, "Presented with the facts, a moral agent can describe them in non-moral words, and express his commitment to an evaluative principle, or evaluative framework, through his own choice of criteria for the use of such [moral] terms as 'good.' "[66]

However, the reason moral terms cannot be derived from nonmoral or empirical terms has nothing to do, according to Murdoch, with the logic of suppressed premises noted earlier. In this sense it is not a strictly logical matter. Rather it arises from the need of the linguistic analysts to guarantee a particular view of morality and moral freedom. "Why can moral terms not be defined in non-moral terms?" Murdoch asks; "the answer to this question is given by the world picture which goes with the current [analytic] view, and whose purpose at this point is to safeguard a certain conception of freedom."[67] The analytic view of moral language, in other words, is part of a cluster of assumptions that portrays the moral life of the individual as "a series of overt choices which take place in a series of specifiable situations."[68] Moral judgments are made on the assumption that all agents apprehend the same objective world of facts, and therefore that valid moral reasons are reasons that would objectively specify the situation "in terms of facts available to disinterested scrutiny."[69] This assumption provides the warrant for the analytic claim about the universalizability of moral judgments. Since there exists an empirical world of objective facts available to each of us, any agent can come up with reasons that will be valid "for all others placed as he."[70] Moral differences amount to differences in the choice of criteria for what an agent regards as "good" or "right," rather than differences in one's initial vision of the facts themselves. In short, this view of moral language guarantees that values are a function of what the agent *chooses*, rather than a function of his or her initial understanding and interpretation of the facts.

Murdoch's critique of these assumptions amounts to a wholesale reinterpretation of the notion of "moral fact." She does not, of course, wish to quarrel with the view that "moral arguments may proceed by appeal to facts,"[71] or that a scrutiny of the facts is the appropriate place to begin in moral reflection. Nor, as Diamond notes, is Murdoch denying "that there are situations in which some view of the facts can be agreed on by every-one."[72] What Murdoch *is* arguing for is a radically different understanding of how "facts" are related to moral concepts. The analytic argument defines moral concepts as "factual specification plus recommendation."[73] What this definition overlooks is that any argument about the facts "take[s] place within a moral attitude where some sovereign concept decides the rele-vance of the facts and may, indeed, render them observable."[74] Moral con-cepts are not merely a function of what an agent chooses to regard as valuable; they are, more deeply, a function of the agent's moral being, the texture of his or her personal vision or consciousness. Morality is bound up with our deepest conceptual attitudes and sensibilities about the world, which determine the facts from the very beginning. "We differ not only because we select different objects out of the same world," Murdoch writes, "but because we see different worlds."[75]

This view of moral concepts dramatically recasts the initial problem of the relation between facts and values. On Murdoch's view of the matter, "the prohibition on defining value in terms of fact loses much of its point,"[76] since there are no longer perceived to be any neutral facts "be-hind" the values from which they can be improperly derived.[77] Or to put the point linguistically, there are no pure empirical facts available to all rational agents apart from moral concepts. Moral concepts, in other words, are not mere attitudes about the facts, but are a way of apprehending the facts rooted in a moral vision. They are not reducible to "lines drawn round separable factual areas,"[78] but are "more like a total difference of *Gestalt*."[79] Differences in moral concept, then, will indicate not only a change in one's evaluation of the facts but also a change in the very perception of what counts as "fact." It follows from this that moral concepts are not limited to the primary words "good" and "right," but must include a much wider range of secondary moral words or "specialized concepts" that communi-cate an agent's inner life. Once this conclusion is reached, the idea of the agent's freedom changes accordingly. Freedom no longer consists "in being able to lift the concept off the otherwise unaltered facts and lay it down elsewhere, but in being able to 'deepen' or 'reorganize' the concept or change it for another one."[80] On this view, freedom appears less as a matter of choice and looks more like "a mode of reflection which we may have to achieve"[81] through an attention to the moral being of ourselves and others.

Thus far, we have considered Murdoch's critique of the first three com-ponents of the linguistic analysts' argument against naturalism: the ar-gument against metaphysical entities, the logical argument about sup-pressed premises, and the argument about the meaning of moral terms in relation to nonmoral terms. The fourth component of the argument, which might be referred to as the "liberal" argument, is already implicit in Mur-doch's critique of the third component, since it involves an argument "in-volving an appeal to our experience of morality, which support[s] the various details of the analysis—the notion of choice, arguing, referring to facts, judging a man by his conduct, and so on."[82] Murdoch contends that what some analytic philosophers claim to be arguing on purely philosophical or logical grounds must be interpreted, at least in part, to be their own version of what morality is like, based on their own particular experience of morality.

> [M]odern philosophers have tended to take their stripped, behavioristic and non-conceptual picture of morality as the only possible picture because they have joined the anti-metaphysical argument and the logical argument to a *moral* argument of a different type—a moral argument which properly belongs in the propaganda of liberalism.[83]

Behind both the argument against metaphysical entities and the argument against the derivation of values from facts lie the moral assumptions of liberal morality.[84] In fact, "much of the impetus of the argument against naturalism comes from its connection with, and its tendency to safeguard, a Liberal evaluation."[85]

At the core of Murdoch's argument is her claim that in spite of what they profess, the linguistic analysts do not themselves escape their own type of "naturalistic fallacy." That is, their own supposedly neutral analysis of morality contains suppressed *moral* assumptions. If our own liberal ideals confirm the dominant view of morality held by the linguistic analysts, it is because the analytic view is in fact *derived* from liberal premises:

> We, in our society, believe in judging a man's principles by his conduct, in reflecting upon our own values and respecting the values of others, in backing up our recommendations by reference to facts, in breaking down intuitive conclusions by argument, and so on. Our morality is, on the whole, conceptually simple. We approach the world armed with certain general values which we hold *simpliciter* and without the assistance of metaphysics or dogmatic theology—respect for freedom, for truth, and so on. We study the facts, and we make our choices in the light of the facts and our values. Our disagreements among ourselves concern the application of principles—our disagreements with other societies concern what principles to hold.[86]

The linguistic analysts believe they have articulated a neutral model of what any morality must be like because "the key concepts of our general social morality . . . have become practically unconscious and are taken for granted."[87] But the view presented by the analytic philosophers is not a universally applicable model of any morality whatsoever, but rather only "a satisfactory presentation of the morality most commonly held in England."[88]

The analytic argument against naturalism is thus neither a purely philosophical nor a purely logical matter. Rather it is motivated, in part, by an essentially liberal claim that morality has its source in the human agent, and not in some metaphysical framework or transcendent state of affairs. The analytic view reflects the liberal assumption that morality "should be flexible and argumentative, centred upon the individual, and that no alleged transcendent metaphysical realities, such as God, or History, or the Church, should be allowed to overshadow the moral life."[89] This description, which the analysts elevate to the level of a universal definition of morality, rules out those types of morality that emphasize quite different aspects of moral and human experience than those affirmed by liberal values. To illustrate this point, Murdoch contrasts two types of moral view:

> There are people whose fundamental moral belief is that we all live in the same empirical and rationally comprehensible world and that morality is the adoption of universal and openly defensible rules of conduct. There are other people whose fundamental belief is that we live in a world whose mystery transcends us and that morality is the exploration of that mystery in so far as it concerns each individual. It is only by sharpening the universality model to a point of extreme abstraction that it can be made to cover both views.[90]

Analytic philosophers fall into the first category, but this represents simply one version of morality among others. The second category of views is held by those "whose morality is not conceptually simple, but metaphysical and dogmatic."[91] These include "types of moral attitude in other ways very dissimilar; certain idealist views, certain existentialist views, certain Catholic views,"[92] as well as "Communist" or Marxist views.[93] Murdoch argues for the inclusion of these minority views in moral philosophy precisely by exposing the liberal bias of the linguistic analysts' arguments.

The conclusion that Murdoch draws from this analysis is that, since the linguistic analysts cannot claim that their conception of morality is universal on purely logical or philosophical grounds, their argument does not constitute a definitive refutation of naturalism, only a moral view that disagrees with naturalism. Far from refuting naturalism, the analytic view "merely summarises a non-naturalistic moral attitude."[94] Naturalism is not a philosophical error or a logical fallacy, but is rather "a different system of concepts"[95] that cannot be made to fit the analytic model of morality as a matter of choice and argument. Thus Murdoch reinterprets "naturalism" as a positive moral view that provides an alternative and a challenge to the analytic view of morality and moral reflection. Whereas the Liberal moralist "sees the agent as central, solitary, responsible, displaying his values in his selection of acts and attitudes," the true naturalist "(the Marxist, for instance, or certain kinds of Christian) is one who believes that as moral beings we are immersed in a reality which transcends us and that moral progress consists in awareness of this reality and submission to its purposes."[96]

The incisiveness of Murdoch's critique of analytic philosophy should not be underestimated. As Diamond comments, Murdoch was attempting

> to articulate a *totally different kind of contrast* between approaches to morality . . . She had tried to show that a view of *what we are as moral agents* could itself be a moral view; and that a view of *what the world is like* could be a moral view. . . . The issue, as framed by Murdoch, concerned the very idea of a mode of understanding of the world as *itself* a kind of moral belief.[97]

Murdoch took precise aim at what at the time were the cornerstones of analytic philosophy: its assumptions of ethical neutrality and universality. Murdoch's rather bold position was that "the supposed ethical neutrality of moral philosophy is illusory. She does not use the word 'ideological,' but her argument could be said to show the ideological character of moral philosophy: It works to exclude certain moral conceptions which it makes appear as logical confusions, discoverable to be confusion by neutral analysis."[98] Murdoch showed that the analytic model of morality is not neutral but is itself a substantive moral conception based on liberal premises. As a result, the anti-naturalistic argument appears at least in part as a disguise for a substantive moral view based on "liberal-scientific assumptions." Murdoch's exposure of these assumptions makes it possible to include alternative moral (and religious) views in the study of ethics, as well as the data of the inner life associated with differences in moral vision, belief, and concept which previously had been excluded from moral philosophy.

The remainder of this chapter will assess the constructive implications of Murdoch's retrieval of metaphysics and her critique of the anti-naturalistic argument for three central features of her ethics: the method of her moral philosophy (Section I.C), her conception of the human agent in relation to a metaphysical framework (Section II), and her defense of moral realism (Section III).

I. C. Picturing the Human: Theory, Language, and the Method of Moral Philosophy

Murdoch's critique of the anti-metaphysical and anti-naturalistic arguments raised some powerful objections to the underlying philosophical method of analytic philosophy. The question must now be raised of how to characterize Murdoch's own philosophical method. Given her argument for the inclusion of metaphysical beliefs in ethical inquiry, her critique of the descriptive-evaluative distinction, and her understanding of moral concepts as having a "shaping role" in our thought,[99] what sort of philosophical method does she herself defend as appropriate?

In order to answer this question, we need to return to the deeper anthropological concerns underlying Murdoch's critique of analytic ethics. The elimination of metaphysics and the critique of naturalism are problematic for her because they diminish moral philosophy's ability to picture the complex reality of human beings. This concern emerged forcefully in Murdoch's exposure of the disguised liberal premises of linguistic analysis, which (under the cover of ethical neutrality) promoted a particular view of moral rationality, freedom, and agency in its very procedures, while excluding other models of morality and agency as dogmatic and nonuniversal. This constriction of morality to a single model is the primary target of Murdoch's own philosophical method. "Philosophers have been misled," she writes,

> not only by a rationalistic desire for unity, but also by certain simplified and generalised moral attitudes current in our society, into seeking a single philosophical definition of morality. If, however, we go back again to the data we see that there are fundamentally different moral pictures which different individuals use or which the same individual may use at different times. Why should philosophy be less various, where the differences in what it attempts to analyse are so important?[100]

Murdoch's own procedure offers an expanded definition of the phenomena of human moral experience that can be included in the study of ethics. These phenomena are no longer restricted to those operations of moral rationality related to choice and action; they can now include what Murdoch calls the "texture" of a person's being or "their total vision of life."[101] This is displayed not only in people's explicit choices, evaluations, and modes of conduct, but more subtlely, "in their mode of speech or silence, their choice of words, their assessments of others, their conception of their own lives, what they think attractive or praise-worthy, what they think funny: in short, the configurations of their thought which show continually in their reactions and conversation."[102]

A philosophical method that includes such phenomena in its analysis will not pretend or even aspire to be ethically neutral; rather it will be one that self-consciously embraces the shaping, figurative role of consciousness and language in our construals of the world. Its motivation, unlike the disguised neutrality of linguistic analysis but similar to the metaphysical ethics of the past, is avowedly normative. "I think it would be a pity," Murdoch writes, "if just because we realize that any picture [of morality] is likely to be half a description and half a persuasion, we were to deny ourselves the freedom in the making of pictures and the coining of explanatory ideas which our predecessors have used in the past."[103] Moral philosophy should attempt to find "a satisfactory method for the explanation of our morality and that of others"[104] by inventing "new and persuasive concepts in the course of offering a description"[105] of human moral existence.

The centrality of moral concepts to Murdoch's thought suggests that her philosophical method will be deeply "linguistic," but in a way that differs considerably from linguistic analysis. As noted earlier, moral concepts are for Murdoch not merely specifications of the facts combined with recommendations arising from the agent's preferences or choice of value criteria. Rather, they represent a particular apprehension or grasp of the facts according to the moral vision of the agent. As Diamond puts it, "fundamental moral differences . . . are [for Murdoch] frequently or indeed usually conceptual differences."[106] This understanding of moral concepts provides the basis for Murdoch's discussion of "what sort of philosophical method should now be used in the study of morals and politics."[107] Rather than abandoning the so-called linguistic method, Murdoch in fact takes moral language and the creation of moral concepts with deep seriousness.

> [T]he notion that moral differences are conceptual (in the sense of being differences of vision) and must be studied as such is unpopular in so far as it makes impossible the reduction of ethics to logic, since it suggests that morality must, to some extent at any rate, be studied historically. This does not of course imply abandoning the linguistic method, it rather implies taking it seriously.[108]

Taking the linguistic method seriously means more than simply engaging in an analysis of the concept "good," which had been at the center of modern analytic ethics since G. E. Moore. Moore was the source of the prohibition against defining moral terms in nonmoral terms in the first place, in his insistence that "good" is a kind of movable label or "nonnatural property" that can be affixed to any state of affairs the agent chooses. After Moore, the kind of descriptive or speculative discussion that was once considered the essence of metaphysical morality gives way to a concentration on act and choice.[109] "Moral language is taken as closely related to choice—that it recommends to action is its defining characteristic—and all this can then be offered as an analysis of the meaning of the word 'good'. 'This is good' equals 'choose this.' "[110]

The problem with Moore's view is that morality is not just a matter of choice and action; it also a matter of thought and perception. "How we see and describe the world is morals too," Murdoch writes, "and the relation of this to our conduct may be complicated.[111] By reducing morality to the analysis of choice-guiding words such as "good," the linguistic analysts cannot do justice to what Murdoch calls the conceptual *background* of our choices—that area of speculation, daydreaming, personal stories, and fables about ourselves that precede and inform our choices and actions. By ignoring this inner region of human moral being, the linguistic method ignores precisely what Murdoch believes should be its primary object, namely, the subtleties and complexities of the full range of moral concepts used by individual agents:

> There are situations which are obscure and people who are incomprehensible, and the moral agent . . . may find himself unable to describe something which in some sense he apprehends. Language has limitations and there are moments when, if it is to serve us, it has to be used creatively, and the effort may fail. When we consider here the role of language in illuminating situations, how insufficient seems the notion of linguistic moral philosophy as the elaboration of the evaluative-descriptive formula. From here we may see that the task of moral philosophers has been to extend, as poets may extend, the limits of the language, and enable it to illuminate regions of reality which were formerly dark.[112]

This creative and extended use of moral concepts necessarily includes not only "good" but also those secondary moral terms that we commonly use to describe our own being and that of others (e.g., brave, funny, pessimistic, vulnerable, arrogant, open-minded, manipulative, and so forth). "It is in terms of the inner complexity of such concepts that we may display really deep differences of moral vision."[113]

In sum, Murdoch agrees with the linguistic analysts that an important task of moral philosophy is "the analysis of contemporary moral concepts, through moral language."[114] Where she differs from them is in her suggestion that this task has been "too narrowly conceived."[115] The single-minded focus on the concept of "good," together with the impulse to reduce morality to a universal formula, has resulted in a certain myopia in ethics: "We have not considered the great *variety* of the concepts that make up a morality."[116] Taking the linguistic method seriously means abandoning the search for universal formula and entering "the cloudy and shifting domain of the concepts which men live by."[117] These concepts, like the beings who produced them, rarely have the clarity or certainty of logic and are subject to historical change.

Murdoch articulates the central concern motivating her philosophical method in a passage that could well serve as an epigram of her thought as a whole:

> The difficulty is, and here we are after all not so very far from the philosophers of the past, that the subject of investigation is the nature of man—and we are studying this nature at a point of great conceptual sensibility. Man is a creature who makes pictures of himself and then comes to resemble the picture. This is the process which moral philosophy must attempt to describe and analyse.[118]

This statement articulates the crucial assumption underlying Murdoch's conception of both the method and substance of ethics: ethics is properly the study of human beings in the process of moral transformation. Because human beings are the peculiar beings they are, creatures who "make pictures of themselves and come to resemble the picture," ethics cannot be a science on the model of the natural sciences, or proceed solely by the canons of deductive logic: "it is not possible in principle to translate propositions about men making decisions and formulating viewpoints into the neutral languages of natural science."[119] Rather, the method of moral philosophy must take into account the peculiar capacity of human beings to reflect on themselves, to imagine who they are and who they might become by forming and revising their ideas about themselves in accordance with certain strong evaluations. As Charles Taylor puts this point, human beings are "self-interpreting animals,"[120] and both Taylor and Murdoch would agree that modern ethical thought has ignored this fact in adopting some of the assumptions and aspirations of natural science.

Murdoch's appeal to metaphysics in the context of describing the method of ethics is thus intended to complicate and deepen our apprehension of the complexity and variety of human moral existence, rather than to provide a universal formula for morality. In this respect metaphysics—like nearly everything in Murdoch's philosophy—is an instrument of her concern to provide an adequately realistic portrayal of human individuals. This is important to Murdoch not simply for philosophical reasons but also for moral and political ones. As the form of philosophical discourse that studies the real, metaphysics must, in her view, seek to represent the unique value of individuals in order to prevent their disappearance into totalizing systems of thought.[121] Given this concern for the reality and value of the individual, the next question we must pose is how Murdoch pictures the individual in relation to the metaphysical framework she is defending. Having contested the analytic arguments against both metaphysics and naturalism, Murdoch is able to conceive ethics as part of a larger substantive account of reality and human existence, and to conceive the self not merely as a choosing agent but also as a being with mysterious inward depths who finds itself encompassed by a moral world. Murdoch's attempt to picture the self within such a framework provides the formal condition for her challenge to the subjectivism of analytic and existentialist ethics by establishing the context within which an objective or realist understanding of the good can be articulated.

Section II. Situating the Self: Metaphysics and the Individual

The central question posed by Murdoch's retrieval of metaphysics is the following: "Is morality to be seen as essentially and by its nature centred on the individual, or as part of a general framework of reality which includes the individual?"[122] This is the context in which she poses the question of the individual in relation to the source of morality. The empiricist tradition, as discussed earlier, had taken it for granted that morality is not dependent on any kind of metaphysical framework or background, but must be completely self-contained.[123] Moral values are not conceived as having their source in any framework independent of the human will. The linguistic analysts remain within this general empiricist tradition in their refusal to picture morality as part of a more systematic metaphysical account of the nature of reality. Indeed, both the anti-metaphysical and the anti-naturalistic arguments of the linguistic analysts *preclude* thinking of morality as part of such a framework or as issuing from some kind of metaphysical background. By contesting both of these arguments, Murdoch provides the philosophical opening for picturing morality as part of "a general framework of reality which includes the individual." Her rebuttal of the anti-metaphysical and anti-naturalistic arguments leads her to conclude that "in answering the question concerning whether morality is to be centred on the individual, we have been influenced partly by our own [liberal] moral outlook and partly by our philosophical empiricism into assuming that it is of the *essence* of morality to be centred in this way."[124] In exposing the assumptions underlying this claim, Murdoch demonstrates that there may be valid alternative moral outlooks that conceive a different locus for morality.

In order to make this point, Murdoch distinguishes between two types of morality: the Liberal view, which is in effect a distillation of the analytic view that morality is centered in the self (a view shared and amplified by existentialism, as we will see in Chapter 4); and the Natural Law view, which includes "Thomists, Hegelians, Marxists—and less reflective persons who are camp followers of these doctrines."[125] The contrast between the Liberal view and the Natural Law view is a key descriptive contrast in Murdoch's thought that will function as a constant reference point in the chapters that follow. These function as ideal types that contrast two different views of the relation between moral agency and a metaphysical framework.

The central difference between the Liberal view and the Natural Law view concerns the way in which the self is pictured in relation to the locus of morality. On the Natural Law view,

> The individual is seen as held in a framework which transcends him, where what is important and valuable is the framework, and the individual only has importance, or even reality, in so far as he belongs to the framework. . . . Here the individual is seen as moving tentatively *vis-à-vis* a reality which transcends him. To discover what is morally good is to discover that reality, and to become good is to integrate himself with it.[126]

For the Natural Law moralist, morality is a matter of conforming oneself to a framework that is the source not only of moral value but also of the agent's identity: the individual only has importance *or even reality*, Murdoch says, insofar as he or she belongs to the framework. For the Natural Law moralist, "there is no axiom of discontinuity"[127] between the moral agent and the framework around him or her. Morality is not a matter of choice, but of conforming oneself to a larger whole whose value does not depend on the imputation of value by the agent.

From the Liberal point of view, on the other hand, the freedom and identity of the moral agent always remain "over against" any structure that encompasses him or her. Morality is a matter of the freedom to choose one's values, rather than acknowledging that the source of values may lie outside oneself. Thus for the Liberal, no matter how "grandiose the structure may be in terms of which a morality extends itself, the moral agent is responsible for endowing this totality with value."[128] Liberal morality thus has its source in the individual autonomous agent, who creates value by his or her choices. Morality is located precisely at the "*point of discontinuity* between the chosen framework and the choosing agent,"[129] and thus in the activity of choice itself.

The positing of an essential continuity between the moral agent and the framework on the Natural Law view brings out an important consequence of this view for moral agency. Just as the Natural Law view extends the field of the moral outward, beyond a narrow concern with the agent and the agent's choices toward a larger framework, so it also extends the domain of moral inquiry inward, toward the unseen background of our actions in human thought and feeling. Natural Law morality has as its corollary a conception of the self as a being with mysterious inward depths that are irreducible to its outward acts and choices. These depths reflect the mysteriousness of the reality outside the agent in which he or she is immersed. Murdoch describes the agent on the Natural Law model as "ruled by laws which he can only partly understand. He is not fully conscious of what he is. His freedom is not an open freedom of choice in a clear situation; it lies rather in an increasing knowledge of his own real being, and in the conduct which naturally springs from such knowledge."[130] This view contrasts strikingly with the Liberal picture of the agent as "able to attain by reflection to complete consciousness of his situation," and as "entirely free to choose and responsible for his choice."[131] Liberal morality is in fact virtually reducible to the agent's choice, "whereby he shows which things he regards as valuable."[132] Implicit in the distinction between Liberal morality and Natural Law morality, then, is a correlative distinction between the public or outward nature of morality and moral subjectivity on the former model and the relative inwardness, privacy, and even mysteriousness of moral subjectivity on the latter.

In sum, Murdoch's articulation of a metaphysical framework shifts the locus of value from the solitary value-creating agent to the framework itself as the source of objective moral claims. In this respect, Murdoch's description of the Natural Law model represents the precondition for her challenge to the subjectivistic voluntarism of analytic and existentialist ethics. Without a conception of morality that can acknowledge the moral significance of the world outside the self, she believes, there appears to be no way to keep moral claims from collapsing into the human will. However, we have not yet addressed the question of the norm that is to guide moral agency within such a framework.

I begin to answer this question in Section III by introducing the subject of moral realism and the idea of the good in Murdoch's philosophy. My discussion will be metaethical, focusing on the good as the formal norm of Murdoch's ethical system, and reserving a full discussion of the content of this norm until Chapter 5.

Section III. A. Metaphysical Realism and Cognitivism in Ethics

"Morality, goodness, is a form of realism."[133] This forthright assertion of Murdoch's metaethical position in *The Sovereignty of Good* can be understood in two senses. First, it is a substantive claim about the proper *content* of the moral norm. Morality involves the struggle against selfish illusion or personal fantasy, "the tissue of self-aggrandizing and consoling wishes and dreams which prevents one from seeing what is there outside one," especially "the existence of other people and their claims."[134] Goodness is the remedy to egoism in the form of attention to the needs of others and to the real world beyond the self. In a second, formal sense, the assertion that morality is a form of realism is a claim about the objective *structure* of morality. The moral norm "cannot be reduced to psychological or any other set of empirical terms";[135] rather it is connected to ideas such as truth, perfection, certainty, and necessary existence. The good does not denote any particular value in this sense, but represents the condition for human valuing, the framework or context within which human beings pursue any good whatsoever. This formal aspect of Murdoch's realism will be my concern in this section. I begin by situating Murdoch's realism in the context of analytic ethics and its prevailing metaethical theory, noncognitivism. This highlights what is at stake in her attempt to defend a cognitivist metaethic as the justificatory background for her moral realism.

Murdoch's attempt to rescue the concept of goodness and to underscore its relation to the concepts of truth and knowledge is a direct response to what she regards as the reduction and impoverishment of the concept of the good in the hands of the linguistic analysts. "The concept of 'goodness', for reasons which it would be interesting to investigate, is no longer a rich and problematic concept. Whereas the concept of 'truth', for instance, contains tangles and paradoxes the unravelling of which would show us really interesting features of the modern world."[136]

The notion of the good has lost its richness, Murdoch believes, because it has come to be perceived as a function of human choice and will rather than as an object of knowledge, desire, and love. The good is no longer conceived metaphysically as "attached to the substance of the world" or as a value which we discover in the world. Rather, the good has become "a mere value tag of the choosing will"[137] or "an empty box into which we put whatever takes our fancy."[138] By conceiving goodness in terms of reality or truth, Murdoch hopes to retrieve some of the richness and complexity it possessed before Moore made his definitive break with metaphysical ethics. Goodness is indefinable not for reasons connected with human freedom and choice, as Moore and his successors argued, but rather because understanding goodness partakes of "the infinite difficulty of the task of apprehending a magnetic but inexhaustible reality."[139]

In pointing out the disjunction between questions of truth and questions of goodness (that is, between knowledge and morality) in analytic ethics, Murdoch identified a distinguishing feature of non-cognitivism. Many contemporary realist theories of the good, including Murdoch's, can be interpreted as a critical response to non-cognitivism. As the name implies, non-cognitivism is the view that moral terms and propositions are not knowledge-bearing, and thus answerable to the norm of truth, but rather express some subjective disposition, preference, or affect of the agent. As Sabina Lovibond puts it, non-cognitivism holds that "there is no truth about values, whether in morals, politics or art."[140] Its central claim is that

> there is no such thing as moral cognition or knowledge. The reason there is no moral knowledge, according to this view, is that knowledge logically requires a real object set over against the knowing subject: but there is no objective moral reality; consequently, as far as morals are concerned, there is nothing to know.
>
> An alternative way of stating the non-cognitivist position is in terms of answerability to truth. Moral judgements, it is claimed, lack truth-status—they are not the sort of utterance which can be true or false—because there is nothing in the world which *makes* them true, in the way that the physical condition of the world makes remarks about material objects true.[141]

As this passage makes clear, the crucial underpinning of non-cognitivism is the distinction between fact and value, which rests on an understanding of truth and verification drawn from the empirical sciences. "[T]he only objectively real entities, qualities or relations are those referred to in natural-scientific discourse, or in other kinds of discourse reducible thereto."[142] There can be no truth about values, in other words, because the truth of judgments of value cannot be demonstrated with reference to facts in the empirical world as studied by the natural sciences. Facts are the only things which are perceived to have "impersonal validity,"[143] while values become "something of which individuals are the ultimate arbiters."[144] Moral judgments are not warranted "by the actual obtaining of a certain state of affairs which they declare to obtain, but by some phenomenon which, pending a better use for the word, can be called 'subjective'," such as personal desires, attitudes, or decisions.[145] Non-cognitivism thus relegates judgments of value to the status of subjective affects and dispositions, rather than considering them as cognitive claims that are responsive to the critical norms of truth and validity.

As we saw earlier, Murdoch rejects both the fact-value distinction and the reduction of ethics to empiricism which underlie this distinction. Against the view that moral judgments lack truth-status, she insists that human beliefs and judgments of value—aesthetic, moral, religious, or otherwise—are not merely "opinions" or subjective exclamations, but fundamental modes of knowledge and explanation which refer meaningfully to the world. They are not, in other words, merely a function of the agent's preferences, reactions, or choices, but are genuine "discoveries" of the world with cognitive value. This point is central to Murdoch's realist challenge to subjectivism. Both Murdoch and Lovibond agree that the subjectivism of analytic ethics is a direct consequence of its most essential feature—namely, its *voluntarism*. For Lovibond, voluntarism might even be regarded "as the crux of the non-cognitivist theory of ethics."[146] On the empiricist assumptions of this view of ethics, morality cannot be a matter of knowledge, so it must be a function of the will. Value "does not belong inside the world of truth functions, the world of science, and factual propositions. So it must live somewhere else. It is then attached somehow to the human will, a shadow clinging to a shadow."[147] Value has only a contingent existence; it is a mere "shadow" with no objective reality apart from the will, which creates value through its choices. The result, Murdoch believes, is "the sort of dreary moral solipsism which so many so-called books on ethics purvey."[148] As long as value claims are conceived as a function of the will and detached from our knowledge of the real, there will be no way to avoid subjectivism about the good.

By conceiving the idea of goodness as connected primarily with questions of truth and knowledge rather than the will, Murdoch shifts the ground of the theory of the good from the voluntarism of analytic ethics to a cognitivist conception influenced by a Platonic understanding of the good. This shift is significant because it indicates an attempt to link moral claims to a standard that is objective to the agent, rather than tied to the agent's preferences. Value concepts, precisely because they are a function of the agent's knowledge, "are not moving about on their own as adjuncts of the personal will"; rather, they are "patently tied on to the world, they are stretched as it were between the truth-seeking mind and the world."[149] This is preeminently the case with the concept of the good, which Murdoch locates in the reflexive "space" that exists between the truth-seeking mind and the world. Goodness unites value and cognition in the evaluative activity of consciousness.

III. B. Introduction to the Idea of the Good

Murdoch's main constructive discussions of the concept of the good occur in texts that take religion—or more accurately, the relation between religion and morality—as their primary subject matter. These include her famous essay "On 'God' and 'Good'" from *The Sovereignty of Good*; her second Platonic dialogue in *Acastos* titled "Above the Gods: A Dialogue About Religion"; and her interpretation of the ontological proof of Anselm in *Metaphysics as a Guide to Morals*. Because of its complexity and length, I have reserved a discussion of the latter text for Chapter 5.

The religious context of Murdoch's arguments about the good is significant for at least two reasons. First, it represents a direct challenge to analytic philosophy's relegation of religion to the realm of unproven metaphysics. By defending metaphysical concepts against the verificationism of linguistic empiricism, Murdoch thereby provided grounds for defending the cognitive status of religious concepts and beliefs from the same critique. Second, Murdoch often acknowledged that philosophy and religion traditionally shared a common goal, the defeat of the ego by fostering techniques to overcome selfishness and to enlarge one's perception of reality and others. Her suggestion that religion and morality might be closely related in their conception of the moral life as a pilgrimage from appearance to reality was intended to thwart the analytic claim of moral neutrality and to reassert the task of moral philosophy as "an attempt to make us morally better."

More strategically, Murdoch uses religious concepts and arguments as the nearest and perhaps most familiar paradigm for what an "objective" morality might look like, one that acknowledges a standard of value that resists collapse into "the selfish empirical consciousness."[150] Her realism is thus marked by the attempt to construct arguments about the good that are analogous, in some measure, to those used to defend a religious construal of an objective moral norm. In "On 'God' and 'Good,'" for example, she argues that moral philosophy "should attempt to retain a central concept which has all [the] characteristics" traditionally associated with God.[151] The most appropriate proof for such a concept would be some form of the ontological argument, which proceeds by showing that the nonexistence of God (or Good) is impossible, that it *cannot not* exist. In "Above the Gods: A Dialogue about Religion," Murdoch makes the similar argument that the Good, like God, is "about what's *absolute*, what *can't* not be there. If we conceive it at all we see that it must be real."[152] These arguments are meant to suggest that the good is neither optional nor relative, but exists necessarily as the "absolute background" or fundamental condition of human knowledge and existence.

The Platonic background to Murdoch's understanding of the good is in the end more decisive than her scattered theological references to God. For her, "Good is a concept about which, and not only in philosophical language, we naturally use a Platonic terminology."[153] The primary Platonic images Murdoch used to describe the good is the image of the sun, an image which can be construed in two ways: as the light which makes knowledge possible and as the source of that light itself. Murdoch refers to both aspects of the sun metaphor when she asks, "We see the world in the light of the Good, but what is the Good itself? The source of vision is not in the ordinary sense seen."[154] This dual image of the sun and its light designates two important and related elements of the formal concept of good in Murdoch: the first I call the transcendental aspect of the good; the second I call the good as ideal standard of perfection. The transcendental aspect of the good represents the condition for the possibility of knowledge; the good as ideal standard represents the distant goal of perfection which is implicit in all human activities. Put differently, the transcendental aspect of the good emphasizes the internal relation of the good to human life ("all our life proves it"); whereas the good as ideal standard emphasizes the objectivity of the good, its distance from the desire and will of the agent ("it's terribly distant, farther than any star"). These two features represent in conceptual terms something that Murdoch often describes in spatial terms. The good is both "the closest thing. . . . And the farthest thing";[155] it "shin[es] from outside existent being and yet also emerg[es] from deep inside the soul."[156] Human life is, as it were, stretched between these two poles.

As a transcendental notion, the good corresponds to Plato's description of the Form of the Good in the *Republic*, which Murdoch describes as "an enlightening and creative first principle. (The light of the Good makes knowledge possible and also life.)"[157] "The sun represents the Form of the Good in whose light the truth is seen; it reveals the world, hitherto invisible, and is also a source of life."[158] The Good is "the light which reveals to us all things as they really are."[159] On Plato's picture, the light of the good shines from beyond the created world, and from beyond the realm of the Forms themselves, as the fundamental ordering principle of the universe. R. C. Cross and A. D. Woozley, in their commentary on the *Republic*, describe the analogy between the sun and the good as follows:

> Just as, then, in the visible world the Sun is the cause of light which
> enables visible things to be seen and of sight which enables the eye to

see, though it itself is neither light nor sight, so in the intelligible world the Form of the Good is the cause of truth, which enables the Forms to be known, and of knowledge, which enables the mind to know, though it itself is neither truth nor knowledge (508e).[160]

Such a description of the good, as the authors remark, has led some critics to assert that the Form of the Good is in fact "empty,"[161] since it itself is neither light nor sight, neither truth nor knowledge, but the source of these. We might put the same point more positively by saying that this is just what it means to say that the good is a "formal" notion, the necessary condition for vision and knowledge. Plato himself describes Goodness as "not the same thing as being, but even beyond being, surpassing it in dignity and power" (*Republic*, 509b). It does not represent any particular being or value, but rather is the ground or source of all being and value.

Murdoch develops this transcendental aspect of the good in "Above the Gods: A Dialogue about Religion." The dialogue takes place among a gathering of friends after a religious festival and centers on the query posed by Socrates, "Could there not be a good religious way of life without the supernatural beliefs?"[162] The discussion turns on the question of whether belief in a personal God, the supernatural, and other "mythological" aspects of religion are necessary to it, or whether there might be a way to sustain religion without its mythological supports. Murdoch's fictional Plato answers that true religion does not traffic in false images created by the human mind, such as a god whose existence might be "thought away" like that of a material object. Rather religion is about "what's *real* and necessarily *true*,"[163] rather than about what might just as well be otherwise. "Religion isn't just a feeling, it isn't just a hypothesis, it's not like something we happen not to know, a God who might perhaps be there isn't a God, it's got to be necessary, it's got to be certain, it's got to be proved by the whole of life, it's got to be the magnetic centre of everything."[164] And further: "If it's not everywhere, in the air we breathe, it isn't what I mean. If it's something whose non-existence is possible it isn't what I mean! It's to do with life being a whole and not a lot of random choices. Religion must be proved by the whole of life. . . . If it's anything it must be everything."[165]

Socrates asks Plato to clarify himself: "What is this 'it' that you're certain of in this special unique way, which isn't God and which has to exist and is proved by everything and is seen in the clear light beyond the shadows?"[166] Plato answers, "Good." When Socrates presses him, "By 'good' do you mean virtue?" Plato replies, "Virtue under a necessity to which everything points."[167] The good, on this account, is not an object of sense, nor is it merely an abstract concept that human beings have invented; it is rather the fundamental background of human life. When the sophist of the group, Antagoras, asserts skeptically that either the Good "is a thing existing outside us like God, or it's a picture inside us which some people choose to play about with,"[168] the fictional Plato answers:

> Of course Good doesn't exist like chairs and tables, it's not either outside or inside. It's in our whole way of living, it's fundamental like truth. If we have the idea of value we necessarily have the idea of perfection as something real. . . . People know that good is real and absolute, not optional and relative, all their life proves it. . . . We can think everything else away out of life, but not value, that's in the very—ground of things.[169]

Unlike Plato's account in the *Republic*, Murdoch's account of the good in this dialogue does not depend on an idealist metaphysic or on a division between the sensible and intelligible worlds. The crucial feature of the good in *Acastos* is its connection with "what's *real* and *necessarily* true,"[170] but unlike the Platonic account, this connection does not depend on the positing of an intelligible or supernatural world. As the character Acastos himself says, "It's all got to be *now* and *here*."[171] Further, this description links the concept of value to human life considered as a whole. There is no human experience apart from the good, since all of human life is lived "under the aspect" of the good, or in its light. The concept of good serves, therefore, to delimit the boundaries of the real for human existence; it is what Charles Taylor might call an "inescapable framework." This is the formal sense of the correlation between the notions of self and good in Murdoch's thought; the self "only has importance, or even reality, in so far as [it] belongs to the framework" of the good.

Because the good is not a being, but rather the ground of all being, not an object we can see, but rather that which makes seeing possible, we cannot know the good as we know other things. "The Good itself is not visible."[172] Knowing the good in this transcendental sense would be like trying to look directly at the sun. "It is *difficult* to look at the sun," Murdoch writes, "it is not like looking at other things. . . . We do not and probably cannot know, what it is like in the centre."[173] "The source of vision is not in the ordinary sense seen."[174] How, then, is this transcendental good known? Murdoch describes the problem as follows:

> Asking what Good is not like asking what Truth is or what Courage is, since in explaining the latter the idea of Good must enter in, it is that in the *light* of which the explanation must proceed. . . . And if we try to define Good as X we have to add that we mean of course a good X. If we say that Good is Reason we have to talk about good judgment. If we say that Good is Love we have to explain that there are different kinds of love. Even the concept of Truth has its ambiguities and it is really

only of Good that we can say 'it is the trial of itself and needs no other touch'. And with this I agree.[175]

On this analysis of the concept, good is the background concept implicit in our definitions of other concepts. We cannot describe what we mean by Reason or Love, for example, without assuming some notion, respectively, of good judgment or good relations with another person. Good, on the other hand, can only be explained in terms of itself; in order to define it, we refer to other things that we already consider good. In this sense, the good is indefineable, or "self-justifying." (As Murdoch puts it above, "it is the trial of itself and needs no other touch.") This logical feature of the good points to its status as a formal concept that functions as the condition of human moral existence. The good is not merely a removable "tag" that can be applied to a variety of objects according to the agent's preference, but a concept that is definable only in terms of itself.

The form of philosophical argument or proof that Murdoch believes is most suited to explain the transcendental aspect of the good is the onto-logical proof. As we will see in Chapter 5, Murdoch's version of the proof in *Metaphysics as a Guide to Morals* is a reconstruction of Anselm's *Proslogion*, which she reads through Plato. But her indebtedness to Plato is already evident in these earlier texts: "Plato's connection of the good with the real (the ambiguous multiform phenomenon of the ontological proof) is the centre of his thought and one of the most fruitful ideas in philosophy."[176] Murdoch has already given us several clues in *Acastos* that this is the form of argument with which she is working. The character Plato asserts repeatedly that the existence of the good is certain or necessary, and that people know "instinctively"[177] that good is real and absolute. In fact, a condensed form of the proof might be Plato's comment in *Acastos* that "if we have the idea of value we necessarily have the idea of perfection as something real."[178]

Murdoch appeals explicitly in *The Sovereignty of Good* to the theological application of the ontological proof. In the essay "On 'God' and 'Good,'" she attempts to apply theological arguments and analogies to the concept of good in order to bring out what she considers essential features of the concept. As in *Acastos*, the attributes of perfection and certainty or nec-essary existence figure prominently as components of the good. "These attributes," Murdoch writes, "are indeed so closely connected that from some points of view they are the same. (Ontological proof.)"[179] Murdoch appeals to the ontological proof to explain the way in which certainty and perfection seem to "attach themselves" to the idea of the good.[180] However, Murdoch seems to undermine her own argument when she suggests that the ontological proof is not strictly speaking a proof at all, but rather a statement of faith or belief:

> If considered carefully . . . , the ontological proof is seen to be not exactly
> a proof but rather a clear assertion of faith (it is often admitted to be

appropriate only for those already convinced), which could only confidently be made on the basis of a certain amount of experience. This assertion could be put in various ways. The desire for God is certain to receive a response. My conception of God contains the certainty of its own reality. God is an object of love which uniquely excludes doubt and relativism.[181]

The certainty of God or good offered by the proof, Murdoch contends, will not make sense apart from a faith in its reality. An all-encompassing faith in the reality and certainty of goodness is what furnishes the proof of the concept.

Murdoch acknowledges that this argument will hardly satisfy the rigorous requirements of analytic philosophers "who might remark that one might just as well take 'I *know* that my Redeemer liveth,' as asserted by Handel, as a philosophical argument."[182] From an analytic perspective, the ontological proof gives us no way of knowing that certainty about the good is not merely a form of *subjective* conviction that could be explained in psychological or empirical terms.[183] Indeed, as Murdoch presents the proof here, the analytic philosopher has a point. It is not clear at this juncture whether the proof represents anything more than an intuitive certainty verging on "wishful thinking." Murdoch nearly concedes this point when she suggests that:

> The virtuous peasant knows [that the good is real], and I believe he will go on knowing, in spite of the removal or modification of the theological apparatus, although what he knows he might be at a loss to say. This view is of course not amenable even to a persuasive philosophical proof and can easily be challenged on all sorts of empirical grounds. However, I do not think the virtuous peasant will be without resources.[184]

Morality, Murdoch seems to suggest, presupposes a natural and inarticulate faith in the reality of goodness, as the example of the virtuous peasant attests. The ontological proof presumes this faith rather than strictly proves it. As we will see in Chapter 5, however, Murdoch provides stronger arguments in *Metaphysics as a Guide to Morals* than she does in "On 'God' and 'Good.'" There, the idea of intuitive certainty is not reduced to the inarticulate faith of simple peasants (shades of Tolstoy), but is explained in the terms of the logic of transcendental arguments.

There is however another route to the good that Murdoch sketches here, one that relies on the experience of beauty and perfection in art, love, and other human activities as "clues" to the structure of the concept. The transcendental aspect of the good thus alternates with a second formal meaning of the term in Murdoch's exposition. The good functions not only transcendentally, as the fundamental and necessary condition for human knowing, but also as a transcendent object that guides the direction of our knowledge. This represents the other aspect of the metaphor of the sun noted earlier—as the "magnetic centre" toward which knowledge strives. The good in this sense represents the ideal standard by which we measure our knowledge of the real as we come to know it in diverse forms of human activity.

Both formal aspects of the good are characterized by the attribute of perfection. As a transcendental concept, as we saw in *Acastos*, the good *necessarily* implies perfection: "If we have the idea of value we necessarily have the idea of perfection as something real." The very idea of the good, considered transcendentally, includes perfection as part of its structure. This is not an empirical argument, but an argument based on the ontology of the concept of the good: the most real thing is the most perfect. As an ideal standard, on the other hand, the good implies perfection because of empirical features of the activity of knowing:

> A deep understanding of any field of human activity (painting, for instance) involves an increasing revelation of degrees of excellence and often a revelation of there being in fact little that is very good and nothing that is perfect. . . . We come to perceive scales, distances, standards, and may incline to see as less than excellent what previously we were prepared to 'let by'. . . . The idea of perfection works thus within a field of study, producing an increasing sense of direction.[185]

This sense of "directedness" toward an ideal of excellence is the most distinctive feature of this aspect of the good, implying the notions of perfectibility and progress. The good as an ideal standard of perfection requires the notions of temporality and of the individual. Though the standard of perfection is itself "indestructible," it is apprehended by human beings only progressively and by degrees. Individuals will find different ways to embody this excellence. "One may of course try to 'incarnate' the idea of perfection by saying to oneself 'I want to write like Shakespeare' . . . ," Murdoch comments, but in the end, "one has got to do the thing oneself alone and differently."[186]

In both of its formal aspects, as transcendental condition and as ideal standard, Murdoch holds that the good remains fundamentally mysterious or indefinable. As a transcendental concept, the good cannot be known because it is the condition for knowledge, rather than an object of knowledge. As an ideal standard, too, the idea of perfection itself remains "non-representable";[187] but we can recognize perfection through its exemplars in works of art and other instances of beauty, which serve as "pointers" in the direction of the highest excellence. At the very least, then, we know that there are degrees of perfection and that the good lies in a certain direction. We know, for example, that "the very great are not the perfect";[188] that even Shakespeare, though almost a god, is not perfect.[189] "We see differences, we sense directions, and we know that the Good is still somewhere beyond."[190] In the end, the ideal of perfection remains mysterious; it "refers us to a perfection which is perhaps never exemplified in the world we know . . . and which carries with it the ideas of hierarchy and transcendence."[191] The good "lies always beyond, and it is from this beyond that it exercises its *authority*."[192]

Murdoch illustrates her argument about the good as an ideal of perfection through the example of art as well as other human activities, including intellectual disciplines and human love. Great art is evidence of the reality of goodness as perfection, because it exemplifies in a concrete way the "steepness" of the ascent to a distant standard, the discipline required to reach perfection, and the unattainability of the goal. But it is impossible to talk about the way in which great art "teaches" us about perfection without bringing in the relation of knowledge to love and desire. The knowledge required to understand the good as the standard of perfection is not mere idle contemplation; rather, learning requires an effort of the entire person to understand an inexhaustible reality that exists beyond his or her grasp. The good, in this sense, "draws us like a magnet."[193] "The idea of perfection moves, and possibly changes, us (as artist, worker, agent) because it inspires love in the part of us that is most worthy. One cannot feel unmixed love for a mediocre moral standard any more than one can for the work of a mediocre artist."[194]

Murdoch's point can be illustrated using her own example of an activity that can teach us the nature of perfection, the example of learning a language. She describes the task as one in which

> the goal is distant and perhaps never entirely attainable. My work is a progressive revelation of something which exists independently of me. Attention is rewarded by a knowledge of reality. Love of Russian leads me away from myself towards something alien to me, something which my consciousness cannot take over, swallow up, deny or make unreal.[195]

Because of its difficulty and unattainability, the standard of perfection remains an ideal that cannot be reduced to or absorbed by the subjectivity of the agent. Perfect knowledge of a foreign language remains a distant and objective ideal that motivates the student to greater discipline and rewards with increasing knowledge.

This chapter has presented the formal outlines of the three interrelated themes of Murdoch's moral thought. The central axis of her ethics is the correlation between a notion of the self or consciousness and an idea of the good within the frame of metaphysical realism. The next two chapters will elaborate this central axis by showing that the two formal aspects of the good correspond to formal features of the self. The transcendental aspect of the good is correlative to a picture of the self as a being whose cognitive processes always presuppose some notion of value. The good as an ideal standard, on the other hand, functions as an implicit principle of moral knowledge that guides cognition toward perfection as embodied in concrete exemplars in the field of human practices. Human cognition is thus not only evaluative in nature but also internally structured by qualitative distinctions and degrees of value. The formal correlation between self and good will be the subject of Chapters 3 and 4, while the normative theory of the good will be the subject of Chapter 5.

3

THE CRITIQUE OF CONSCIOUSNESS
IN EXISTENTIALISM AND
LINGUISTIC BEHAVIORISM

In the last chapter, I tried to show that Murdoch's retrieval of metaphysics and her defense of moral realism provide the condition for relating knowledge and morality by establishing a formal correlation between notions of self and good. The purpose of the present chapter and the one following it is to clarify Murdoch's substantive account of the moral self, focusing especially on her claims about consciousness. These two chapters are crucial in establishing the book's general thesis that the importance of Murdoch's thought for contemporary ethics lies in her effort to redescribe the moral self and its integral relation to the good. To the extent that she succeeds in this effort, she may be said to articulate a "moral ontology"[1] in which the self is conceived as situated within a "space" or framework of questions about the good.

The retrieval of such an ontology seems to indicate that Murdoch would favor Natural Law moralities over Liberal moralities which assert the agent's autonomy from any overarching framework. In fact, this feature of Murdoch's thought helps to account for the attractiveness of her position to contemporary critics of liberalism, narrative ethicists, and others who seek to articulate a more "situated" view of the self. However, the way in which Murdoch conceives the moral self as an individual renders this claim problematic. Contrary to first impressions, Murdoch cannot be regarded unambiguously as a Natural Law moralist, as these chapters (especially Chapter 4) will show. Although she affirms a metaphysical framework as including the individual, such a framework should not be thought of as wholly absorbing the individual. Rather than rejecting the Liberal view of morality completely, Murdoch tries to preserve one of its fundamental claims—that the value and integrity of the individual is irreducible to any overarching structure in which it is situated.

In order to make this argument, the present chapter will need to consider Murdoch's critique of two philosophical positions that she believes offer reductionistic accounts of the moral self: Sartrean existentialism and what she called linguistic "behaviorism."[2] Both of these philosophies may be considered instances of the Liberal view because they reject an encompassing framework for moral agency. But just as importantly, in Murdoch's view, they fail to portray the complex reality of human individuals. There are two fundamental issues at stake in Murdoch's critique of these philosophies: neither provides an adequate account of the nature and role of consciousness in morality; and both misunderstand the nature of freedom. The argument of the chapter proceeds through these elements of Murdoch's critique. Section I analyzes Murdoch's relation to Sartre. Section II examines Murdoch's critique of linguistic behaviorism as represented by Stuart Hampshire and others. As noted, Murdoch's constructive response to these philosophies and her own account of moral subjectivity will be more fully developed in Chapter 4.

Section I. A. The Existentialist Self: Consciousness, Freedom, and Value

Murdoch's most extended treatment of Sartre's philosophy can be found in her early monograph, *Sartre, Romantic Rationalist*.[3] In this work, Murdoch presents what she believes to be the essential paradox or dilemma of Sartre's moral and political thought:

> As a European socialist intellectual with an acute sense of the needs of his time Sartre wishes to affirm the preciousness of the individual and the possibility of a society which is free and democratic in the traditional liberal sense of these terms. This affirmation is his most profound concern and the key to all his thought. As a philosopher however he finds himself without the materials to construct a system which will hold and justify these values.[4]

In spite of his concern to defend the individual and its freedom in the face of every form of totality, Murdoch argues, Sartre's essentially liberal affirmation of the value of the individual is not adequately supported by his philosophy as a whole. As a political liberal, Sartre wishes to affirm the value of the individual existent as the self-determining creator of its own values. Yet having abandoned any belief in God, Nature, or History,[5] which have traditionally provided the constitutive background for conceptions of the self, Sartre's defense of the individual is left "without the support of any background faith, religious or political."[6] "It is as if only one certainty remained," Murdoch writes, "that human beings are irreducibly valuable, without any notion of why or how they are valuable or how the value can be defended."[7] This sets the first problem for Murdoch's own account of the moral self—that is, a defense of the individual that is grounded in a larger ontology of value.

Murdoch's criticism of Sartre is focused on two related conceptual issues: his description of consciousness and his conception of freedom. Sartre's description of human consciousness in *Being and Nothingness* is ordered by two central dualisms. The first dualism is between consciousness (the for-itself or *être-pour-soi*) and the objects of consciousness or things (the in-itself or *être-en-soi*); the second dualism is between consciousness and an ideal totality to which it aspires (*être-en-soi-pour-soi*). Murdoch summarizes this picture as follows:

> Consciousness is negation, nothingness; it makes itself by negating the given, the brute thingy world, on one side—and it makes itself also by aspiring, on the other side, toward an ideal completeness. So consciousness is both *rupture* (the break with the given) and *projet* (aspiration to totality); both these characteristics Sartre equates with freedom and the latter he connects with value. Freedom, considered as negation and project, is the main character of human consciousness.[8]

I examine each of these dualisms and their correlative notions of freedom in turn.

The first dualism pictures consciousness as a rupture from or negation of the world of objects. In *Being and Nothingness*, Sartre argues that the for-itself (consciousness) establishes itself only in terms of and against the in-itself (the given). That is, the for-itself determines itself precisely as a lack of being, or nothingness: "The concrete, real in-itself is wholly present to consciousness as that which consciousness determines itself not to be";[9] consciousness "determines its being by means of a being which it is not."[10] This privative nature of consciousness as nihilation or rupture means that from the very beginning, consciousness is incomplete. For precisely "what the for-itself lacks is the self—or itself as in-itself."[11] Thus consciousness as rupture is constituted both as a negation of what is other than itself and as a lack or privation of the very being it negates.

Murdoch describes the characteristic "nothingness" of consciousness in relation to the solid world of objects as a contrast between the "flickering, unstable, semi-transparent moment-to-moment 'being' of the consciousness, the shifting way in which it conceives objects and itself," with "the solid, opaque, inert 'in-themselvesness' of *things* which simply are what they are."[12] In concrete terms, this means that consciousness has no stable being of its own, but rather "flickers" among different degrees and qualities of awareness, from a reflective state of "open self-awareness toward a more opaque and thing-like condition."[13] Consciousness thus moves continually between transparent self-reflection (by which it appears most distinct from the opaque world of things) and an unreflective grasping of the world (by which it appears at its most "thing-like").

Since consciousness itself has no being, but is rather a flickering translucence, it aspires to an ideal or stable state of being characterized by identity, purity, and permanence. In other words, consciousness is not only constituted in contrast to the opacity of contingent matter; it is also constituted on the other side as a *transcendence* toward a condition of perfect stability and completion.[14] This aspiration (*projet*) by which consciousness seeks to transcend its own lack of being signals the second dualism by which Sartre describes human reality. Consciousness aspires to a condition of stability that will not render it opaque (like the in-itself) but in which it will retain its essential translucence or reflectiveness. This state would combine the transparency of the for-itself with the solidity of the in-itself in an ideal synthesis that Sartre calls *être-en-soi-pour-soi* (being-in-itself-for-itself). The task of all human projects will be to struggle to effect this ultimately impossible synthesis. As Sartre writes in *Being and Nothingness*, the for-itself is a perpetual project of founding itself qua being and a perpetual failure of this project.[15]

Sartre gives us a concrete portrait of these aspects of consciousness in his philosophical novel *Nausea*, which Murdoch calls "a sort of metaphisical [*sic*] poem on the subject of the two dualisms."[16] The narrator of *Nausea*, Roquentin, reports a series of experiences in which he feels his consciousness becoming thing-like; that is, it appears to partake of the character of the *être-en-soi*, or contingent matter. At certain unpredictable moments—in a cafe, in a park—Roquentin becomes "afflicted with a dreadful sense of the contingency of the world, the brute nameless thereness of material existence. He feels himself as an empty nothing which has been crowded out of the opaque world of objects."[17] Gradually, the meaning of ordinary things—the root of a chestnut tree, a glass of beer—seems to withdraw from the physical objects themselves, to the point where the world now appears as a "swooning abundance"[18] of brutely existing matter that is devoid of meaning. At such moments, consciousness ceases to be an active, mobile, flickering entity; rather, it becomes identified with the gluey inertness of things themselves. This is what Sartre describes as "nausea"; or as Murdoch calls it, a "sweetish sort of disgust"[19] that attends the disturbing immersion of consciousness in the viscous substance of things.

Yet this experience, in which consciousness threatens to lose its mobility in the *être-en-soi*, is counterbalanced by the experience of transcendence toward an ideal state that is the subject of Sartre's second dualism. Roquentin expresses this aspiration by being "haunted by thoughts about melodies and circles which seem to have a perfect satisfying intelligible mode of being which lift them out of the fallen world of existence."[20] In contrast to the imperfection and contingency of brutely existing matter, Roquentin yearns for a perfect mode of being. "His ideal mode of being, to which he often recurs in thought, is that of a mathematical figure—pure, clear, necessary and non-existent."[21] Roquentin hopes to attain this ideal condition by creating a work of art, but this is only one form such a project can take. For Sartre, Murdoch argues, what is important is not the content of our various human endeavors—whether political, intellectual, or aesthetic—as much as the "schematic pattern"[22] that provides the form which our endeavors take. According to this pattern, "*all* value lies in the unattainable world of intelligible completeness"[23] that our projects struggle vainly to fulfill.

Murdoch notes that Roquentin's experience of the senseless contingency of nature (*être-en-soi*), on the one hand, and his dream of a perfect totality (*être-en-soi-pour-soi*), on the other, is a kind of picture of the human predicament and provides the basis for understanding two central tensions in Sartre's philosophy: the tension between freedom and "bad faith," and the tension between freedom and value. A brief analysis of these tensions will help to clarify the nature of Murdoch's criticisms of Sartre's position and her constructive response to it.

According to the terms of the first dualism, freedom as rupture is that which defines the active human consciousness in distinction from the inert world of things; it is the negation by which consciousness is constituted. Since a human being is a being who can realize a nihilating rupture with the world and with itself, the permanent possibility of this rupture is the same as freedom.[24] Thus to the extent that we are conscious self-reflective beings rather than things, we are "condemned" to be free. In *Nausea*, Murdoch notes, Sartre pictures this aspect of freedom in terms of a "dispersion" of the "gluey inertness" that invades Roquentin's consciousness to the point of nausea. Freedom is "the mobility of the consciousness, that is our ability to reflect, to dispel an emotional condition, to withdraw from absorption in the world, to set things at a distance."[25] Freedom is thus related to the *transparency* of consciousness, its ability to reflect on itself and to avoid becoming immersed in the world of objects.

By the same token, it is in terms of a "solidification" or "immobilization" of the normally active and shifting consciousness, its tendency to become inert and thinglike, that Sartre pictures the *denial* of freedom to which he gives the name insincerity or bad faith. Murdoch describes this notion as "the more or less conscious refusal to reflect, the immersion in the unreflectively coloured awareness of the world, the persistence in an emotional judgment, or the willingness to inhabit cosily some other person's estimate of oneself."[26] Bad faith finds expression in myriad forms, such as "the idolatry of state and family, the 'justification' drawn from position and wealth." It is, in short, "the reification of relations and institutions"[27] whose value is in reality contingent upon human beings *choosing* to find them valuable. Bad faith is the attempt to evade one's freedom by attributing value to the world independently of human subjectivity.

The condition of bad faith is essentially a state of self-deception. As conscious beings, we are condemned to be free; thus the refusal to reflect which characterizes bad faith is itself a choice made in freedom. Accordingly, the "cure" for such self-deception is sincerity, the authentic recognition that human beings create their own values. Roquentin's experience is instructive on this point. His terrifying discovery was that conventional opinions, social classes and institutions, even the very names we assign to the ordinary objects of our awareness are, in reality, arbitrary conventions invented by human beings to keep at bay the brute and senseless contingency of the world. The consciousness that is finally able to see through such conventions may either fall into a nauseous immersion in brute reality, as Roquentin does, or may choose courageously to face the anguish (*angoisse*) that for Sartre is the inevitable burden of taking responsibility for one's own freedom.

The tendency of human beings to fall into bad faith indicates that for Sartre, freedom demands a rejection of all values that are merely "given." To the extent that such values are perceived to exist independently of the human subject, they are falsified. They confront the free reflective consciousness as dead and thinglike rather than as human creations. To prevent this reification of value, Sartre insists that the only legitimate values are those which one chooses self-consciously, with the authentic awareness that one is in fact doing so. Otherwise, consciousness loses its transparent reflectiveness and becomes identified with a false conventionalism.

This analysis points to an important difference between Sartre and Murdoch that will emerge more fully in Chapters 4 and 5 but should be anticipated here. For Murdoch, consciousness and its freedom are not constituted as a rupture with the given world of value, but are rather constituted in integral relation to an order of value that does *not* depend on the self-creating will of the agent. In her view, there exists an objective or antecedent order of value the recognition of which is not symptomatic of "bad faith," but is rather a function of our knowledge of the real. This is in fact the import of Murdoch's transcendental argument for the good: consciousness is not free to *choose* the good in this sense; rather, the good is the very condition for consciousness and its freedom. In sum, while consciousness for Sartre is constituted by the freedom to break from an essentially false world of inert values, Murdoch defines freedom as knowledge of an order of value that is the locus of the real.

A second tension in Sartre's conception of freedom arises when we turn from freedom as rupture to consider freedom as project. Freedom in this sense is defined as the aspiration to realize our chosen values through various projects or endeavors that will give form and stability to our existence. "To value something is to seek through it to achieve a certain stabilising of one's own being."[28] Freedom in this sense is connected to self-transcendence through the pursuit of value. The tension arises because the attempt to achieve stable being in this fashion may lead consciousness into bad faith, and thus threaten the first aspect of freedom as a mobile, reflective negation of the given. Paradoxically, the very attempt to stabilize the being of consciousness by the pursuit of value in diverse human projects may end by immobilizing consciousness in bad faith. "The reflective consciousness . . . still runs the danger of falling into bad faith, that is of losing its tense mobility and degenerating into a 'gluey' unreflective condition."[29] Thus the second dualism marks a deep paradox between freedom and value in Sartre's philosophy: the ideal totality to which we aspire, which is a synthesis of the *être-pour-soi* and the *être-en-soi*, is in fact a self-contradictory state. As Murdoch puts it,

> What we want is the impossible; that is to be a living transparent consciousness and at the same time a stable opaque being; to be both *pour-soi* and *en-soi* at the same time. This, says Sartre, is the aspiration to be God, to be *ens causa sui*, and it is innately contradictory. This . . . is the fundamental form of all our particular projects and ambitions.[30]

The aspiration toward an ideal synthesis of the for-itself and the in-itself is an attempt to combine two opposing conditions: "the firmness of thing-like being (*être-en-soi*), combined with the transparency of consciousness (*être-pour-soi*): a state of complete lucidity and complete changelessness."[31] Only God is able to be *ens causa sui*, entirely self-caused; human beings are condemned to be haunted by the pull of a magnetic totality of value outside themselves which is "patently unattainable."[32]

In seeking to be both *pour-soi* and *en-soi* at the same time, we put ourselves in the contradictory position of using our freedom to negate our freedom, by striving to achieve a God-like condition that is perfectly stable and self-sufficient. Every attempt to stabilize the being of the self by aspiring to some value leads to an immobilization of consciousness that is the very antithesis of freedom. The achievement of value thus appears to be impossible without losing the essentially active or free nature of consciousness, since any value that is realized would no longer be a value but would become a *thing*. Murdoch summarizes the general dilemma posed by the Sartrean paradox between freedom and value as follows:

> The picture of man which Sartre offers is of a being constantly threatened by a deadening and solidifying of his universe—a fall into the banal, the conventional, the bourgeois, the realm of *Mauvaise foi*—who may rise out of this in search of a living totality but forever in vain. Such a being is at his best, his most human, when he is by an effort of sincerity breaking his bonds; yet such a moment can never be held or stabilised. . . . All achievement deadens and corrupts—living value only resides in active affirmation or the rebellious struggle.[33]

This view appears to leave us with the impossibility of ever incarnating our values in our projects, or of achieving a permanent coincidence of freedom and value. Human life is, in Sartre's phrase, a "useless passion" in which all our projects are equally in vain.[34] No project, no value ultimately satisfies, since every attempt to achieve value through our various endeavors only "tends to fall dead into the region of the reified."[35] Thus the task of authentic human existence is to struggle ceaselessly to preserve our freedom through a perpetual revolt against existing values, in the name of an ideal value that can never be concretely embodied.

Sartre's account of the paradox inherent in the human attempt to transcend itself in pursuit of an unattainable value raises a second important point of contention between Murdoch and Sartre. Again, this point will emerge more clearly in Chapters 4 and 5, but is useful to note here. Just as Sartre's account of freedom as a rupture from the world of value is countered by Murdoch's transcendental idea of the good as constitutive of human consciousness, so his account of freedom as project may be compared to Murdoch's understanding of the good as an ideal standard of perfection. In one respect, there is an obvious similarity between Sartre and Murdoch on the latter point: both thinkers affirm that transcendent value exerts a "magnetic pull" on human life. Indeed, Murdoch's idea that human beings continually strive for perfection without ever being able to reach it echoes some of the vain aspiration of Sartre's view of freedom as project.

The difference, however, is that for Sartre the tension between freedom and value sets up an inescapable conundrum, because the attainment of value would simultaneously negate the reflective ability of consciousness to break free from any value. The pursuit of perfection always threatens consciousness with bad faith, in Sartre's view; the two aspects of freedom always threaten to negate one another. For Murdoch, by contrast, no fundamental paradox exists between the two aspects of consciousness that are correlative to her two aspects of the good. The good is both the formal or transcendental condition for our pursuit of any value whatever and the ideal standard that guides all of our projects. Murdoch's image of human life as "stretched," as it were, between these "near" and "far" aspects of the good does not generate a sense of futility, as in Sartre's view; rather, it provides an encompassing context in which value is shown to be inescapable in human life. For Murdoch, in short, human consciousness is understood as constituted by a realm of value, rather than existing in irresolvable tension with it.

Taken as a whole, then, Murdoch's critique of Sartre centers on the way in which he pictures human consciousness as "divided" between the empty movement of freedom, on the one hand, and an unattainable realm of value, on the other. This split leaves the Sartrean self in a perpetual state of resistance to or separation from value, without any way to construct an authentic normative framework beyond the momentary acts of its own freedom. In Murdoch's view, such a framework is crucial to the idea of the individual. Sartre's account thus leaves an important question unanswered: what does his account of consciousness imply for his understanding of the individual? The problem has particular urgency for Sartre if we read him, as Murdoch does, as "a European socialist intellectual" whose concern to affirm the value of the individual and the possibility of a free and democratic society is "the key to all his thought."[36] If all of our projects are equally futile, as Sartre's analysis suggests, how can he affirm the key political values that are his most profound concern? His account of consciousness means that no value—political or otherwise—can ever attain the force of a practical program without falling into the dynamics of inauthenticity and bad faith that his view of freedom is intended to avoid. From this perspective, it appears that Sartre cannot derive a constructive moral and political philosophy from the ontology he presents in *Being and Nothingness*.

Murdoch suggests that Sartre himself sees the dilemma posed by his own account of freedom, and is not content to leave us with only a "stoical defiance"[37] in the face of our inability to incarnate value in our projects. For this reason, he proposes a possible solution to the impasse of freedom and value in the conclusion of *Being and Nothingness*, where he asks: what if freedom were to take *itself* as a value, thereby ending the "reign of value" according to which human aspiration is judged to be a perpetual failure? If we cease to conceive human life as haunted by a transcendent value (*être-en-soi-pour-soi*), and instead take "the self-aware unillusioned consciousness"[38] as the source of all value, we might escape the dilemma in which ideal value is unrealizable and freedom remains an empty aspiration.

Sartre promised to provide an answer to these questions in his next book, a work on ethics which was not to appear for decades.[39] But Murdoch suggests that Sartre attempts to escape the dilemma posed by his own philosophy in his political and literary writings, where he describes freedom in markedly different terms than he does in *Being and Nothingness*. In these writings "we find Sartre speaking of freedom in much more universalistic and Kantian terms . . . more like what it means in talk about social democracy and liberalism."[40] In other words, Sartre appears in these works to embrace a substantive liberal democratic conception of freedom that is linked to an affirmation of the value of the individual. The question that this development in Sartre's thought poses for Murdoch is whether this new conception of freedom helps to resolve the tension between freedom and value entailed in his view of consciousness. In other words, is Sartre's new conception of freedom supported by a revised understanding of consciousness that situates it within a larger ontology of value?

I. B. A Possible Solution to the Paradox of Freedom and Value

In order to answer these questions, Murdoch turns from *Being and Nothingness* to Sartre's development of the concept of freedom in two slightly later works, *What is Literature?* (1947) and *Existentialism is a Humanism* (1948). A consideration of these texts, Murdoch believed, reveals an incoherence or ambiguity between Sartre's definition of freedom in the ontology of *Being and Nothingness* and his attempts to give freedom a liberal political content. Specifically, Sartre appears to conflate three distinct senses of freedom in these works: (1) freedom as the constitutive feature of human consciousness (i.e., as rupture); (2) freedom as our response to a work of art (newly introduced in *What is Literature?*); and (3) freedom as an ideal state of society (i.e., political freedom or *liberté*, which represents one type of project).[41]

Murdoch argues that Sartre offers a more substantive conception of freedom and value in *What is Literature?* Although the meaning of freedom as the characteristic mobility of consciousness (i.e., as rupture) is still presupposed in this text,[42] Sartre now attempts to define the *content* of freedom in the context of an analysis of the relation between the writer and his reader. As Murdoch notes, freedom "is no longer a fruitless drive toward stability which anything might appear to satisfy, but a particular *disciplined activity* which is contrasted with other less admirable ones."[43] Sartre argues that the literary work created by the writer can only be realized or completed through the act of reading. The work of art does not exist on its own, to be discovered subsequently by the reader; rather, it exists precisely in and through the activity of reading. Thus, it presents itself not as an existing fact, but as "a task to be discharged; from the very beginning it places itself on the level of the categorical imperative."[44] In this way, the work of art is an absolute end or value that demands the freedom of the reader's creative act. Sartre writes:

> Since the creation can find its fulfillment only in reading . . . , all literary work is an appeal. To write is to make an appeal to the reader that he lead into objective existence the revelation which I have undertaken by means of language. And if it should be asked to what the writer is appealing, the answer is simple. . . . The writer appeals to the reader's freedom to collaborate in the production of his work.[45]

But the freedom demanded by the work of art is of a particular kind; it involves a certain "*purging* of the emotions"[46] of both author and reader, an attempt to dispel a purely subjective response to the work. Although Sartre acknowledges that a writer creates a work of art through the creation of emotion in the reader, if he writes solely for this purpose, the work "is no longer anything but a means for feeding hate or desire."[47] Further, although the reader, too, has an emotional response to a literary work, such feelings "have their origin in freedom."[48] That is, the reader's response is borne of the *generosity* that the reader lends to the author in freedom, which is "a perpetually renewed choice to believe"[49] in the work of art. Thus Sartre writes, "reading is a pact of generosity between author and reader"[50] in which both parties make a free decision to transform their emotions into free emotions that will reveal the work as an absolute value or end. In this way, a "dialectical going-and-coming" is established between the author's appeal to the reader's freedom and the reader's response to this appeal, with the result that "my freedom, by revealing itself, reveals the freedom of the other."[51]

Murdoch argues that Sartre describes freedom in this context as a kind of "spiritual discipline" in which the engaged writer addresses an audience of free readers, both of whom generously withdraw themselves from their emotions in order to disclose the value of the work. To the extent that the act of literary creation presupposes the freedom and mutual respect of those engaged in it, it aims at being a kind of "city of ends"[52] that harmonizes the will of all. The freedom involved in the creation and consumption of literary works, Murdoch writes, involves "a setting aside of *selfish* considerations, a respect for the autonomy of another's . . . creative power, which leads on to a respect for the autonomy of all other men."[53] This reference to the Kantian idea of a kingdom of ends is a clue to the change that the concept of freedom has undergone in Sartre's thought. First, Sartre appears to have moved from a purely descriptive idea of freedom as the structure of human consciousness in *Being and Nothingness*, to something closer to freedom as a regulative idea in *What is Literature?* "Sartre seems now to be saying that if we make a proper exercise of our freedom, which will involve our taking mankind as an absolute end, we shall tend toward a harmony in willing."[54] Second, Sartre is now treating freedom not merely as the reflective movement of the solitary consciousness, but rather as a substantive value that can only be realized collectively—that is, in the "generous" exchange between writer and reader mediated through the work of art. Third and finally, Sartre's idea of freedom as a disciplined purging of one's emotions in order to disclose the value of the literary work seems to acknowledge that value can in fact be realized in human projects (e.g., literature) and can exist independently of the self. In this respect, freedom no longer seems to be in tension with value, but is identified as the value *par excellence* which literature both demands and calls into being.

Sartre further develops the social and political aspects of this notion of freedom in his pamphlet *Existentialism is a Humanism*. In the context of a discussion of the existentialist dictum that "existence is prior to essence," Sartre argues that "the first effect of existentialism is that it puts every man in possession of himself as he is, and places the entire responsibility for his existence squarely upon his own shoulders."[55] This much was already clear from *Being and Nothingness*. But now we find Sartre making the further claim that this does not mean that every man is responsible only for himself, but also that he is responsible for all of humanity.[56] "When we say that man chooses himself, we do mean that every one of us must choose himself; but by that we also mean that in choosing for himself he chooses for all men. . . . In fashioning myself I fashion man."[57] The true sense of existentialist responsibility, and the anguish of freedom that results from it, is that in every decision and commitment, one chooses not only what one will be, but "is thereby at the same time a *legislator* deciding for the whole of mankind."[58] As Murdoch comments, "This Kantian argument with its implicit social conclusions seems a long way from the heroic solipsism of *L'Etre et le Néant*."[59] Sartre appears to have moved from a description of freedom as the general characteristic of human consciousness to an explicitly political argument for a form of the ideal society in which the freedom of all could be realized. In this way, "Sartre is able to preach social democracy as if it were deducible from existentialism."[60]

But Murdoch argues that political imperatives cannot in fact be deduced from the reductionistic picture of consciousness that Sartre gives us in *Being and Nothingness*. Sartre's attempt to break the impasse between freedom and value by developing a more substantive liberal conception of freedom fails, in Murdoch's view, because it does not succeed in solving the problem of our "divided being." In order to connect the purely formal notion of freedom as the reflective movement of consciousness in *Being and Nothingness* with the substantive sense of political freedom that he wants to defend in *Existentialism is a Humanism*, Sartre would have to assume "a more stable conception of human nature" than his ontology provides.

Although Murdoch does not elaborate on precisely what she means by "a stable conception of human nature," her criticism may be stated as follows. As long as Sartre's conception of consciousness is riven by the tensions and paradoxes I have described, he cannot be said to have a concept of the individual strictly speaking. For Murdoch, the concept of the individual requires an understanding of consciousness as integrally related to value. This is perhaps what she means by "human nature": a normative conception of the human, as opposed to the paradoxical depiction of the human condition that Sartre provides. Although Sartre himself might sense the limitations of his own ontology, his new and more explicitly political definition of freedom does not solve the problem because it has no corollary in his view of consciousness. If freedom as rupture was correlative to one aspect of consciousness (as transparent being), and freedom as project was correlative to another (as striving toward transcendent value), what is the corollary in consciousness to freedom as a liberal political value? Murdoch's point is that this notion of freedom requires a fuller account of consciousness in relation to a social world of others, and also as capable of realizing stable values (e.g., works of literature, political democracy, and so forth) without falling into bad faith.

I. C. Murdoch and Sartre on the Individual

In spite of Murdoch's persistent criticism of Sartre, her attitude toward existentialism remained ambivalent. This ambivalence is rooted in the fact that Murdoch in fact shared a deep sympathy with Sartre's underlying liberal assumptions about the value of the individual and its freedom, even though she believed that his philosophy failed adequately to support these values. Like many members of her generation, Murdoch was drawn immediately after WWII to the moral and political passion of existentialism, its "ethic of resistance" to political and social tyranny. Sartre's picture of "the heroic consciousness, the individual self, inalienably and ineluctably free, challengingly confront[ing] the 'given', in the form of existing society, history, tradition, other people"[61] resonated with the experience of many people in Europe in the aftermath of the war. Murdoch's concern for the integrity of the individual human being was forged in this political and cultural context, and she remained deeply preoccupied in her writings with the problem of freedom as it pertains to the irreducibility of the individual to any form of totality, and to the self-transcending nature of the human.

This aspect of Murdoch's relation to Sartre becomes apparent if we briefly examine her position in relation to the Marxist response to existentialism. She agrees in some measure with the charge made by the Marxist critic George Lukacs that existentialism amounts to nothing more than a "politics of adolescence"[62] that favors a state of perpetual rebellion over a concrete political solution that would work toward the achievement of a new social order. In order to combat the constant threat of bad faith, the Sartrean ideal of sincerity presupposes a continual *resistance* to existing values (the state, the family, social conventions, class distinctions, etc.), in the name of a disillusioned awareness that all such values and norms are the creation of human freedom. "Sincerity is not a *state* of being,"[63] Murdoch writes, but a ceaseless act of rebellion against the alienation of human freedom in the mass of ossified values and institutions. Thus Murdoch believes that the Marxists were correct when they claimed that

> a powerful reason for the popularity of existentialism is that it makes a universal myth of the plight of those who reject capitalism but who cannot adjust themselves to the ideal of socialism and who seek a middle way. . . . To put it in Sartrian jargon, they reject the opaque brutish world of capitalist institutions and values, they are outside, or conceive themselves as outside, this *être-en-soi;* yet the ideal totality which they yearn for, the *en-soi-pour-soi* of socialism, is impossible, since all achievement corrupts. . . . So they are left in the middle, empty and lonely and doomed to continual frustration.[64]

On this reading, the reason for Sartre's failure to develop a coherent substantive conception of freedom within a practical political program becomes more obvious: a workable ethical and political solution cannot be built on what is in effect a philosophy of perpetual rebellion. In the end, Murdoch writes, "The general impression of Sartre's work is certainly that of a powerful but abstract model of a hopeless dilemma, coloured by a surreptitious romanticism which embraces the hopelessness."[65]

On the other hand, Murdoch ultimately defended Sartre against his Marxist critics in one crucial respect. Sartre's philosophy, she believed, expresses "an obstinate and denuded belief, which clings to certain values even at the expense of seeming to make them empty. . . . [W]hat Sartre wishes to assert is precisely that the individual has an absolute importance and is not to be swallowed up in a historical calculation."[66] In contrast to Marxism, which insists on the socially and historically conditioned nature of the individual, Sartre depicts the human being "in the moment-to-moment flux of this thoughts and moods, where no consistent pattern either of purposeful activity or of social condition can easily be discerned."[67] Sartre is willing to pay the price of a denuded or solipsistic view of the self for the sake of what is for him a more urgent value. He "wishes at all costs to withdraw his man to a point at which he is independent of what seems to him the inhuman determinism of the modern world, the realm of the economist and the sociologist—even if it means depicting him as an empty shell."[68] Thus by stripping the individual of any kind of social, historical, or metaphysical framework and by defining freedom as an abstract ideal, Sartre hopes to protect the individual from any sort of "totalizing" explanation that would threaten the individual's value.

This fundamental point of sympathy between Murdoch and Sartre is crucial for Murdoch's own constructive moral anthropology. Indeed, Murdoch believes that Sartre's failure is "a symptom of a dilemma in which we are all involved,"[69] namely, that it now seems impossible for us "either to live unreflectively or to express a view of what we are in any systematic terms which will satisfy the mind. We can no longer formulate a general truth about ourselves which shall encompass us like a house."[70] This sets the first task for Murdoch's own account of the moral self: to articulate a defense of the individual that does not, like Sartre's, strip the self of any supporting conceptual structure, but rather grounds the self in a larger ontology of value. The essential question that Murdoch's early work on Sartre raises for our understanding of her ethics is whether it is possible to defend a view of the agent as embedded within a larger framework, without necessarily forfeiting or "losing" the individual in the totality. This will be the burden of Murdoch's position.

Further, we have seen that Sartre was unable to defend a substantive liberal notion of freedom by the terms of his own ontology, and thus was left with an abstract notion of freedom as "reflective awareness." The second problem for Murdoch's theory of the self will be to articulate a co-

herent understanding of freedom that can find a place within a nonreduc-
tionistic account of consciousness in relation to value. Murdoch develops
a notion of freedom as part and parcel of an overall theory of the moral
agent that situates the agent within a context defined by the existence of
others. Freedom, for Murdoch, is directly related to our knowledge of and
respect for others within a complex moral world. I take up these matters
in my exposition of Murdoch's constructive position in the next chapter.
But first we must complete the second half of Murdoch's critique by turning to the other reductionistic account of the moral agent against which
she defines her position, linguistic behaviorism.

Section II. A. Linguistic Behaviorism and the Disappearance of Mind in Moral Philosophy

Recall that both existentialism and linguistic behaviorism are important
for Murdoch's position because they underscore the dependence of her idea
of the individual on a particular understanding of consciousness. While
Sartre at least acknowledges the importance of consciousness in his account of human moral being, Murdoch believes that an adequate concept
of the individual requires that consciousness be understood as constituted
by its relation to value. This is the core of her argument that the self is
integrally related to the good. But Murdoch's quarrel with linguistic behaviorism goes deeper, in a sense, because it rejects the moral value of
consciousness altogether. This requires Murdoch to defend the notion of
consciousness itself and to show how it is in fact central to moral agency.
In doing so, she will also need to defend a view of moral freedom that is
intended to challenge the noncognitivism of both existentialism and linguistic behaviorism.

Murdoch presents a powerful critique of what she calls "the
existentialist-behaviorist view"[71] of the moral agent in the three essays
collected in *The Sovereignty of Good*. As its name implies, this view combines
an existentialist conception of the self as a solitary agent who exercises
his or her freedom as an act of the will, with a behaviorist view of the
meaning of moral language as dependent on public contexts and conventions.[72] The pervasive influence of this view on modern moral theory had
in Murdoch's view rendered certain aspects of the moral life "non-
expressible" or inarticulable, while exaggerating the importance of other
aspects.[73] In particular, philosophers associated with the existentialist-
behaviorist view (including Stuart Hampshire, R. M. Hare, and A. J. Ayer)
embraced a picture of morality and moral agency that emphasized discrete
decisions, actions, and public conduct, as opposed to the privacy of our
inner thoughts, imaginings, and states of mind. Against what she per-

ceived to be this narrowing of morality to the outward behavior of agents, Murdoch attempted to produce "if not a comprehensive analysis, at least a rival soul-picture which covers a greater or a different territory," and makes "new places for philosophical reflection."[74] A central feature of this new moral psychology is a defense of the notion of consciousness, which is threatened by linguistic behaviorist currents in modern moral philosophy which seek to reduce morality to action or conduct.

The existentialist-behaviorist view as Murdoch presents it in *The Sovereignty of Good* must be understood in the context of important currents in analytic philosophy of mind, especially the philosophy of Gilbert Ryle and the view of meaning associated with the verification principle of British empiricism.[75] Murdoch had already described the central features of this view and its genealogy in several early essays, including "Vision and Choice in Morality," "Nostalgia for the Particular," and "Thinking and Language," which prepare the ground for many of the arguments found in *The Sovereignty of Good*. I draw freely on these early essays in the following pages in order to supplement the view presented several years later in *The Sovereignty of Good*. Here, as elsewhere, my concern is systematic rather than strictly exegetical. This means that I will be returning to certain texts and arguments discussed in Chapter 2 in order to build a coherent picture of Murdoch's understanding of the moral agent.

In "Vision and Choice," Murdoch describes the "current view" of morality held by Hampshire, Ayer, Hare, and others, as follows:

> the moral life of the individual is a series of overt choices which take place in a series of specifiable situations. The individual's 'stream of consciousness' is of comparatively little importance, partly because it is often not there at all (having been thought to be continuous for wrong reasons), and more pertinently because it is and can only be through overt acts that we can characterise another person, or ourselves, mentally or morally.[76]

The central operative distinction underlying this description of the agent is between the private sphere of thoughts, beliefs, imagination, and intentions and the public sphere of choice, behavior, and action. Morality is a matter of making choices and recommendations based on facts that are the same for all agents, and moral terms amount to "an objective definition of a certain area of activity plus a recommendation or prohibition."[77] The inner life of the individual agent, his or her quality of consciousness or private state of mind, is less important or even irrelevant on this picture, since morality is a matter of prescribing universal judgments based on a disinterested scrutiny of the facts for agents who inhabit the same public world.

One of the most significant features of this view of morality is that it guarantees a particular conception of moral freedom as essentially freedom of choice. In common with the more general Liberal view of morality, it "displays the moral agent as rational and responsible and also as free."[78]

> On the current view the moral agent is free to withdraw, survey the facts, and choose again. There is, moreover, an open field for argument of an empirical fact-investigating kind among those who have similar principles. This view is Kantian in atmosphere: moral beings, or those of them who can communicate, live in the same world. It is also Humian: only carelessness and inattention, that is habitual and traditional attitudes, separate us from "the facts."[79]

Such a view of freedom safeguards the autonomy of the moral agent, since the agent relies on his or her own reason to survey the facts and then chooses according to principles that any other similarly placed rational agent may reach. Morality must overcome "habitual and traditional attitudes" that might obscure an objective view of the facts and thus impede rational choice. Such attitudes include anything that would separate the agent from the public world of facts shared by all, such as religious beliefs, personal visions of the world derived from one's experience, private myths, or stories about oneself.

The philosophical background to this picture of the agent can be found in the psychology presented by Gilbert Ryle in *The Concept of Mind*, which helped to bring about what Murdoch refers to as "the disappearance of mind"[80] in modern moral philosophy. This background is important, because Murdoch argues that modern moral philosophy has taken epistemological arguments presented by Ryle, Wittgenstein, and others, and drawn moral consequences that do not necessarily follow from these arguments. The epistemological arguments and Murdoch's critique of them will be considered first, while the explicit moral consequences will be considered in the next section.

On Murdoch's reading of Ryle, the mind is not described as "a set of inner entities such as faculties and feelings, which are open to introspection"; rather, we must speak of "observable actions and patterns of behaviour."[81] Under the influence of this view,

> Recent philosophy has concentrated upon the task of resolving "the mind" into sets of identifiable activities, where the problem is first, how to isolate and identify such of these activities as are purely introspectible ones, and second, how to assess the importance of these inner proceedings as criteria for the application of words descriptive of the mind.[82]

At its core, the behaviorist argument radically questions the status of what is "private" in human consciousness. The introspectible content of the mind, or "mental event," is held to be suspect, for two reasons: "partly because we do not need it and partly because we cannot find it."[83] We do not need it, the argument goes, because "such an entity cannot form part of the structure of a public concept";[84] we cannot find it, because "such an entity cannot be introspectively discovered."[85]

Until very recently, Murdoch notes, the private mental event was thought to be necessary "partly to constitute the stuff and contents of the mind and be the guarantee of the intelligent character of action, and partly to provide a world composed of recurrent and intrinsically meaningful entities which should also be the basis of language."[86] Both of these functions of the mental event have been called into question by developments in the philosophy of mind. First, Murdoch notes Wittgenstein's argument that "what determines the use of words about the mind are features of the overt context; the rigidity that creates meaning lies in the social framework and not in the relation to an inward utterance."[87] We learn the meaning of mental words by observing how they are used in the conduct of others, not by referring to our own inner experiences.[88] The meaning of the concept "red," for example, can only be known or identified by the "public schemata" that I have learned.[89] " 'Red' cannot be the name of something private. The structure of the concept is its public structure, which is established by coinciding procedures in public situations."[90] The notion of the private mental event literally is devoid of sense, since the meaning of such entities depends on its public context. As Wittgenstein put it, "there are no 'private ostensive definitions.' "[91] Thus we no longer need such an entity to guarantee the meaning of language or as a referent for making our outward actions intelligible: both of these depend on the conventions and rules of public language.

Second, we no longer need the notion of the private mental event, according to this argument, because it is now held that "acts of meaning (for instance in the form of images) do not necessarily accompany intelligent uses of words and that even if they did they would only be rendered unambiguous by the use which we made of them."[92] In other words, we now recognize that we do not need to depend on a repeatable inward experience in order to use a concept correctly. The inward act of meaning is not an identifiable core experience; rather, the act of meaning is identified or justified by how it is used. We may, for example, use the word "red" correctly without necessarily understanding the imagery of color or knowing what a private experience of "red" is like. "What matters," says Murdoch of this view, "is whether I stop at the traffic lights."[93] The meaning of "red" depends upon the public fact of its use in this context, not on my private experience of "red." In short, private experiences cannot furnish the criterion for the meaning of concepts such as "red," since even identifying such entities in the first place requires "the rigidity supplied by a public test."[94]

The criterion of meaning implicit in this argument is associated with the verificationism of British empiricism. According to this criterion, inner experiences are "justified" or verified by their public context, which is subject to empirical observation:

> The notion of meaning which goes with strict justification (or verification) demands an observable or identifiable something which shall by a universal convention be that which justifies the use, and this is to be detected from an objective impersonal standpoint. From such a standpoint "the mind" is inevitably seen as divided between obscure private communings about which nothing can be said, and overt cases of intelligent, etc., conduct; and the language which this investigation illuminates is a public symbolism taking its sense from an open network of social conventions.[95]

Linguistic behaviorism has drawn two conclusions from this view of meaning: first, that because mental terms are learned in public contexts and justified by their public use rather than by an inner experience, such experiences therefore do not exist; second, that "what goes on in our heads" is irrelevant to the meaning of mental terms.[96] In both cases, the private realm of the individual agent is discredited in favor of the public realm of shared social conventions, which determine meaning and provide the criterion for understanding conduct.

Murdoch's criticism of both of these assumptions in her early essays helps to shed light on her constructive position about the importance of a notion of consciousness to the idea of the individual. On the first point, Murdoch argues that "an ontological approach [to the idea of the private mental event], which seeks for an identifiable inner stuff and either asserts or denies its existence, must be avoided."[97] Rather than looking for empirical proof that such "inner stuff" exists, Murdoch argues that it is enough that we *think* of our thoughts as inner events; this idea is crucial to how we understand ourselves as individual selves. "[W]e need and use the idea that thoughts are particular inner experiences," she writes. "This is an idea which connects up with our notion of the privacy and unity of our 'selves' or 'personalities.' "[98] In this sense, the idea of the private mental event is "a necessary regulative idea" that supports our conception of ourselves as individuals; a strict verificationist test which seeks to prove or disprove the existence of such phenomena is simply beside the point.[99]

On the second point, Murdoch insists that meaning simply cannot be reducible to overt or public meaning in all cases. For example, there is a sense of inner or private meaning according to which I might object that "what I meant" when I said something was quite different from the overt meaning of my statement. Murdoch writes: "Imagine a people who *really* held that what happened 'in their heads' was irrelevant to the use of words such as 'decide.' "[100] Mental events such as "having an idea" or "solving a problem" or "making a decision"[101] are private phenomena whose meaning is not reducible either to a physical concomitant (as a feeling like anger or jealousy might be) or to their public display or consequence. In other words, "certain remarks about the mind do seem to refer to particular mental events, and to suggest that such remarks are really about behaviour is to suggest a radical alteration of their sense."[102]

On both points of contention, Murdoch is insisting that the notion of ourselves as unified individuals requires the idea of consciousness. The experience of "thinking" as something that goes on "inside" us, the notion that our minds are a mysterious and private region the contents of which are not observable by others—these ideas are indispensable to our most basic understanding of ourselves as human individuals. Without these notions, it is difficult to identify what it is that distinguishes human beings from one another at the level of mental contents. If the meaning of mental events is determined by their outward context or by public criteria, there seems to be no room for any notion of a purely "private" meaning that is the product of a particular individual mind.

So far, our discussion of linguistic behaviorism has concentrated on its epistemological presuppositions rather than its moral consequences. In the next section I turn to a consideration of the effects of the linguistic behaviorist argument on moral philosophy strictly speaking.

II. B. The Moral Consequences of Linguistic Behaviorism

The epistemological discussion in analytic philosophy about the status of what goes on in the mind had a vast impact on modern moral philosophy, in Murdoch's view. Its effect was to encourage a *moral* behaviorism that discredited the entire inner region of thought and introspection as not only epistemologically dubious but also morally irrelevant.[103] Murdoch believed that moral philosophy extended the linguistic behaviorist criticism of the idea of private meaning to the sphere of morality without justification. For example, she writes that Wittgenstein "does not make any moral or psychological generalizations"[104] from his argument there are no private ostensive definitions: "Wittgenstein is not claiming that inner data are 'incommunicable', nor that anything special about human personality follows from their 'absence', he is merely saying that no sense can be attached to the idea of an 'inner object'."[105] Further, Wittgenstein "does not apply this idea to moral concepts, nor discuss its relation to mental concepts in so far as these form part of the sphere of morality."[106] Philosophers such as Hampshire, Hare, Ayer, Ryle, and others who have discredited the moral status of consciousness on the basis of linguistic behaviorist arguments have therefore done so without adequate warrant.

Murdoch challenges the linguistic behaviorist view by first calling our attention to the great diversity of phenomena that make up the inner realm. In focusing on the existence and status of the private mental event, the linguistic behaviorist view has neglected a whole range of mental phenomena associated with the agent's individual character or moral being. These include "private stories, images, inner monologue"[107] that the agent may or may not choose to make public, as well as "overt manifestations of personal attitudes, speculations, or visions of life such as might find expression in talk not immediately directed to the solution of specific moral problems."[108] Murdoch notes that even Ryle conceded the existence of "mental images, speeches uttered to oneself, and perhaps more obscure occurrences which ask for metaphorical descriptions."[109] But he argued that these events "are in no way privileged, either as being causes of more outward activity or as being the hidden core or essence of individual minds."[110] Murdoch insists on the contrary that such phenomena of the inner life of consciousness are essential to the idea of the individual, and that they play a crucial role in morality.

Murdoch develops her critique of the moral consequences of linguistic behaviorism in the essay in *The Sovereignty of Good* titled "The Idea of Perfection." She focuses her analysis specifically on Stuart Hampshire's work as indicative of the influence of linguistic behaviorism on moral philosophy.[111] For example, she describes Hampshire's view of the moral agent in *Thought and Action* as

> an object moving among other objects in a continual flow of intention into action. . . . Actions are roughly instances of moving things about in the public world. . . . The inner or mental world is inevitably parasitic upon the outer world. . . . Further: thought and belief are separate from will and action. . . . Thought as such is not action but an introduction to action.[112]

Murdoch interprets Hampshire to mean that the purpose of thought is to serve as a preparation for action by surveying possibilities and clarifying the agent's intentions: "We should aim at total knowledge of our situation and a clear conceptualization of all our possibilities."[113] The inner life is only morally relevant to the extent that it performs this function.

> Thought and intention must be directed towards definite overt issues or else they are merely day-dream. . . . What is 'inward', what lies in between overt actions, is either impersonal thought, or 'shadows' of acts, or else substanceless dream. Mental life is, and logically must be, a shadow of life in public. . . . Morality is a matter of thinking clearly and then proceeding to outward dealings with other men.[114]

Thought aims at gaining an impersonal and objective knowledge of the options or choice of goods confronting the agent, so that the will—which is the center of the personality and the locus of the agent's freedom—can perform the overt action of choice. This emphasis on the will explains Murdoch's reference to this view as "existentialist-behaviorist."

The separation in Hampshire's moral psychology between thought (as a preparation for choice) and the will (as the agency of choice) is a central feature of the existentialist-behaviorist view. The moral agent is divided between impersonal thought and a personal will. Thought is impersonal because its activity is guided by the impersonal logic of mental words and thus assumes an objective or neutral standpoint, whereas the will is personal because it is the seat of the agent's subjectivity and is defined by its freedom to choose independent of the strictures of logic: "Will does not bear upon reason, so the 'inner life' is not to be thought of as a moral sphere. Reason deals in neutral descriptions and aims at being the . . . ideal observer."[115] The result of this distinction between thought or reason and the will is a particular conception of moral freedom, which Murdoch describes as follows:

> What I am doing or being is not something private and personal, but is imposed upon me in the sense of being identifiable only via public concepts and objective observers. Self-knowledge is something which shows overtly. Reasons are public reasons, rules are public rules. Reason and rule represent a sort of impersonal tyranny in relation to which however the personal will represents perfect freedom. Morality resides at the point of action. What I am 'objectively' is not under my control; logic and observers decide that. What I am 'subjectively' is a foot-loose solitary, substanceless will. Personality dwindles to a point of pure will.[116]

Freedom on this view is a function of the will's ability to escape (leap out of) the impersonal logic of linguistic convention by the act of choosing. Freedom is related neither to the agent's own private being nor to his or her ability to use language in particular ways associated with the agent's own individual character.

Murdoch calls the view of meaning implied in Hampshire's existentialist-behaviorist position "the genetic analysis of mental concepts."[117] According to the genetic analysis, we learn the meaning of a mental concept such as "decision" by observing the conduct that goes with deciding.

> How do I *learn* the concept of decision? By watching someone who says 'I have decided' and who then acts. How else could I learn it? And with that I learn the essence of the matter. . . . A decision does not turn out to be, when more carefully considered, an introspectible movement. The concept has no further inner structure; it *is* its outer structure.[118]

On this genetic view, there is no difference in this context between the mental concept of "decision" and the physical concept of "red" that I noted earlier: both owe their meaning to a public criterion rather than to a core experience. Although the linguistic behaviorists concede that a sense can be given to the idea that deciding means "I said some words to myself," they insist that in order to determine whether this was really a decision, I must "examine the context of my announcement rather than its private core."[119] On this view, Murdoch observes, "That I decided to do X will be true if I said sincerely that I was going to and did it, even if nothing introspectible occurred at all. And equally something introspectible might occur, but if the outward context is entirely lacking the something cannot be called a decision."[120]

This understanding of what it means to "decide" is based entirely on what one overtly says or does and discounts any private mental operation as nonverifiable. What is important for morality are actions rather than " 'what goes on inwardly' in between moments of overt 'movement.' "[121] But Murdoch objects that there is far more at stake for our picture of the moral agent in the case of mental words such as "decision" than in the case of "red." In brief, the linguistic behaviorist image of moral agency is "both alien and implausible"[122] because it does not do justice to our most basic and ordinary sense of what it means to decide or deliberate as an individual thinking consciousness. "Surely there is such a thing as deciding and not acting? Surely there are *private* decisions? Surely there are lots and lots of objects, more or less easily identified, in orbit as it were in inner space? It is not, as the argument would seem to imply, silent and dark within."[123] A genetic analysis fails sufficiently to illuminate the actual phenomenon of deciding because it cannot account for the idea that something occurs privately in an individual consciousness which may not achieve outward expression. The verificationist view of meaning "breaks down" in the face of the concept of the individual, Murdoch suggests, and requires us to "attempt a new description" of the inner region.[124]

Murdoch classifies the different types of attitude that the moral philosopher might adopt towards this inner region as follows:

> It may be held that these elusive activities (e.g., deciding, private story-telling, inner monologue) are irrelevant to morality which concerns definite moral choices and the reasons therefor. It may be held that these activities are of interest in so far as they make choices and their reasons more comprehensible. It may be held that these activities can be regarded as being themselves moral acts resulting from responsible choices and requiring reasons.[125]

Each of these three positions, Murdoch observes, would be compatible with the linguistic behaviorist view of the relation between thought and action. By contrast, her own position on the moral status of consciousness constitutes a radical break with linguistic behaviorist assumptions: "[F]inally, it may be held that these activities are themselves direct expressions of a person's 'moral nature' or 'moral being' and demand a type of description which is not limited to the choice and argument model."[126] Murdoch's view of moral agency aims to redeem thought or consciousness as a moral sphere whose description and justification do not depend solely on its connection to overt actions. The integrity of the individual moral agent depends on preserving this inner region of privacy and meaning. This is perhaps the single most important insight linking Murdoch's diverse writings over the course of her career, so much so that nearly forty years after the publication of her first essays on this subject, she writes in *Metaphysics as a Guide to Morals*: "Our present moment, our experiences, our flow of consciousness, our indelible moral sense, are not all these essentially linked together and do they not *imply* the individual?"[127] It is precisely the inner life of consciousness that distinguishes human beings as individuals and renders them capable of valuing and choosing one course of action over others.

In conclusion, Murdoch's argument against linguistic behaviorism brings out with even greater force than her critique of Sartre the integral connection in her thought between the concept of the individual and the idea of consciousness. The Sartrean account of the moral self, in spite of its deficient ontology, nevertheless leaves us with a picture of the "heroic *individual*," constantly re-creating himself or herself in the face of a deadening fall into conventional value. The linguistic behaviorist self, by contrast, appears more as a functionary of linguistic codes than as an individual in any traditional sense of the term. Indeed, linguistic behaviorism's tendency to reduce the mind's complex mental operations to the public rules of the "moral language game" threatens the very thing that distinguishes individuals from one another: the notion of a private realm of meaning particular to each person. In this respect, linguistic behaviorism offers a more radical challenge for Murdoch than does existentialism, because it requires her to defend the notion of consciousness itself.[128] This will be the constructive task of her moral psychology, which is the subject of the next chapter.

4

MORAL AGENCY, CONSCIOUSNESS, AND THE CONCEPT OF THE INDIVIDUAL

In her last and widest-ranging philosophical work, *Metaphysics as a Guide to Morals*, Murdoch writes that "consciousness or self-being [is] the fundamental mode or form of moral being."[1] Morality is inseparable, in other words, from the activity of a thinking, evaluating consciousness whose inner reflection forms much of the substance of moral activity. This claim about consciousness runs against the stream of voluntaristic forms of ethics since Kant, which identify the will as the center of human moral being and the source of value-creating power. More specifically, Murdoch's theory of consciousness brings together two things that have been severed in post-Kantian ethics: knowledge and morality, or cognition and value. The disjunction between these represents at the level of moral psychology the theoretical disjunction between fact and value represented in the debate over naturalism in Chapter 2.

In this chapter I turn from an exposition of Murdoch's critique of existentialism and linguistic behaviorism as reductionistic accounts of the moral self to an analysis of her constructive response to these philosophies. In developing an account of her moral psychology, I examine what I take to be Murdoch's two central claims about consciousness: first, that consciousness is "the fundamental mode of moral being" and is structured in correlation with an idea of the good; and second, that consciousness is constituted in relation to a larger moral ontology in which others are paradigmatic of the real. The first claim concerns the internal structure of consciousness itself and answers the linguistic behaviorist rejection of consciousness as morally insignificant. The second claim addresses Sartre's argument that consciousness is constituted in paradoxical tension with value or the good.[2]

The argument of the chapter will proceed as follows. In Section I, I analyze Murdoch's first claim by showing that the activity of consciousness is itself a moral activity and is integral to the idea of the individual as a moral being. In Section II, I consider Murdoch's second claim about consciousness to show that her account overcomes the deficiencies of Sartre's dualistic conception of consciousness by situating moral consciousness against a background of relations to others in a moral world. In Section III, I address Murdoch's theory of the individual as she formulates it in a series of essays on liberal theory and literature. These writings help to situate Murdoch's position midway between the Liberal view and the Natural Law views of moral agency, rather than unambiguously supporting the latter (see Chapter 2). I conclude the chapter by showing that Murdoch's insistence on the moral significance of consciousness enables her to relate three crucial elements of her ethics: cognitivism; the idea of the individual; and the concept of freedom.

Section I. Consciousness as the Mode of Moral Being

The articulation of a "working philosophical psychology"[3] was a central interest of Murdoch's thought for forty years, and is perhaps the greatest source of her influence on ethical inquiry. She has suggested that her philosophy as a whole might be considered "a kind of moral psychology"[4] rather than as a systematic philosophical position per se. This psychology is centered on recovering a philosophical description of the mind or consciousness as a bearer of value or moral being and not merely a neutral surveyor of the facts. The recovery of such a view is the guiding theme of her wide-ranging reflections on art, morality, and religion in her Gifford Lectures, *Metaphysics as a Guide to Morals*, as well as her influential earlier work, *The Sovereignty of Good*. In both works, Murdoch attempts to rescue the notions of consciousness and private meaning from philosophers, linguistic philosophers, and others who by various strategies seek to do away with the individual self as a "moral centre or substance."[5]

Although Murdoch's explicit claim that "consciousness or self-being [is] the fundamental mode or form of moral being"[6] is specific to *Metaphysics as a Guide to Morals*, the same essential conviction lies behind her critique of the existentialist-behaviorist view that dominates *The Sovereignty of Good*. While both of these texts defend a notion of consciousness as basic to moral agency and the idea of the individual, the more recent work does so in the context of recent Wittgensteinian and poststructuralist linguistic theory rather than in response to thinkers such as Ryle and Hampshire. Further, *Metaphysics as a Guide to Morals* moves beyond the argument of *The Sovereignty of Good* by showing more directly how aspects of moral subjectivity are correlative to aspects of the good. For these reasons, I will leave the discussion of *Metaphysics* for Chapter 5, where I will take up the idea of consciousness as it relates to the concept of the good in the reflexive structure of Murdoch's ontological proof.

In *The Sovereignty of Good*, Murdoch attempts to refute the linguistic behaviorist claim that the inner life of consciousness is irrelevant to morality by developing an alternative account of moral agency. Against the view that "morality is choice, and moral language guides choice through factual specification,"[7] she argues that morality also has to do with vision—that is, with our complex apprehension of ourselves and the world, which cannot be reduced to a rational scrutiny of the facts. Our choices are a function not only of our will but also of our knowledge and vision, which includes the quality of our perceptions and states of mind. Moral language is no longer seen merely as a practical pointer of our choices, but rather as an instrument of an individual's unique perception of the world.

The centerpiece of Murdoch's critique of the arguments of Hampshire and others can be found in the essay "The Idea of Perfection," where she presents a now famous example of concrete moral deliberation involving a mother and her daughter-in-law. As Martha Nussbaum has noted, Murdoch's decision to use an example of this sort is itself indicative of her attempt to broaden the realm of the relevant data of ethical inquiry to include the activity of self-consciousness.[8] Specifically, Murdoch believes that what happens in a quite ordinary situation of a mother reflecting privately on her son's choice of a wife is in fact an example of moral *activity*, even when no real "action" takes place. The example is thus expressly designed to call into question the linguistic behaviorist assumptions about the status of mental activity or introspection and its ostensible relation to outward conduct. In the following pages, I present the example in full and summarize the essential points of Murdoch's analysis in order to bring out her response to behaviorism.

> A mother, whom I shall call M, feels hostility to her daughter-in-law, whom I shall call D. M finds D quite a good-hearted girl, but while not exactly common yet certainly unpolished and lacking in dignity and refinement. D is inclined to be pert and familiar, insufficiently ceremonious, brusque, sometimes positively rude, always tiresomely juvenile. M does not like D's accent or the way D dresses. M feels that her son has married beneath him. Let us assume for purposes of the example that the mother, who is a very 'correct' person, behaves beautifully to the girl throughout, not allowing her real opinion to appear in any way.[9]

By describing a situation in which an agent's inward feelings remain private or hidden to observers, Murdoch is already questioning the linguistic behaviorist claim that such "mental contents" cannot be said to exist in any meaningful way unless they are verified by their outward expression. In order to underline the fact that "whatever is in question as *happening* happens entirely in M's mind,"[10] Murdoch's example further stipulates that

D and her husband may be imagined to have moved away, or that D is now dead.

> Time passes, and it could be that M settles down with a hardened sense of grievance and a fixed picture of D, imprisoned (if I may use a question-begging word) by the cliche: my poor son has married a silly vulgar girl. However, the M of the example is an intelligent and well-intentioned person, capable of self-criticism, capable of giving careful and just attention to an object which confronts her. M tells herself: "I am old-fashioned and conventional. I may be prejudiced and narrow-minded. I may be snobbish. I am certainly jealous. Let me look again."[11]

Already, in this passage, Murdoch introduces the language of vision to describe what goes on in M's mind. M has a fixed "picture" of D—that is, a mental image that has no relation to her actions toward D. M realizes that in order to reevaluate D she must "look" at this image again, giving it her full "attention" in the light of her scrutiny of her own motives. The result of this process is that gradually, M's vision of D alters. It is essential to Murdoch's point to emphasize that the change that occurs "is not in D's behaviour but in M's mind."[12] "D is discovered to be not vulgar but refreshingly simple, not undignified but spontaneous, not noisy but gay, not tiresomely juvenile but delightfully youthful, and so on. And as I say, *ex hypothesi*, M's outward behaviour, beautiful from the start, in no way alters."[13] If M's perception of D does not show in her outward behavior, what status are we to give this inward mental activity? How are to describe the status of M's changing perception of D?

A defender of the linguistic behaviorist view might argue that M's change of mind about D has only hypothetical status, since M's conduct does not reflect any outward change, thus leaving us with no way to verify whether there is in fact any "introspectible material" in M's mind.[14] Or the linguistic behaviorist might argue that, even if it is conceded that M has introspectible material in the sense that she formed visual images of D, "talked to herself" about D, and so forth, "the identity and meaning of these statements is a function of the public world. She can only be thought of as 'speaking' seriously . . . if the outer context logically permits."[15] Further, since there is no outward change in M's behavior to correspond to the alleged inner change of mind about D ("no sequence of outer events of which the inner can claim to be shadows"), it is doubtful that we can claim that M's changing inner perception of D counts as an "activity."[16] On a linguistic behaviorist interpretation of Murdoch's example, then, "the idea of M as *inwardly* active turns out to be an empty one. There is only outward activity, ergo only outward moral activity, and what we call inward activity is merely the shadow of this cast back into the mind."[17]

This refusal to consider what is happening in M's mind as morally significant activity is precisely what Murdoch contests. "[T]he idea which we are trying to make sense of," she writes, "is that M has in the interim been *active*, she has been *doing* something, something which we approve of, something which is somehow worth doing in itself. M has been morally active in the interim: this is what we want to say and to be philosophically permitted to say."[18] The linguistic behaviorist analysis defines M " 'from the outside in.' "[19] That is, she is defined by her movements, which are a function of her will, while her inner acts do not seem to belong to her or to form "a continuous fabric of being."[20] Conversely, Murdoch attempts to describe M "from the inside out" by attempting to describe the nature of M's inward deliberation about D.

Murdoch's description of M's activity presents several significant points of contrast between her own account of the moral agent and the existentialist-behaviorist view as represented by Hampshire. These include: (1) the role of vision in morality; (2) the nature and function of moral language; (3) the notion of privacy as irreducible to individual deliberation; and (4) the progressive nature of the activity of moral reflection. I will discuss each in turn. First and most important, as I have already noted, M's activity is one about which we use the language of vision. This is the first indication that Murdoch understands moral perception as analogous to aesthetic perception, a view that persists throughout her ethics. M "takes a second look" at D in order to try to be fair to her; she begins to "see her differently"; she may "brood on visual images of D."[21]

> [I]s not the metaphor of vision almost irresistibly suggested to anyone who, without philosophical prejudice, wishes to describe the situation? Is it not the natural metaphor? M *looks* at D, she attends to D, she focuses her attention. M is engaged in an internal struggle. She may for instance be tempted to enjoy caricatures of D in her imagination.[22]

On the existentialist-behaviorist view, the agent is identified with the "empty choosing will,"[23] and morality is defined as action, movement, and conduct rather than vision. "There is no moral vision. There is only the ordinary world which is seen with ordinary vision, and there is the will that moves within it."[24] In Murdoch's example, however, M's moral being resides "not simply in her moving will but in her seeing knowing mind."[25] Moral activity is not merely outward action, but also takes place in the mind "in between the occurrence of explicit moral choices."[26]

This contrast between the activity of vision and the activity of the will is crucial to Murdoch's moral psychology. Whereas the existentialist-behaviorist view affirms the priority of the will and emphasizes choice as the paradigmatic moral activity, Murdoch's picture shifts the center of gravity in the moral agent to the larger complex of intellect, vision, and imagination that is the omnipresent *background* to our choices. As she puts the point more recently in *Metaphysics*: "We may judge a man's virtue by his actions, but also demand or hope to know the 'substance' which lies behind them, as in our own case we apprehend a value-bearing base of being from which actions spring."[27] This retrieval of a notion of consciousness as the *condition* for moral choice entails a radical departure from the existentialist-behaviorist conception of free choice as an unconditioned leap of the will. Rather, for Murdoch, freedom is always situated within a larger complex of values, and conditioned by some prior notion of the good. Thus, while both linguistic behaviorism and Sartrean existentialism treat the good as an "empty box" to be filled in by what the will chooses, Murdoch understands the good as an antecedent "background" that constitutes moral consciousness internally. More pointedly, this understanding of consciousness as the background or "value-bearing base" of moral action is correlative to Murdoch's transcendental aspect of the good, as we will see in Chapter 5.

The second point of contrast with linguistic behaviorism is that Murdoch's description of M's activity represents a different view of the nature and function of moral language. M's change of heart about D might be described in terms of "the substitution of one set of normative epithets for another."[28] For example, M stops thinking of D as "tiresomely juvenile" and instead sees her as "delightfully youthful." It is an important feature of this activity that it requires a wide range of what Murdoch calls "the secondary moral words" that describe persons and situations in their particular details, rather than "the primary and general ones such as 'good.' "[29] Once morality ceases to be conceived merely as choice and action and is conceived also as thought and vision, it will require not only choice-guiding words such as "good" and "right," but also an "elaborate normative vocabulary"[30] to aid moral vision. Moral language in Murdoch's example is thus an instrument of the individual's knowledge of herself and the world, rather than determined by a public context on which all agents can agree.

In this respect, Murdoch sets herself apart from those who defend the priority of "ordinary language" or of impersonal linguistic codes over individual users of a language, a position she identifies with linguistic behaviorists but also, more recently, with certain poststructuralist thinkers as well as linguistic philosophers in the tradition of Wittgenstein.[31] Against this view, Murdoch insists that an individual's use of language cannot be reduced to any established code of linguistic meaning. Although she recognizes that moral language is *learned* publicly, that we develop a moral vocabulary in the presence of others, and that understanding others depends in large part on learning the meaning of words in a shared context,[32] Murdoch insists that we put our publicly learned concepts to private uses. "Of course, in a general sense, language must have rules," she writes in *Metaphysics*. "But it is also the property of individuals whose inner private consciousness, seething with arcane imagery and shadowy intuitions, occupies the greater part of their being."[33]

The third contrast with the linguistic behaviorist account is related to the preceding point about language. In Murdoch's view, the idiosyncratic nature of our use of moral language is directly indicative of the irreducibly private and personal nature of M's deliberation about D. Because moral vision and the use of moral language is highly individual, another person engaged in a similar reflection about D would not think about her precisely as M does. "M's activity is peculiarly *her own*. Its details are the details of *this* personality; and partly for this reason it may well be an activity which can only be performed privately. M could not *do this* thing in conversation with another person."[34] In contrast to the linguistic behaviorist argument that mental events must be verified by linguistic rules or by the observation of the agent's conduct, in the case of M's deliberation about D, "there is an activity but no observers."[35] This privacy is in fact essential to how the activity is constituted; M's reflections about D reflect her own particular moral vision, personal history, and moral temperament. M's reasons for changing her image of D may not be public reasons, shared by other rational agents; rather, they are reasons based on her particular relation to D and her own individual moral being. Murdoch writes: "Reasons are not necessarily and *qua* reasons public. They may be reasons for a very few, and none the worse for that. 'I can't explain. You'd have to know her.' "[36] Murdoch's analysis of the inevitable privacy of our language use thus calls into question "the would-be timeless image of reason"[37] that has been presumed in modern moral philosophy. Language is uttered "in spatio-temporal and conceptual contexts,"[38] in the presence of varied listeners and varied cultural and other objects. Our understanding of others is not guaranteed by an appeal to public reasons; rather, "We learn through attending to contexts . . . and we can only understand others if we can to some extent share their contexts. (Often we cannot.)"[39] Moral reasoning involves the elaboration of a moral vocabulary in the context of particular acts of "looking" with others, and sharing such a vocabulary means that one must overcome the privacy in some measure that is a constitutive feature of individual minds.

The fourth and final point of comparison with the linguistic behaviorist view is that, unlike the momentary activity of the will in moral choice, the activity of looking is essentially progressive, continuous, and fallible; it implies an ideal end-point which may never be reached.[40] The change in M's perception of D is not instantaneous, but gradual and uneven: M may enjoy creating wicked caricatures of D in her mind before arriving at a more just and compassionate view. And once she arrives at this view, there is no guarantee that M's perception of D may not change again, simply by virtue of the fact that the activity of understanding another human being is necessarily an open-ended process. "Morality," Murdoch writes, is essentially connected with change and progress."[41]

M confronted with D has an endless task. Moral tasks are characteristically endless not only because "within," as it were, a given concept our efforts are imperfect, but also because as we move and as we look our concepts themselves are changing. To speak here of an inevitable imperfection, or of an ideal limit of love or knowledge which always recedes, may be taken as a reference to our "fallen" human condition. . . . Since we are neither angels nor animals but human individuals, our dealings with each other have this aspect.[42]

The idea of perfection that is implied in the progressive and fallible nature of M's moral reflection on D is centrally important to Murdoch's notion of consciousness. This is because it introduces into the notion of consciousness a perfectionist ideal that structures consciousness according to a hierarchy of values on the basis of which we evaluate persons, states of minds, and courses of action. As I will argue in Chapter 5, this aspect of consciousness is correlative to Murdoch's second aspect of the good— namely, the good as perfectionist ideal or standard. Thus, as illustrated in the example, M's reflection about D strives to be "just" and "compassionate" based on an implicit ideal of clear vision present in her consciousness, and in reference to which she weighs her own mental states against various images of D in her mind.

A further significant implication of the existence of an implicit standard of perfection in M's moral deliberation about D is that it indicates a shift in the "root metaphor" of moral activity from the rational objectivity of the scientist to the creative vision of the artist. This shift has been enormously influential in contemporary ethics, and it has important consequences for understanding the type of moral realism that Murdoch embraces. The linguistic behaviorist view, like the philosophical empiricism on which it is founded, assumes the existence of a hard objective world of facts. It replaces "the old impersonal atom-world of Hume and Russell" with an "impersonal language-world" governed by logical rules. We know the meaning of a word, including value terms, on this view, "through being rational and knowing ordinary language."[43] Mental concepts can be analyzed by tracing their meaning back to their "genesis" not in the mind, but in "the rulings of an impersonal public language."[44] We learn the meaning of such terms by observing their use by others and the accompanying conduct.

On Murdoch's view, however, the progressive and highly individual nature of moral thinking means that "Knowledge of a value concept is something to be understood, as it were, in depth, and not in terms of switching on to some given impersonal network."[45] The concept of love, for example, requires more than simply understanding how the word "love" is used in public contexts or observing how people who say they love each other behave. Rather, we have to learn the meaning of moral words such as "love" gradually, not only through the given rules of ordinary language but also through our inward experience of love, our knowledge of ourselves and others. Moreover, what we believe to be love may change throughout our lives. As we learn such concepts, "A deepening process, at any rate an altering and complicating process, takes place."[46] Moral concepts thus imply an ideal limit of understanding that can never be reached, since that limit is inevitably conditioned by the privacy and personal history of each individual.

Murdoch believes that morality on the empiricist or scientific model cannot do justice to what human beings are actually like. What causes problems for empiricism is precisely "the conception of persons or individuals, a conception inseparable from morality."[47] "[S]ince we are human historical individuals the movement of understanding is onward into increasing privacy, in the direction of the ideal limit, and not back towards a genesis in the rulings of an impersonal public language."[48] The introduction of the idea of progress or perfection into the functioning of moral concepts and value terms implies a view of the moral agent as historical human individual rather than as rational agent or neutral observer. In any given example of an individual's moral deliberation, "the activity in question must remain a highly personal one upon which the *prise* of 'the impersonal world of language' is to say the least problematic: or rather it is an activity which puts in question the existence of such an impersonal world."[49] In the case of a man reflecting, for example, on whether what he is feeling can be considered "repentance," his inquiry is of course subject to certain public rules of language use governing the meaning of "repentance."[50] Yet at the same time, his reflection reveals him "making a specialized personal *use* of a concept. Of course he derives the concept initially from his surroundings; but he takes it away into his privacy. Concepts of this sort lend themselves to such uses; and what use is made of them is partly a function of the user's *history*."[51] The notions of privacy and history are integral to the notion of the individual and radically challenge the empiricist basis of modern behaviorist moral philosophy. "The idea of 'objective reality,' for instance, undergoes important modifications when it is to be understood, not in relation to 'the world described by science,' but in relation to the progressing life of a person."[52]

Murdoch's emphasis on moral vision and on the private and imaginative use of moral language in our reflection about the world deals a serious blow to the linguistic behaviorist ideal of rational choice and presents an alternative conception of moral realism and objectivity. Linguistic behaviorism had been suspicious of the notion of the inner or private mental event in part because "it would separate people from 'the ordinary world of rational argument.'"[53] But, Murdoch insists, "the unavoidable contextual privacy of language already does this, and except at a very simple and conventional level of communication there is no such ordinary world."[54] Morality has been defined as observable conduct in a world of facts accessible to all rational observers because linguistic behaviorism conceives moral rationality on the model of scientific rationality, the language of which "tries to be impersonal and exact and yet accessible for purposes of teamwork . . . in relation to definite practical goals."[55] On Murdoch's view, however, moral rationality is more like aesthetic perception than it is like science.[56] The work of vision and imagination, which are the very substance of our inner reflection, builds up a world which is in part our own private creation.

> Each of us lives and chooses within a partly private, partly fabricated world, and . . . it is false to suggest that we could, even in principle, "purge" the world we confront of these personal elements. Nor is there any reason why we should. To be a human being is to know more than one can prove, to conceive of a reality which goes "beyond the facts" in these familiar and natural ways.[57]

Murdoch's aesthetic view of morality does not assume an objective world of facts apart from the activity of an individual thinking consciousness. Rather, it assumes that the moral world is always already constituted by an individual mind that is internally structured in relation to a background of value and an implicit idea of perfection.

The implications of this understanding of moral realism can be illustrated by returning to the case of M and D. What is the "objective reality" about D? What would be missing if M's deliberation about D consisted only of a survey of the facts of D's behavior; or an attempt to identify "impersonal reasons" for adopting a particular attitude toward D; or a use of concepts guided only by conventional meanings of the terms? Murdoch insists that understanding any particular reality requires a disciplined reflection that elicits one's whole moral being, and that seeks to go beyond the observable "facts" of the object to which one is attending. Through the creative and personal use of descriptive terms, mental images, moral concepts, and other forms of inner reflection, M's understanding of the "facts" about D are shaped by her own particular moral vision and temperament. In this respect, M maintains a certain independence from "science and . . . the 'world of facts' which empiricist philosophy has created in the scientific image."[58] Her freedom resides not in the capacity of her will to choose a course of action on the basis of clear and neutral facts; rather, it resides in her ability to *see* the facts in a new context, or to discover new facts as suddenly relevant to her deliberation. "Moral concepts do not move about *within* a hard world set up by science and logic," Murdoch writes. "They set up for different purposes, a different world."[59]

We have now seen that Murdoch establishes the moral significance of human consciousness by suggesting that some conception of value is internal to consciousness itself. The example of M and D in *The Sovereignty of Good* reveals that a formal notion of the good is implied in the very activity of consciousness, both as a transcendental background that renders all of our perceptions "moral" and also as an implicit ideal of perfection that guides the progressive nature of moral deliberation about specific persons, courses of action, and states of mind. Thus we have succeeded in explicating Murdoch's first major claim about consciousness, that "consciousness is the mode of moral being."

Section II. Consciousness in Relation to an Ontology of Value

I now take up her second major claim about consciousness—namely, that consciousness is related to a larger ontology of value. While Murdoch does not state this claim explicitly, it has been implicit in her retrieval of metaphysics, her critique of the fact-value distinction, and her support of a cognitivist and realist metaethic. My task now is to show that a conception of the good structures the individual's relation to this larger ontology or framework, including the reality of others. The question that first needs to be addressed is the following: How does Murdoch's insight into the moral structure of human consciousness in *The Sovereignty of Good* provide the basis for her conception of the individual's relation to others and to a morally structured world?

This question first arose in the context of Murdoch's critique of Sartre. Murdoch had attempted to overcome the reductionism of Sartre's dualistic notion of consciousness and its separation from the realm of value by situating moral consciousness against the background of its relations to others within a moral world. My claim is that her understanding of consciousness as structured by transcendental and perfectionist aspects of the good may be read as her response to Sartre's division of consciousness into rupture and project. Rather than picturing consciousness as severed from or in perpetual tension with value, Murdoch insists on a fundamental correlation between consciousness and value. This correlation provides the basis for a moral ontology that includes the reality of others as the paradigmatic locus of value. As we will see, the reality of others is for Murdoch the preeminent instance of knowledge of the real, a knowledge that shatters the moral solipsism of the ego and connects the self with the good. In sum, the aim of Murdoch's moral psychology is not only to demonstrate that "consciousness is the fundamental mode of moral being" but also that "the fundamental mode of moral being is the individual in conscious relation to others." In order to make this argument, I must return briefly to the two major points of contention between Sartre and Murdoch: his dualistic account of consciousness, and the tension this sets up between freedom and the realization of value.

Recall that Sartre divides consciousness into two aspects and correlates these to two senses of freedom. Both as rupture and as project, consciousness is defined over against any antecedent order of value rather than conceived as integrally related to such an order. As rupture, consciousness is constituted as a negation of the given world of brutely existing things as well as reified values which have become "thinglike." Freedom in this first sense depends on the ability of consciousness to reflect upon and avoid immersion in the immobilizing substance of contingent reality. As project, consciousness aspires not to negate but to transcend the given world altogether and to stabilize its own being by seeking a perfect world beyond the realm of brute existence. Freedom in this second sense is pursued through the attempt to incarnate value in various human projects or endeavors that will unify consciousness with itself. The problem is that the very attempt to realize stable value undermines the ability of consciousness to maintain its freedom from the deadening world of things, social values, and conventions. All human aspiration carries the threat of "bad faith"— the reliance on dead or inherited values rather than the authentic creation of value through perpetual resistance to the given world. Thus the two aspects of consciousness and of freedom are in direct conflict with one another in Sartre's account, since the fulfillment of freedom as project only comes at the expense of freedom as rupture. There is no way for consciousness to stabilize its being through the pursuit of value without losing its freedom to negate the dead world of value against which it defines itself.

Murdoch's understanding of consciousness as structured by the two aspects of the good resolves the dualism of Sartrean consciousness and the paradoxical relation to value that follows from it. First, with respect to consciousness as rupture, Murdoch argues that Sartre's picture still assumes the same division between fact and value that she consistently attacks throughout her philosophy. Consciousness is seen as creating its own values through an act of will that negates the "factic" world of things and reified values. In contrast, Murdoch argues that we do not *impose* value on a morally neutral world of facts by an act of will. Rather, the world is already constituted as a moral world through our perception, which is a function of the ordinary operation of consciousness. As I will argue in Chapter 5, Murdoch's understanding of the reflexive nature of consciousness means that our perception of value is not an imposition on a neutral world of fact, but a product of an interpretive engagement between mind and world mediated by moral language and individual perception. In this respect, the importance of vision for Murdoch's moral psychology is that it breaks down the strict division between fact and value that is characteristic of voluntarist philosophies such as Sartre's. For Murdoch, the moral structure of human consciousness means that the individual exists within a moral reality. This is the import of her transcendental argument for the good as it relates to consciousness. The good is not merely a "label" that the will attaches to neutral objects of its own choosing; it is the prior condition for consciousness and its freedom. In sum, while consciousness for Sartre is constituted by the freedom to break from an essentially false world of inert values, Murdoch defines freedom as knowledge of a moral world in which the self is already situated.

Second, with respect to consciousness as project, Murdoch argues that the human aspiration to self-transcendence through the pursuit of value is not the self-contradictory and wholly futile effort that Sartre imagines it to be. Rather, the pursuit of perfection is in fact an integral component of the activity of consciousness that does not conflict with freedom. Just as Sartre's account of freedom as a rupture from the world of value is countered by Murdoch's transcendental idea of the good as constitutive of human consciousness, so his account of freedom as project may be compared to Murdoch's understanding of the good as an ideal standard of perfection implicit in consciousness.

In one respect, an obvious similarity exists between Sartre and Murdoch on this point: both thinkers affirm that transcendent value exerts a "magnetic pull" on human life. Murdoch's insistence that human beings continually strive for perfection without ever being able to reach it echoes some of the futility of Sartre's view of freedom as project. Her description of the progressive nature of moral reflection affirms that our vision is guided by the existence of an ideal end point of love or knowledge *which always recedes*. But Murdoch insists that the endless nature of the moral task does not entail the negation of our freedom. On the contrary, freedom involves choosing within a moral world that is already structured by degrees of value, rather than seeking to transcend this world by a creative leap of will.

It is now possible to see how Murdoch's account of consciousness presents a way out of the paradox inherent in Sartre's account of the human attempt to transcend itself in pursuit of an unattainable value. For Murdoch, no fundamental paradox exists between the two aspects of consciousness that are correlative to her two aspects of the good. As a transcendental idea whose formal character is perfectionist, value is part of the very substance and texture of consciousness. In this respect, the world we see is already a morally structured world that contains our values. Murdoch contests Sartre's dualism by showing that value is inescapable in human life. While Sartre describes human being as a "useless passion" whose pursuit of transcendent value is heroic in the same measure that it remains unfulfilled, Murdoch presents a more modest image of human beings (think of the mother-in-law in the M and D story) as engaged in a progressive struggle to see justly, honestly, and compassionately within a complex moral world. The exercise of freedom involves the struggle for knowledge and right vision within this world rather than a leap of the will outside of it. Human consciousness is understood as integrally related to a realm of value, rather than existing in irresolvable tension with it.

Murdoch's account of consciousness thus succeeds in showing not only that consciousness is internally structured by a notion of value (against the linguistic behaviorist account), but also that consciousness exists within a morally structured world keyed to the agent's vision and not merely the value-creating will (against the existentialist account). The task now is to show how the existence of others within this morally structured world becomes the primary locus of value in Murdoch's moral ontology. This will require us to turn from the notion of consciousness to the idea of the individual. The existence of individuals encountered in the social world becomes the paradigmatic occasion in Murdoch's thought for a transformative encounter with the real. In order to make this transition, we must return briefly to Sartre's own struggle with the idea of the individual and then consider Murdoch's response to that effort.

Sartre, as I noted, was not unaware of the deficiencies in his own ontology with respect to a defense of the individual and its freedom. His attempt to resolve the paradox of freedom and value in his later works was intended to address this problem. In these works Sartre sought to give substantive content to the idea of freedom in order to end the impasse in which the pursuit of value ends in the denial of human freedom. His new understanding of freedom breaks from his previous definitions to the extent that it presupposes a social understanding of human being engaged in collective projects, including political ones. Yet Sartre's attempt to redefine freedom and thereby resolve the tension in his own thought fails because there is no corollary in his view of consciousness to support this new understanding of freedom. Freedom in the liberal sense Sartre wishes to give it requires a more fully developed idea of the human individual than his view of consciousness is able to provide, one that recognizes the self's relation to others and allows for the realization of value in human projects without an inevitable fall into bad faith.

Murdoch answers this deficiency in Sartre's thought by providing, in effect, the missing corollary to a substantive conception of freedom in her view of consciousness. This corollary can be found by showing that the two aspects of consciousness in fact *imply* a notion of the individual as the paradigmatic locus of value. That is, within the moral structure of consciousness provided by the transcendental and perfectionist aspects of the good, the individual stands out as the most real and the most valuable thing when considered as both the subject and the object of moral attention. In the example of M and D we saw that Murdoch insisted on the irreducibly private, historical, and unique nature of every individual consciousness and its activity. Against the linguistic behaviorist assumption that our use of moral concepts is a matter of following the rules of the public language game, Murdoch asserts that moral thinking is always done by individuals who use language according to their own history, temperament, and perception. Every act of moral thinking is thus the product of a unique consciousness. This is why Murdoch asserts that "the conception of persons or individuals, a conception inseparable from morality,"[60] presents difficulties for the linguistic behaviorist view. Instead of picturing moral reflection as a search for impersonal reasons for action on which all agents can agree, Murdoch understands it as the activity of an individual consciousness whose reasoning emerges from a complex of public and private perceptions.

Further, Murdoch's insistence in the example of M and D on the progressive nature of the moral task means that the activity of moral thinking is not only carried out *by* unique individuals (as the subject of morality); it is also directed *at* individuals (as the object of morality). In contrast to the linguistic behaviorist emphasis on the public nature of moral reasons shared by all participants in the moral language game, Murdoch argues that moral vision should strive to grasp the particular rather than the universal. "The central concept of morality is 'the individual' thought of as knowable by love,"[61] she writes. Progress in understanding moral concepts does not move in the direction of increasing generality, but rather in the direction of increasing depth, privacy, and particularity. Thus the idea of the individual and the idea of perfection are connected.[62] Perfection is measured by our ability to perceive individuals: " 'reality' and 'individual' present themselves to us in moral context as ideal end-points or Ideas of Reason."[63] Knowledge of the individual is the highest goal of moral understanding, and is identified with knowledge of reality.

In this way, Murdoch shows that the activities of perception and evaluation that are endemic to the ordinary functioning of consciousness imply a notion of the individual as both the subject and the object of morality. Of the two aspects of consciousness, however, the perfectionist aspect is more important than the transcendental aspect in this context, since it affirms that morality is centered on individuals as the most important *object* of knowledge and vision. This is especially important because it provides an answer to Sartre in the implication that consciousness is severed neither from a realm of value nor from the existence of others. The connection Murdoch draws between the idea of the individual and the idea of perfection suggests that within the intentional structure of consciousness itself, there is already a striving toward the other (the individual, the real, the good) as the ideal end point of moral understanding. Consciousness is in a very real sense oriented toward knowledge of the individual other to the extent that it is structured by an ideal of perfection. This view of consciousness represents the missing corollary to the definition of freedom that Sartre was attempting to articulate in his later works because it points toward an implicit affirmation of the social nature of human beings. Freedom is understood not as a leap without any content, but rather as a substantive value enacted within a moral world of others that one strives to know in all its depth and particularity. Reconceiving freedom in this way lends support to a defense of the individual as situated in a social world of other individuals who are the preeminent object of moral understanding.

Taken as a whole, Murdoch's view of consciousness succeeds in addressing the deficiencies of Sartre's view of the moral self as individual.

She has provided an analysis of consciousness that is not divided, as Sartre's was, between two conflicting definitions of freedom that sever it from a realm of value. Rather, Murdoch's understanding of consciousness as correlative with two aspects of the good situates the self within a moral world. Further, she has shown that the human aspiration to realize value through the pursuit of perfection does not necessarily conflict with human freedom, as Sartre insisted. For Murdoch, the perfectionist orientation of consciousness toward knowledge of the individual is itself an aspect of freedom.

In spite of these advances, however, two important issues remain to be addressed in order to gain a thorough understanding of Murdoch's view of the individual. First, we need to ask how Murdoch's emphasis on the concept of the individual is worked out in her ethics with respect to the relations among moral selves in a social world. How does she justify her view that the individual is the paradigmatic locus of value in the moral world? The second and related issue has to do with gaining a more precise understanding of the kind of freedom Murdoch attributes to individuals when pictured within such a framework. The question, in brief, is whether Murdoch's view of freedom can answer the threat articulated in Sartre's notion of "bad faith." If, as Murdoch proposes, freedom is conceived not as the ability to create value, but rather as knowledge of a moral world that already contains our values, she appears to fall into what Sartre saw as the danger of thinking that our values are "given in the nature of things." Sartre's view of freedom was intended to affirm the human capacity to negate or transcend conventional values in the face of every social or political totality that presents its values as authoritative. What resources, if any, does Murdoch give the individual to transcend his or her situation and call certain values into question?

These questions will require a consideration of Murdoch's writings on liberalism, since that is the context in which she works out her theory of the individual and his or her relation to others. These writings strongly suggest that a residue of Sartre's worry about freedom and bad faith persists in Murdoch's theory of the individual. In spite of her criticism of Sartre on many points, Murdoch in fact remains preoccupied with the problem of freedom as it pertains to the question of the individual in the social world.

Section III. A. Introduction to Murdoch's Theory of the Individual

Murdoch articulated her theory of the individual in a number of highly original essays written in the period following her work on Sartre that address the meaning of the concept of the individual in the western liberal tradition. Taken together, these essays advance the argument that the liberal tradition in its modern theoretical and literary expressions has failed adequately to grasp the reality of the human individual. "We have never solved the problems about human personality posed by the Enlightenment,"[64] Murdoch writes in an early essay. "What we have never had, of course, is a satisfactory Liberal theory of personality, a theory of man as free and separate and related to a rich and complicated world from which, as a moral being, he has much to learn."[65] This quotation indicates the fundamental tension that Murdoch is seeking to preserve in her own position: a view of the individual as free, but also related; as separate, but also situated in a moral world that is an object of knowledge. Although she agrees with Sartre that the concept of the individual and its freedom rest in some measure on the capacity to resist or act against the values given by one's social context or community, Murdoch nevertheless believes that a defense of the individual requires the support of an ontology that recognizes the reality and value of others in a moral world. This contextualization of the individual in a moral world of others means that Murdoch understands the freedom to resist social convention not as a matter of will or decision, as Sartre does, but rather as a matter of moral knowledge.

Modern attempts to portray human individuals fail, in Murdoch's judgment, to preserve this necessary tension between the self's freedom and its situatedness in a moral world of others. She argues that the idea of the person or individual may be menaced from either of two directions. Either we fail to see the individual because we are enclosed in a solipsistic world and neglect the reality and independence of others;[66] or we fail to see the individual "because we are ourselves sunk in a social whole which we allow uncritically to determine our reactions, or because we see each other exclusively as so determined."[67] The first danger Murdoch calls "neurosis," which she relates to the construction of self-absorbed myths or fantasies that inflate the importance of the self and obscure the reality of others. The second danger she calls "convention," which she relates to the loss of the individual in the face of a larger social totality. This descriptive contrast or conceptual dyad constitutes a recurring trope in Murdoch's moral theory that often overlaps with other oppositional pairs and figures, as we will see. She traces these twin dangers in modern thought and attempts to articulate a conception of the individual that avoids both.

In the case of neurosis, the danger to the concept of the individual is that the self is inflated to the point of becoming a world unto itself, with no reality or value existing outside it. Murdoch associates this danger especially with Hegel and Romanticism, and also with Sartre (whom she called a "romantic rationalist"). In the case of convention, the danger to the concept of the individual is that the self is diminished in relation to a larger authoritative whole that encompasses all reality and value. The two types are actually two sides of the same coin. In one case, the self becomes the whole of reality; in the other, the self is eclipsed or shrunk in relation to the social totality. Murdoch wants to avoid both extremes by defending a conception of the individual as a separate being that is related to, but not overcome by, a complex social reality.

Murdoch regards her two primary opponents, linguistic behaviorism and existentialism, as succumbing to one or the other of these dangers. Linguistic analysis, with its emphasis on the public rules of the moral language game, represents the surrender to convention. It pictures the agent "as a being subject to rules, surrounded by a civilized society, surrounded in short by the network of ordinary language, that is, for these purposes, by the network of moral conceptual activity at its most common and universally accepted level."[68] Ordinary Language Man—the conceptual "persona" Murdoch uses to depict the moral agent on this view—is surrounded by a structure of concepts and linguistic rules that provide him with the "practical pointers" needed to express his choices. The network of moral words and concepts is "the instrument of commendation whereby we point out what is to be chosen."[69] Yet in spite of the fact that the agent is immersed in this moral language game and is therefore conceived as participating in something outside himself, Murdoch argues that he is socially isolated nevertheless: "the presence of others is felt, if at all, simply as the presence of rational critics."[70] "As a moral agent he is completely free, choosing between acts and reasons on his own responsibility."[71] In this respect, Ordinary Language Man also does not escape a certain kind of solipsism, since the existence of others is only morally relevant in the minimal sense that the network of moral language implies a social activity in which its users participate.

The existentialist agent, on the other hand, represents the surrender to neurosis. Like Ordinary Language Man, he is depicted as "totally free and self-sufficient."[72] As portrayed by Sartre, for example, the moral agent "is simply the center of an extreme decision, man stripped and made anonymous by extremity."[73] Whereas Ordinary Language Man is at least a participant in the linguistic conventions of a community, the neurotic existentialist self dramatizes his situation in a self-absorbed myth.[74] Thus he never confronts anything other than aspects of himself that must eventually be absorbed into his own consciousness. In this respect, Totalitarian Man, as Murdoch calls this conceptual persona, is a descendant of the Hegelian self:

> In the world inhabited by Totalitarian Man there are other people, but they are not real contingent separate other people. They appear as organized menacing extensions of the consciousness of the subject. A potentially or apparently separate center of significance is necessarily a menace to a Hegelian, something to be internalized in a battle of consciousnesses just as discrepant centers in oneself are overcome by reflection.[75]

Thus both Ordinary Language Man and Totalitarian Man are pictured as fundamentally alone. Ordinary Language Man is surrounded by the network of language, but his freedom and self-sufficiency are not challenged by the claims of other people. Totalitarian Man is faced only with "menacing extensions" of his own consciousness, rather than with real separate others. Both philosophies tend toward solipsism, Murdoch concludes, since neither is "concerned with anything real outside ourselves" or "provides us with a standpoint for considering real human beings in their variety."[76] Both fail, therefore, to provide a moral ontology that relates the individual to the real world of other people.[77]

We can conclude from this analysis that what Murdoch is seeking is not merely an affirmation of the self as a social being. In different ways, both neurosis and convention already do that by acknowledging the presence of others, albeit inadequately. Rather, she is seeking a more radical affirmation of the existence of individual others, not as mere extensions of the neurotic self, nor as mere functionaries of a public code of meaning, but as separate and unique beings. Such an affirmation of the individual other *as* other lies at the very core of both art and ethics: "The enemies of art and of morals, the enemies that is of love, are the same: social convention and neurosis."[78] Thus, a central element in Murdoch's theory of the individual will be an articulation of the meaning of love as it relates to the knowledge of diverse individuals as the primary object of moral attention. She formulates this insight in the context of the liberal tradition and its expression in the art form of the novel.

III. B. The Case of Liberalism: Tolerance and the Reality of Other People

Murdoch regards the central tension in the philosophical inheritance of the modern west as a kind of tug-of-war between a Liberal emphasis on the separateness and autonomy of the individual, represented especially by Kant, and a Romantic urge to overcome or absorb the individual in a larger organic unity, associated especially with Hegel's philosophy. We have observed this dyadic contrast between Kant and Hegel (or more accurately, between what these thinkers signify to Murdoch) at several points in earlier chapters. Throughout her writings, the point of the contrast is to bring into sharper focus what she perceives to be the dangers to the concept of the individual. In "The Sublime and the Beautiful Revisited," for example, Murdoch argues that the Liberal emphasis on the value and integrity of the individual was endangered by the infusion of Romanticism into the Kantian tradition via Hegel. Hegel's gift to the Romantic movement, and one "from whose effects we have not yet recovered," is the view that "there is only one being in the Hegelian universe, the whole which cannot allow anything outside itself and which struggles to realize all that is apparently other."[79] Murdoch calls for the detachment of liberalism from Hegel's "corrupting" influence, and her constructive position may be read as the attempt to articulate a theory of the liberal individual that avoids the problems of both Kant on the one hand, and Hegel on the other.

This assessment of Hegel marks a departure from Murdoch's apparent embrace of Hegel as a Natural Law moralist noted in Chapter 2. Specifically, it lends support to my claim that Murdoch is not unambiguously a Natural Law moralist, but is attempting to preserve important insights of the Liberal view as well. This is especially evident in light of the important (albeit ambiguous) role played by Kant in her thought. Kant's moral philosophy occupies a central position in Murdoch's account of liberalism, since she believes that it contains "both the initial strength and the later weakness of the Liberal theory of personality, which is to such an extent also the Romantic theory of personality."[80] The weakness of Kant's liberalism is that he fails to recognize others as unique individuals, but rather only as rational agents. As Murdoch interprets Kant, the basis of our respect for others is not their individuality, but rather the universal reason that all rational agents share. This, she argues, is the seed for the later degeneration of Kantian liberalism into Romanticism, which neglects the particularity of individuals for the sake of some larger value or unity: "We respect others," on Kant's view, "not as particular eccentric phenomenal individuals, but as co-equal bearers of universal reason."[81] In this sense, the subject of Kantian morality is not the individual as a particular, unique being, but rather the individual as rational citizen subject to the moral law. As Murdoch puts it in another essay, "Kant does not tell us to respect whole particular tangled-up historical individuals, but to respect the universal reason in their breasts. In so far as we are rational and moral we are all the same."[82]

On the other hand, the strength of Kant's liberalism lies in what Murdoch calls his "agnosticism"—that is, his recognition that reason is powerless ever to comprehend the whole of reality, including the reality of individuals, who remain opaque to themselves and to one another. On Kant's view, Murdoch writes, "we do not *know* reason in ourselves or others, in the same way that we know material objects. Not being purely rational we are not transparent to ourselves."[83] Interestingly, Murdoch believes that Kant's theory of the sublime, which is a powerful expression of this agnosticism, provides an opening for a proper recognition of the reality of others. The sublime may be interpreted as an acute recognition of the fact that "others are, to an extent we never cease discovering, different from ourselves."[84] The true sublime in Murdoch's view is captured in the sight "not of physical nature, but of our surroundings as consisting of other individual men,"[85] a spectacle of the real that always escapes totalization by reason or imagination. This agnostic limit on our ability to know others fully is also expressed in Murdoch's claim in *The Sovereignty of Good* that knowledge of the individual is an ideal end point that always re-cedes.[86]

Hegel's philosophy, has the advantage over Kant's of acknowledging the importance of history in a conception of moral identity, and of connecting freedom with the knowledge of oneself as a participant in a progressing social and historical reality. This conception of the self as part of a larger whole that is the source of value is a feature of what Murdoch has affirmed as the Natural Law view of morality, elements of which are present in *The Sovereignty of Good*. Yet Hegel's thought lacks precisely that feature that attracts Murdoch to Kant's liberalism—namely, an agnostic tolerance of the limits of reason to know the whole of reality, including the reality of other people. "Hegel pictured reality in terms of a developing range of historical and psychological concepts and implied that complete knowledge of it was possible. Reason was not ultimately defeated; it could close the circle of knowledge: no agnosticism here, no sense of limit."[87] In the He-gelian universe, there may be conflict among individuals, but such conflict is in effect "the mutual misunderstanding of parts of the whole,"[88] rather than a real conflict between dissimilar others. From the point of view of the whole, what appears to be conflict is in fact "the self locked in struggle with itself and evolving as a result of the struggle."[89] Thus we see in Hegel's influence what Murdoch believes is the beginning of the decline of the liberal tradition: in the Hegelian system the individual "is not ulti-mately an independent irreducible entity at all,"[90] but only a passing mo-ment in the absolute. On this view, there is no longer any meaningful distinction to be made between the individual and the reality that encom-passes the individual.

With the influence of Hegel and Hegel's Romantic descendants on the liberal tradition, Murdoch argues, the original stream of Kantian liberalism was prevented from ever achieving the kind of radical acknowledgment of the reality of other people that is central to her position and implicit in Kant's own view. Yet this overwhelming influence of Hegel was not allowed to go unchallenged. Murdoch divides Hegel's opponents into "those who understand him very well and feel a mixture of love and hate as a result, and those who have never read him and would not understand him if they did."[91] Among the former she notes especially the Kierkegaardian or "ex-istentialist Hegelians, who are pure Romantics," and among the latter "the Hobbesian empiricists, who are Liberals touched by Romanticism at a later stage."[92] Murdoch identifies "the Liberal dilemma as the failure of these two disparate elements to help each other to produce a new post-Hegelian theory of personality."[93]

These two contrasting philosophies, Kierkegaardian existentialism and Hobbesian empiricism, share an important insight that is fundamental to their opposition to Hegel. Both views identify the fundamental unit of re-ality and value as the individual existent rather than the universal essence, the discrete particular rather than abstract whole. Murdoch shares a fundamental sympathy with these positions insofar as they lend philosophical support to her claim that the individual is the paradigmatic locus of value in ethics. Kierkegaard, like Sartre and other modern existentialists, "fought against the swallowing up of the individual human person in the Hegelian system. He fought for the conception of a private individual destiny: the root idea of existentialism, that the individual human existence is not enclosed by a world of essences."[94] Yet in spite of his incisive challenge to Hegel's monism, Kierkegaard remains "profoundly Hegelian. He retained and used with wonderful versatility the clear, dramatic, solipsistic picture of the self at war with itself and passing in this way through phases in the direction of self-knowledge."[95] For this reason, Murdoch holds that even Kierkegaard's critique is not radical enough to overcome Hegel's influence, since the individual is still not yet related to other diverse individuals. Rather, Kierkegaard, oddly enough, may still be described as "totalitarian,"[96] in the sense that he views the essential relation as that of the solitary individual to a deity who between them "enclose the whole of reality."[97]

It is the other group of Hegel's critics, the Hobbesian empiricists, who have the potential to mount an effective critique of Romanticism. Murdoch asserts this even though she concedes that what in fact motivated the liberalism of Hobbes, Locke, and Hume "was not primarily moral or political, it was scientific."[98] "What most of all concerned the empiricists, and what drove their theories onward, was the construction of a picture of the material world, the development of that atomic empiricism which has had so strong a hold on our philosophical imagination."[99] This atomistic picture, which Murdoch criticized in *The Sovereignty of Good*, nevertheless produced a theory of the individual that gave rise to the some of "the most familiar ideas of our Liberalism, ideas we take for granted."[100]

> In the world as envisaged by Hobbes, Locke, and Hume there is a plurality of persons, who are quite separate and different individuals and who have to get along together. Moreover, implicitly for Hobbes and explicitly for Locke, that which has a right to exist, that which is deserving of tolerance and respect, is not the rational or good person, but the actual empirically existing person whatever he happens to be like.[101]

The essential insight of this tradition is the simple but obvious fact that "other people exist,"[102] and that their divergent aims and purposes are to be respected.

This notion of tolerance for diverse individuals was most explicitly developed by J. S. Mill, whom Murdoch takes as exemplary of the type of liberalism she wants to defend. In contrast to the Romantic or Hegelian view, she contends, Mill's individual is not a self-contained unit encompassing a world unto itself, but rather is confronted with a varied society of dissimilar others. In contrast to Kant also, who tried to exclude history and particularity from his notion of the self as a rational agent, Mill took particularity and uniqueness to be the very essence of personality. Surprisingly, Murdoch does not mention Mill's concern for sentience as morally basic to an account of human being. Rather, she contends that what makes a person an individual, on Mill's view, are not those qualities that all persons share as rational agents or as citizens or as sentient beings, but precisely those qualities that differentiate them from one another as unique individuals.[103] Mill turns our attention "towards the real impenetrable human person. That this person is substantial, impenetrable, individual, indefinable, and valuable is after all the fundamental tenet of Liberalism."[104]

Thus Murdoch finds in Mill's thought a conception of the liberal individual that represents a mediating position between Kant's liberalism and Hegel's Romanticism. Although Mill "was indeed touched . . . by the Romantic movement"[105]—his picture of the individual as "eccentric, unique, holy, pregnant with genius"[106] was influenced by Romanticism's emphasis on human creativity and self-fulfillment—what is more significant to Murdoch is what Mill shares with Kant. His conception of the individual is marked by a measure of that "agnostic tolerance" toward the reality of others that Murdoch so admires in Kant and believes is implicit in Kant's theory of the sublime. But Kant's agnosticism is rather "dramatic" in nature while Mill's is "undramatic" and even "commonsensical."[107] For Kant, reason's inability to comprehend the whole in the experience of the sublime is an emotional experience that "rends" us with "a mixture of defeat and victory."[108] Mill's agnosticism, by contrast, is expressed in the calm recognition that "it just is in fact rather difficult to understand other people and to be certain what is the right thing to do: one is fallible, so one must be patient."[109]

The defining feature of the liberalism Murdoch wants to defend is this kind of "undramatic, because un-self-centered" agnostic tolerance that, she suggests, is another name for love.[110] Defined in this way, love is "the apprehension of something else, something particular, as existing outside us."[111] It is "a real apprehension of persons other than [the self] as having a right to exist and to have a separate mode of being which is important and interesting to themselves."[112] Murdoch's defense of liberalism is thus an aspect of her broader intention to articulate a form of moral realism that can defeat subjectivism by recovering the reality of the individual as paradigmatic of an encounter with moral reality generally.

III. C. The Case of Literature: Love and the Creation of Individual Characters

In keeping with her insight that art and ethics are analogous disciplines, Murdoch presents an analysis of twentieth-century literature that closely parallels her analysis of liberalism. She argues that the portrayal of character in the novel partakes of the same tensions as the portrayal of the individual does in moral philosophy and political theory. Accordingly, since both art and ethics face the dilemma of neurosis and convention, they may also share a similar solution. The best novels, like the best theory of liberalism, may be the ones whose authors practice the virtue of love or tolerance in their creation of fictional individuals.

In her analysis of twentieth-century literature, Murdoch classifies the novel into two types that form a pair analogous to the descriptive contrast between neurosis and convention: the first type she calls "crystalline," the second "journalistic."

> The twentieth-century novel is usually either crystalline or journalistic; that is, it is either a small quasi-allegorical object portraying the human condition and not containing "characters" in the nineteenth-century sense, or else it is a large shapeless quasi-documentary object, the degenerate descendant of the nineteenth century novel, telling, with pale conventional characters, some straightforward story enlivened with empirical facts.[113]

Both types fall short of what Murdoch judges to be the standard for the portrayal of individual character in literature, the nineteenth-century novel. The crystalline (neurotic) novel, exemplified by the work of Albert Camus, is "a tight metaphysical object"[114] in which "the hero is alone, with no company, or with only other parts of himself for company."[115] The hero is thus an instance of the neurotic individual who has "swallowed up the entire book"[116] in his own mythlike plight or fantasy. The journalistic (conventional) novel, on the other hand, including certain works of Simone de Beauvoir and Sartre, suffers from the opposite symptom. Rather than having a single character who dominates the entire work, the journalistic novel is "a piece of informative prose"[117] in which conventional characters are used chiefly to comment on current institutions or a particular historical matter, rather than being developed for their own sake. Faced with the choice between the two types, we are left in a dilemma where "we are offered things or truths. What we have lost is persons."[118]

Murdoch associates the crystalline novel with the Romantic tradition, ushered into the modern world by Hegel and reaching its climax in the Symbolist movement in poetry and literature. "We may notice," Murdoch writes, "that with the dominance of what I have called neurotic Romantic literature the real individual has tended to disappear from the novel, and his place has been taken by the symbolic individual who *is* the literary work itself."[119] Instead of characters interacting freely with other characters within a realistically conceived fictional world, the crystalline novel is dominated by the will of the author, who uses the characters in the work "to work out his own salvation"[120] or as "an exercise in self-discovery."[121] In philosophical terms, "Here Hegel is king and the struggle between persons is really a struggle within the mind of a single character,"[122] behind which lurks the personality of the author.

While the neurotic novel thus denies freedom to the fictional individual "by making him merely part of his creator's mind,"[123] the journalistic novel, at the other extreme, hardly attempts to portray characters at all. Such novels, in Murdoch's judgment, "lack creative vitality, and are most concerned with exploration of institutions than with creation of character."[124] This may partly be due to the fact that the nature of society in the twentieth century lends itself to such a treatment. "Whereas society in the nineteenth century was either a reassuring place where one lived, or else an exciting, rewarding, interesting place where one struggled, society today tends to appear, by contrast, as menacing, puzzling, uncontrollable, or else confining, and boring."[125] The structure of nineteenth-century society, fueled by "a profound belief in God [and] a faith in the absolute significance and *unity* of the moral world"[126] provided a powerful support for the individual and a framework for the portrayal of literary character. In the nineteenth-century novel, "Society is real and the human soul is pretty solid too: the mind, the personality are continuous and self-evident realities."[127] By contrast, the individual in the twentieth-century journalistic novel is hardly an individual at all, but rather a "conventional social unit"[128] that lacks the depth and color it might have gained by being surrounded by diverse others in a structured and dynamic social context.

Having thus defined the symptoms of failure in the portrayal of individuals in the modern novel, Murdoch goes on to articulate the positive literary standard by which such failures are to be judged. This standard sheds light on her own normative understanding of the individual in relation to the series of oppositional contrasts she has introduced. The most important thing that the art of the novel can reveal to its readers, "not necessarily the only thing, but incomparably the most important thing," Murdoch writes, "is that other people exist."[129] This is precisely what she believed was missing from the novels of her own time, where the idea of character is either so diffuse that it gets lost in the social commentary of the journalistic novel (convention), or so concentrated that it becomes a symbol rather than a concrete individual (neurosis). Murdoch attributes both flaws largely to the corrupting influence of Romanticism in literature. "That literature must be either play (production of self-contained things) or else didactic (discursive statement of truths) is a fallacy which dates from Kant, and which is of the essence of Romanticism."[130] Indeed, what Murdoch most admires about the novels of the nineteenth century was precisely how "un-Romantic" or "un-Hegelian" they are.[131] "The feature that most interests me in the un-Hegelian nature of those great novels is imply this: that they contain a number of different people."[132]

Unlike either the crystalline or the journalistic novels of our century, the nineteenth-century novel "was concerned with real various individuals struggling in society."[133]

There is in these novels a plurality of real persons more or less natu-
ralistically presented in a large social scene, and representing mutually
independent centers of significance which are those of real individuals.
What we have here may be called a display of tolerance. A great novelist
is essentially tolerant, that is, displays a real apprehension of persons
other than the author as having a right to exist and to have a separate
mode of being which is important and interesting to themselves.[134]

What distinguishes the great nineteenth-century novelists, Murdoch argues, is "the quality of their awareness of others."[135] Walter Scott, Jane
Austen, George Eliot, and especially Tolstoy, she believes, succeeded in creating individual characters who were neither mere symbols of the author's
neurosis nor thinly drawn conventional figures. In this respect, the
nineteenth-century novel succeeds in avoiding both of the dangers that
plague twentieth-century literature:

The great novels are victims neither of convention nor of neurosis. The
social scene is a life-giving framework and not a set of dead conventions
or stereotyped settings inhabited by stock characters. And the individuals
portrayed in the novels are free, independent of their author, and not
merely puppets in the exteriorization of some closely locked psychological
conflict of this own.[136]

The greatest novelists thus display what Murdoch calls "that godlike capacity for so respecting and loving [their] characters as to make them exist
as free and separate beings."[137]

As the references in these passages to values such as tolerance, freedom,
diversity, and respect suggest, the nineteenth-century novel represents a
kind of literary analogue to Mill's liberalism. Indeed, Murdoch writes, " 'tolerance' is a word which links nineteenth-century literature with Liberalism. Here one may see the Liberal spirit at its best and richest, disporting
itself in literature, and not yet menaced by those elements of romanticism
which later proved, if I am right, so dangerous."[138] The nineteenth-century
novel thus displays the very qualities of the liberalism that Murdoch ap-
pealed to in Mill's philosophy. In both liberal moral theory and the art of
the novel, what is required is "that un-dramatic, because un-self-centered,
agnosticism which goes with tolerance."[139]

In her analysis of the liberal tradition and the art of the novel, Murdoch's emphasis on the reality of others provides a supporting context for
the individual through mutual relations of tolerance, love, and respect.
The recognition that "other people exist," which Murdoch emphasizes as
the hallmark of great literature and the guiding insight of liberalism at
its best, is the paradigmatic experience of reality and value in the moral
world. Murdoch's dictum in *The Sovereignty of Good* that "love is knowl-

edge of the individual," becomes the central affirmation of both art and ethics.

III. D. The Liberal View and the
Natural Law View Revisited

In light of the foregoing analysis, Murdoch's descriptive contrast between the Liberal view and the Natural Law view as types of moral theory can now be reevaluated. In Chapter 2, I argued that Murdoch seemed to favor the Natural Law view of the moral agent over what she judged to be the "liberal bias" of analytic moral philosophy. Analytic ethics exemplified the Liberal view in its contention that morality is properly centered on the individual rather than on a general framework of reality that includes the individual. Murdoch's support for the Natural Law view in this context provided the crucial basis for her challenge to analytic moral philosophy and her retrieval of a metaphysical ethic. My analysis of Sartre in Chapter 3 also presented him as fitting the general profile of the Liberal view, and Murdoch's critique of Sartre suggests that she would favor the Natural Law view over the existentialist version of liberal morality as well. In light of my analysis of Murdoch's theory of the individual, however, any simple or unambiguous classification of Murdoch as a Natural Law type of moralist must be tempered by her adoption of central ideas from the liberal tradition in her understanding of the moral agent.

Recall that the Liberal view is characterized by the belief in the autonomy of morals from any kind of metaphysical or theological framework. Further, "however grandiose the structure may be in terms of which a morality extends itself, the moral agent is responsible for endowing this totality with value."[140] This view tends toward solipsism because it pictures the individual and morality as self-contained. Freedom is conceived as a detachment or "leap" of the will in the face of duty or moral choice, rather than a continuous interaction of the agent with a world that already contains value. The agent is pictured as only contingently related to anything that might be considered a "moral world" as well as to other individuals, except insofar as they are considered rational agents like itself.

In contrast, the picture of moral agency that Murdoch presented in *The Sovereignty of Good* contains some of the central elements of the Natural Law view of moral agency. The Natural Law view counters the Liberal view by picturing the individual as enclosed within a larger transcendent framework. Against Kantian and existentialist variants of the Liberal view like Sartre, Natural Law moralists (e.g., Thomists, Hegelians, and Marxists) insist that the self is not "a brave naked will surrounded by an easily comprehended empirical world,"[141] but a complex being with dark and not fully rational motives immersed in a reality that exceeds the self. Here there is no "axiom of discontinuity" between the choosing agent and the chosen framework; indeed the point is that the framework is not so much chosen, as given antecedently to the self. "The individual's choice is less important," Murdoch writes, "and the interest may lie in adoration of the framework rather than in the details of conduct."[142] Instead of a leap of the will, freedom here is closely related to knowledge rather than action, and cannot be achieved apart from one's relations to others and to reality. Freedom does not safeguard the isolation of the agent, but rather relates the agent through knowledge to a moral world as the source of normative claims.

The point I want to stress is that although Murdoch endorses much of the Natural Law view's conception of moral agency and its relation to a larger framework, she ultimately rejects its contention that "the individual only has importance, or even reality, in so far as he belongs to the framework."[143] Murdoch's fundamental sympathy with Sartre on the irreducibility of the individual supports my claim that she cannot be considered a Natural Law type of moralist in the tradition, for example, of Hegel. Indeed her relentless critique of Hegel and Romanticism clearly establishes that Murdoch is fundamentally opposed to this view of the individual's relation to a larger whole. Rather, Murdoch remains close to Sartre in her resistance to the idea of totality as a fundamental threat to the value and integrity of the individual and his or her freedom. In this respect, she wants to preserve one of the fundamental insights of the Liberal view—namely, that the individual must not be absorbed without remainder by *any* framework. This conclusion, however, leaves an important question unanswered: if Murdoch endorses a conception of the individual that is closer to Sartre and the Liberal view than was first thought, what are we to conclude about her understanding of freedom?

Section IV. Consciousness, Freedom, and the Individual

We can answer this question by returning to the problem of whether Murdoch's theory of the individual succeeds in answering Sartre's concern about bad faith. My claim (at the end of Section II) that the echo of a similar worry is evident in Murdoch's own position has been confirmed by her preoccupation with the problem of "convention" in the realm of both art and morals. Like Sartre, Murdoch is concerned to prevent the loss of the individual in a social whole that becomes determinative for its moral identity and freedom. The question is how, if at all, Murdoch has managed to avoid this danger. Answering this question will allow me to draw together several strands of the argument of this chapter and the one preceding it, including: (1) the importance of consciousness in morality; (2) the notion of freedom as related to knowledge and vision; and (3) the idea of the individual.

As we have seen, Murdoch's distinction between neurosis and convention highlights a fundamental tension that she is seeking to preserve in her understanding of the individual. On the one hand, she affirms that the concept of the individual requires some notion of separation or autonomy from a determining social context that is the locus of value; on the other hand, she also insists that freedom is not merely an empty or abstract notion but must be contextualized with respect to an understanding of consciousness as structured by some idea of value. In short, Murdoch's position is consistent with Sartre's on the importance of autonomy, but diverges from Sartre on the relation of consciousness and value. The crucial issue between Sartre and Murdoch remains the issue of how each thinker defines the notion of freedom in relation to consciousness and the individual.

For Sartre, freedom is understood as an absence of constraining forces on one's actions and desires, and as the capacity to remove the will by a leap from social contexts that seek to condition it. This conception of freedom was intended to combat the determinism that Sartre believed was a feature of modern thought, one that threatened the will as an individuating principle operative in discrete acts of moral decision. As Murdoch pointed out, Sartre "wishes at all costs to withdraw his man to a point at which he is independent of what seems to him the inhuman determinism of the modern world, the realm of the economist and the sociologist— even if it means depicting him as an empty shell."[144] The Sartrean individual is able to resist or act against convention because of the will's capacity to separate itself from constraining contexts through the activity of choice and decision.

Murdoch articulates her conception of freedom against a different background and according to different assumptions than Sartre's. The problem for Murdoch is not a determinism that constrains moral choice,[145] but rather the problem of properly orienting one's knowledge of reality according to some notion of perfection. In fact, by shifting the primary metaphor of moral activity from will to vision, Murdoch also indicates a shift in the ground of freedom from choice to knowledge. Underlying both of these shifts is a change in the metaethical assumptions informing her theory. Sartre's view is informed by the theory of noncognitivism, which holds that values are not a matter of objective moral knowledge but are chosen according to a subjectivist principle of will or preference. Murdoch's view, by contrast, is cognitivist in that it affirms that morality is a matter of knowledge undertaken by a thinking consciousness that judges values according to an objective norm of truth or falsity. This shift has important consequences for the question of how Murdoch avoids the danger of convention or its analogue, bad faith. Sartre leaves the individual to engage in a perpetual rebellion against determinism and social convention by choosing its own values, avoiding bad faith via a leap of the will. Murdoch's position attempts to avoid bad faith by affirming some principle of knowledge that allows the agent to criticize value in the moral world. The crucial question is, What is this principle that would allow the Murdochian individual to make specific judgments about other individuals, courses of action, and states of mind?

So far, what we know from our analysis of Murdoch's view of consciousness is that the norm of valid moral knowledge has certain formal characteristics. First, its status is transcendental to the extent that a conception of value is presumed in the very activity of consciousness in the act of knowing. Second, its formal character is perfectionist to the extent that consciousness distinguishes among degrees of value and is oriented toward an ideal *telos* or endpoint. What we do not yet know is the substantive content of this formal idea of perfection. We are not helped in this matter by appealing to the notions of love and tolerance as providing the principle we are seeking. These terms do tell us that Murdoch associates perfection or perfect knowledge with the affirmation of individuals as the primary locus of reality and value in the moral world; but they do not tell us what the actual character or quality of this affirmation is. Thus the problem of valid knowledge is only pushed back another step. If, for example, we say that love is a kind of knowledge that seeks the good of the other, we are still lacking a conception of the good to fill out this definition. Our question is, What norm guides the virtue of love?

What then is the content of the principle that would allow the agent to make specific moral judgments and criticize values in the moral world? An answer to this question will require an inquiry into Murdoch's substantive theory of the good, which will be the subject of Chapter 5. Until then, we do not have an answer to how her position regarding the individual and moral freedom avoids the charge of bad faith. In short, we do not know how the moral agent avoids an uncritical adherence to the social whole, thus adopting a conventional rather than a realist ethic.

5

THE IDEA OF THE GOOD AND THE
TRANSFORMATION OF AGENCY

My principal aim in the last chapter was to present Murdoch's defense of a notion of consciousness as central to morality and to the idea of the individual. In doing so, I sought to establish the fundamental correlation in Murdoch's thought between the notion of the self or consciousness and the idea of the good. This analysis raised important and unanswered questions, however, about the *content* of the notion of value that Murdoch believes is inherent in consciousness, and what kind of freedom is affirmed in her theory of moral knowledge and agency. The present chapter shows how Murdoch's theory of the good attempts to answer these questions.

The success or failure of Murdoch's effort to provide an alternative to what she regarded as the subjectivistic voluntarism of modern ethical theory hinges on her ability to define the content of the idea of perfection implicit in the activity of cognition. That is, we need to understand what it would mean on her view to have acquired "perfected knowledge" of reality. Without a clear articulation of a standard by which to evaluate the quality and veracity of our moral knowledge, Murdoch's moral theory cannot escape the very charge of subjectivism that her metaphysical ethic is intended to address. Thus this chapter will be "synthetic" in its attempt to show how Murdoch's insistence on the primacy of consciousness in morality is critically evaluated by an objective standard of perfected moral knowledge that is grounded in a realist metaphysic. The crucial issue to be addressed is the following: How can Murdoch avoid subjectivism when she insists on a starting point in consciousness? If the good is an inherent feature of consciousness itself, how can it provide a critical principle by which to evaluate consciousness?

Answering this question will require a return to certain metaethical considerations first introduced in Chapter 2, including Murdoch's ontological proof. What is at stake is the issue of what kind of realist and cognitivist Murdoch is and whether her position succeeds in providing an objective and realist standard for moral judgment over its noncognitivist rivals. My contention is that Murdoch's realism can best be understood as a form of "reflexive" or "hermeneutical realism."[1] This means that she will be seeking a criterion of valid moral knowledge in and through the reflexive medium of consciousness itself. In order to trace the significance of this idea as it bears on Murdoch's normative account of consciousness, I also return to important aspects of her moral psychology with the intention of illuminating the norm by which consciousness is evaluated and transformed. In short, I attempt to define the substantive meaning of the term "good" (and the related terms "reality," "truth," and "perfection") as it serves to ground Murdoch's cognitivist metaethic and as the normative principle of moral vision.

The argument of the chapter will proceed as follows. In Section I, I show that Murdoch's relation to G. E. Moore is important for understanding the reflexive character of the realism she embraces. In Section II, I address this issue through a detailed exposition of Murdoch's account of morality as spiritual change—her ethics of vision. Accordingly, I present her critique of egoism and show how selfish vision is transformed through various "techniques of unselfing" that redirect psychic energy toward the real. In Section III, I examine two important aspects of Murdoch's moral psychology through this reflexive lens: her theory of freedom and her theory of moral motivation. Finally in Section IV, I take up the question of whether Murdoch's ethic of vision leaves her open to the charge of intuitionism. I consider Murdoch's own assessment of her ethics of vision in relation to this charge, and her development of a theory of duty and obligation that is intended to answer these deficiencies.

Section I. A. G. E. Moore and the Metaethics of the Good

Recall that in Chapter 2, I presented Murdoch as a cognitivist thinker and introduced the formal dimensions of her theory of the good. The point was to show that Murdoch affirms a realist metaphysic in opposition to what she takes to be the subjectivism of analytic and existentialist ethics. Murdoch's cognitivism and realism can now be brought into sharper focus by framing her theory in relation to G. E. Moore. Moore represents a crucial reference point for Murdoch's theory of the good, but her realism significantly differs from his in being "reflexive" in character. This difference between the two thinkers is related to two other significant differences in their metaethics that bear on the central concern of this chapter: (1) their theories of moral language (i.e., how they answer the question "What is the meaning of the word 'good'?"); and (2) their theories of moral knowledge (i.e., how they answer the question "How do we know what things are good?")

Murdoch identifies Moore's thought as marking a decisive turning point in modern moral philosophy that had disastrous consequences for metaphysical ethics. By distinguishing the question "What is the meaning of the term 'good'?" from the question "What things are good?" Moore set the course for the dominant trend of moral theory in the twentieth century. After Moore, Murdoch argues, both metaphysical ethics and ethical naturalism were held to be untenable, thus opening the door to emotivist, existentialist, and other noncognitivist theories that she believes reduce the good to matters of subjective preference. Without rehearsing Murdoch's detailed refutation of the anti-metaphysical and anti-naturalistic arguments set in motion by Moore (see Chapter 2), it is clear that her moral theory as a whole is as an extended attempt to retrieve versions of metaphysics and naturalism in ethics. By doing so, she renewed the possibility of a realist and cognitivist grounding for moral value.

In spite of Murdoch's contention that aspects of Moore's position had negative consequences for the history of moral theory in this century, her position nevertheless retained certain clear affinities with Moore. Very early in *The Sovereignty of Good*, for example, she defends Moore against his critics and aligns herself with key features of his thought:

> Moore believed that good was a supersensible reality, that it was a mysterious quality, unrepresentable and indefinable, that it was an object of knowledge and (implicitly) that to be able to see it was in some sense to have it. He thought of the good upon the analogy of the beautiful; and he was, in spite of himself, a "naturalist" in that he took goodness to be a real constituent of the world. We know how severely and in what respects Moore was corrected by his successors . . . and let me say in anticipation that on almost every point I agree with Moore and not with his critics.[2]

As this passages indicates, the specific points of agreement between Moore and Murdoch can be summarized as follows: (1) both thinkers are cognitivists who agree that goodness is not a function of the choosing will but a real object of knowledge; (2) they hold that the primary moral faculty for knowing the good is vision or perception; (3) they agree that morality and aesthetics (goodness and beauty) are analogues; and (4) both insist that the concept of goodness is unanalyzable and indefinable (though for different reasons, as we will see).

Given Murdoch's ambiguous assessment of Moore—her rejection of his apparently anti-metaphysical and anti-naturalistic stance, on the one hand, and her defense of him against his later critics, on the other—how are we to assess the relation between the two thinkers? Fundamentally, what is at stake in a comparison of Moore and Murdoch is the question of how a cognitivist metaethical theory conceives the relation between an account of consciousness and a theory of the good. Murdoch's realism contrasts with Moore's to the extent that she conceives the relation between consciousness and the good to be "reflexive" as well as "linguistically mediated." In order to lay the groundwork for this argument, I want to examine the basic features of Murdoch's critique of Moore, especially with respect to her theory of moral language and its underlying epistemological assumptions.

Murdoch argues that Moore's distinction of the question "What does the word 'good' mean?" from the question "What things are good?" marked a breach with metaphysical approaches to ethics because it effected a kind of linguistic and subjectivist "turn" in Anglo-American moral theory.

> It transformed the central question of ethics from the question, "What is goodness?"—where an answer was expected in terms of the revelation of some real and eternally present structure of the universe—into the question—"What is the activity of 'valuing'? . . . The philosopher is now to speak no longer of the Good, as something real or transcendent, but to analyse the familiar human activity of endowing things with value.[3]

Moore himself did not completely abandon the metaphysical question "What is goodness?" He remained a cognitivist in believing that goodness was an object of knowledge, and a naturalist ("in spite of himself," as Murdoch says) in believing it was a real property. Yet by undertaking a linguistic analysis of "good" as an adjective that can be applied to a plurality of things, he opened the door to the noncognitivist understanding of the good as a label of the choosing will (i.e., in voluntarism), or as a simple tag indicating commendation (i.e., in emotivism). Murdoch's metaethical theory of the good is in fact a sustained attempt to refute what she takes to be the voluntarist consequences of Moore's linguistic analysis of "good."

In light of her critique of voluntarism and the "elimination of metaphysics from ethics" after Moore, it is natural to assume that Murdoch's own sympathies lie with the first, metaphysical question, "What is goodness?" With Plato, she seeks an answer to this question that would ground value in the nature of reality. However, a comparison with Moore clarifies the sense in which Murdoch is a "reflexive" rather than a straightforward metaphysical realist. While Moore's understanding of the reality of goodness is grounded in an epistemology of moral properties according to which the good can be directly apprehended through intuition, Murdoch's theory of the good necessarily passes through its own reflexive and linguistic turn with respect to her account of consciousness. That is, instead of simply ignoring the question, "What is the human activity of 'valuing'?" Murdoch seeks to answer the metaphysical question about goodness in and through an account of how the reality of the good is mediated through consciousness and moral language.

This reflexive approach to moral realism can be contrasted with other forms of moral realism that ground the truth-status of moral claims in a principle of knowledge *external* to individual consciousness. Classical realism accomplishes this by claiming that values are conceived as ontologically real and are discoverable by human reason. On this view, moral values are grounded in some conception of the objectively real, such as the order of nature. Other more "pragmatic" versions of moral realism ground the truth of moral claims in the intersubjective agreement among participants in a language game or form of life.[4] On this view, an objective standard of moral judgment is found in the consensus provided by "intellectual authority-relations" within a moral and linguistic community.[5] In contrast to both approaches, reflexive realism affirms the truth-status of moral claims by adopting a starting point *internal* to consciousness and looking for an objective standard through the medium of consciousness itself. That is, reflexive realists argue that the search for an objective standard of truth and value can only proceed by means of the first-person standpoint.[6] The good is discovered through the medium of consciousness as it reflects on itself; yet at the same time, the act of reflexivity reveals the good to be a perfection or "higher condition" that transcends or surpasses consciousness. Thus, reflexive realists argue that the search for the good, to use Charles Taylor's language, involves "the grasping of an [objective] order which is inseparably indexed to a personal vision. . . . The order is only accessible through personal, hence 'subjective', resonance."[7]

The reflexive character of Murdoch's realism becomes evident when we compare Moore's nonnaturalistic theory of moral language to her own, which might be called "nonreductively" naturalistic.[8] This allows me to expose the epistemological presuppositions underlying their views. The basic thesis of naturalism as a theory of moral language is that moral terms (e.g., "good") can be identified with or derived from nonmoral terms (e.g., pleasure, happiness, etc.).[9] Moore rejects naturalism in order to challenge what he regarded as the Utilitarian doctrine that pleasure can be identified as the sole good. By distinguishing the meaning of the term "good" from its content, Moore instituted what has come to be called the "open question argument," according to which (as Murdoch, following Moore, puts it) "it made *sense* always, given any proposition of the form 'X is good', to withdraw thoughtfully and ask—'But is X really good?' "[10] By this method, Moore hoped to show that goodness is not reducible to or identifiable with any natural or nonmoral property such as pleasure, happiness, rationality, and so on, but is a "simple" notion that cannot be further analyzed. Murdoch quotes the relevant passage from Moore's *Principia Ethica* as follows:

> If I am asked, "What is good?' my answer is that good is good and that
> is the end of the matter. Or if I am asked, "How is good to be defined?"

my answer is that it cannot be defined, and that is all I have to say about it. But disappointing as these answers may appear, they are of the very last importance. To readers who are familiar with philosophic terminology, I can express their importance by saying that they amount to this: That propositions about the good are all of them synthetic and never analytic; and that is plainly no trivial matter. And the same thing may be expressed more popularly, by saying that, if I am right, then nobody can foist upon us such an axiom as that "Pleasure is the only good" or that "The good is the desired" on the pretence that this is "the very meaning of the word."[11]

Thus in reply to the question, "What does the word 'good' mean?" Moore answers that one cannot give a definition or explanation of the meaning of "good" because the very grammar of the concept disallows it. The moral term "good" is *sui generis*—that is, it cannot be derived or inferred from nonmoral facts or properties. "Good," as Moore puts it, is "one of those innumerable objects of thought which are themselves incapable of definition, because they are the ultimate terms by reference to which whatever is capable of definition must be defined."[12]

Significantly, Moore supports his argument for the essential indefinability of the moral term "good" by relying on an epistemology of moral properties that compares goodness to the color "yellow."

My point is that "good" is a simple notion, just as "yellow" is a simple notion; that just as you cannot, by any manner of means, explain to anyone who does not already know it, what yellow is, so you cannot explain what good is. . . . We may try to define [yellow], by describing its physical equivalent; we may state what kind of light-vibrations must stimulate the normal eye, in order that we may perceive it. But a moment's reflection is sufficient to show that those light-vibrations are not themselves what we mean by yellow. *They* are not what we perceive. . . . The most we can be entitled to say of those vibrations is that they are what corresponds in space to the yellow which we actually perceive.[13]

On the basis of this analogy, Moore argues that "good" is an adjective that can be used to describe various entities called *the* good, just as "yellow" is an adjective used to describe particular vibrations of light. But we must not confuse the meaning of the adjective "good" as identical with things that are good, since things that are good (e.g., pleasure, happiness, and so on) will also have *other* adjectives besides "good" that apply to them as well.[14] Thus Moore identifies the naturalistic fallacy, in Murdoch's words, as "the mistake of *defining* good, and trying to do so by joining fact and value through a definition such as 'good is happiness', 'good is pleasure',"and so on.[15] He concludes that no *one* thing can be considered good, and that all good things which share the simple property of goodness may, if properly scrutinized, be found also to possess *other* qualities (e.g., being desirable or pleasurable).[16] In sum, Moore's argument about the meaning of the concept "good" depends on an epistemology that separates moral values from natural or nonmoral facts. One cannot infer or derive goodness from the existence of natural facts (e.g., pleasure, happiness, rationality, etc.) because goodness is a *sui generis* property that cannot be reduced or analyzed into further constituent parts.

In contrast to Moore, Murdoch affirms a naturalistic theory of ethics and hence of moral language that does not depend on a sharp distinction between fact and value. She holds that moral terms cannot be entirely segregated from natural or nonmoral facts; they are not *sui generis*. Yet at the same time, Murdoch's naturalism is, in her own words, "inconclusive" and "non-dogmatic" because she does not believe that the good can be wholly *reduced* to some natural fact or state of affairs either (e.g., "human flourishing"). In contrast both to strict naturalism and to nonnaturalism, Murdoch understands moral language as *mediating* the relation between fact and value through the complex interpretive and evaluative activity of moral perception. This is the crucial insight for understanding her as a reflexive realist in relation to Moore.

Murdoch's theory of moral language has already been examined at several points in previous chapters, but must now be placed in this "reflexive" context. Chapter 2 argued that Murdoch sees the distinction between fact and value as depending on an untenable empiricist epistemology that assumes that since all human beings inhabit the same empirical world of objective facts, the moral differences among them are a function of what individual agents *choose.* This view utterly fails in her judgment to acknowledge the way in which any description of the facts is mediated by a set of evaluative concepts that determine even what is to *count* as a relevant fact. This is the burden of her argument against critics of the so-called naturalistic fallacy, including Moore. Moore's position in her view ultimately had the effect of impoverishing the concept of goodness by rendering it a mysterious property or movable "label" detached from the world of natural facts. In response, Murdoch attempts to restore the conceptual richness of this and other moral terms by seeing it in the context of an agent's struggle to apprehend reality by means of a total vocabulary of moral vision. Thus in spite of her critique of the dominance of "the linguistic method" in twentieth-century moral theory, Murdoch's own position takes moral language seriously by focusing on "the inner complexity of moral concepts as the key to deep differences in moral vision."[17]

Further, as we saw in Chapter 4, Murdoch contextualizes the functioning of moral language within a more general psychology of moral consciousness. She uses the example of M and D to illustrate how moral perception and cognition proceed in the life of a developing, unique, fallible human individual via the complex mediation of a full range of descriptive terms and images. Moral language is the instrument of an individual's unique cognitive and evaluative grasp of reality. To the extent that one's moral vocabulary is narrowed or impoverished, one's grasp of the moral world becomes correspondingly less perspicuous and richly textured. The import of Murdoch's emphasis on vision in this context is that she understands moral perception as an activity of conceptual formation and translation *between* fact and value, rather than an analysis of moral terms divorced from natural facts. In contrast to Moore, for whom moral perception is the simple apprehension of a moral "property" of goodness independent of natural facts, Murdoch holds that moral perception is a complex interpretive activity of consciousness in which moral concepts mediate the world of facts to moral vision. On this view, the idea of "objective reality" assumed by empiricism must be understood differently, "in relation to the progressing life of a person"[18] who is possessed of a unique perception of the moral world. Any grasp of the empirical world of natural facts must pass through the unique language-using consciousness of the individual agent.

Given this reflexive account of moral language as the necessary medium of moral vision and knowledge, one must conclude that contrary to first impressions Murdoch is not offering a simple or classically realist account of how human beings know the good. This is not because she believes, as Moore did, that goodness is a mysterious, indefinable property distinct from natural facts and known by intuition (as Moore says, "good is good, and that is an end to the matter").[19] Rather, it is because her position acknowledges the inescapable mediation of moral concepts in an individual's apprehension of the facts. In order to make this point clear, we can compare Murdoch and Moore's understanding of the indefinability of the good as a final measure of the reflexivity of her position.

Moore's understanding of the indefinability of the good is the direct corollary of his empiricist presuppositions and his view that moral terms such as "good" are autonomous or radically distinct from nonmoral or natural facts. Since goodness is understood as a *sui generis* property, there is no need for a complex reflexive theory to explain how we know the good: we perceive it, that is all. Moore can draw an analogy between our apprehension of the property of goodness and our perception of the color "yellow" precisely because his moral theory rests on an empiricist understanding of the distinction between facts and values.

Murdoch's understanding of the indefinability of the good rests on entirely different assumptions. Given the nonreductive character of her naturalism, the good is neither a property that is mysteriously attached to a plurality of goods in the world nor can it simply be derived from natural facts. Rather, the good is grasped as real in and through the interpretive and evaluative activity of an agent's moral perception, which is inseparably indexed to a personal vision. In this respect, Murdoch sees moral concepts as "concrete universals"[20] that partake of the infinite and perfectible nature of an individual's understanding of moral reality. The good is indefinable because reality—reflexively mediated through moral concepts—is mysterious and transcends our complete understanding of it. Murdoch writes, "Good is indefinable . . . because of the infinite difficulty of the task of apprehending a magnetic but inexhaustible reality . . . good partakes of the infinite elusive character of reality."[21] On this view, knowing the good is not an act of immediate intuition, as Moore would have it; rather, it requires the kind of piecemeal, disciplined, and progressive effort of attention to reality that Murdoch describes in her example of M and D. In terms that will be relevant later in this chapter, it involves a concentrated and disciplined effort of selfless *attention*.

Having established that Murdoch's realism is reflexive in relation to Moore's, we can now turn our attention to how Murdoch validates the reality of the good. If the underlying basis for Moore's claim for the reality of goodness is empirical or perceptual, what is the corresponding basis for Murdoch's claim that the reality of the good is known reflexively through the structures of human consciousness and language? Given her rejection of an empiricist grounding for moral knowledge and her reflexive stance on the relation between consciousness and the good, does her account of moral knowledge amount to anything more than a form of subjective intuition? More specifically, does her theory succeed in providing a more objective basis for the reality of the good than an intuitionism based on the apprehension of moral "properties"?

I. B. The Reality of the Good: Murdoch's Ontological Proof

Murdoch makes use of a version of the ontological proof in order to argue that goodness is not a property that inheres *in* objects of moral knowledge; rather, it is the transcendental condition *for* such knowledge. Her proof attempts to avoid the charge of subjectivism at two different but related levels. First, it contains a transcendental argument that seeks to answer the question "what is the meaning of the term 'good'?" by establishing the reality of the good on transcendental rather than empirical grounds. Second, it contains what she calls a "metaphysical" (or perfectionist) argument that seeks to answer the question "what things are good?" by providing an ideal standard by which to judge things good. These two arguments were introduced in Chapter 2, but must now be considered in more depth. Although it is not possible to represent in its entirety Murdoch's extensive treatment of the ontological proof and its history here,[22] I will analyze the two basic interpretive strategies she pursues with respect to Anselm's original proof for the existence of God. These become the basis of her argument that consciousness and the good are correlative terms whose reality is grasped transcendentally and metaphysically.

Murdoch distinguishes two arguments in the classic Anselmian version of the ontological proof: a logical argument about the necessary existence of God, and a metaphysical argument claiming that we can arrive at the idea of God by discovering a hierarchy of perfection in the created universe. As Arthur McGill has argued, until fairly recently, the standard view of Anselm's proof tended to take the logical argument as primary and rarely developed what Murdoch calls the metaphysical argument.[23] The proof was treated as a self-contained logical argument comprising the argument of chapter II of the *Proslogion* seeking to prove God's existence from an idea of God in the mind. After defining the object of his faith as "something than which nothing greater can be conceived," Anselm showed that this idea must exist in the understanding, since even the fool who denies God can understand the meaning of these words when he hears them. But if this idea exists in the understanding, it must also exist in reality, since this is something *greater* than existence in the understanding alone. Therefore, "something than which nothing greater can be conceived" must exist both in the understanding and in reality.

Stated in these terms, the logical argument is fundamentally reflexive in character. As Charles Taylor has noted, Anselm stands within "that strand of Western spirituality [originated by Augustine] which has sought the certainty of God within."[24] Taylor summarizes the logical argument of the proof as follows:

> [W]e start from the idea in the mind, that of the most perfect being. . . . [T]he underlying intuition is that this is not an idea we just happen to have, but one which must occur to us. The notion that the idea must occur is the properly "Augustinian" intuition: we can only understand ourselves if we see ourselves as in contact with a perfection which is beyond us. But if the idea must be, then the reality must exist, because the notion of a most perfect being lacking existence is a contradiction.[25]

Taylor makes two important points here that are relevant to Murdoch's reflexive understanding of the proof. First, he notes that the proof takes its starting point in consciousness; it seeks to prove the reality of God from an idea of God in the mind. Second, according to the proof the idea of God *must* occur to us, because it the very condition for our consciousness of ourselves as "selves." Thus the form of the proof is distinctive from that of the later cosmological proofs (such as that of Aquinas) because it moves not through the realm of objects, but "through the subject and through the undeniable foundations of his presence to himself."[26] Murdoch makes essentially these same two points as she reinterprets Anselm's argument as a proof for the necessity of the idea of the good, which exists in necessary correlation with a thinking consciousness.[27]

Historically, we should recall, the logical argument has attracted the familiar criticism that it is invalid, since existence is not a predicate. For example, Kant subjected the argument in this form to its most telling criticism by arguing that we cannot think something into existence simply from the conception of it. Existence is not a quality or predicate that *adds* anything to an idea in the understanding. Therefore, there is no contradiction in saying that "something than which nothing greater can be conceived" exists in the understanding alone, since the idea of its existing in reality is not something greater. In short, existence cannot be considered a perfection, the lack of which would render the idea of the most perfect conceivable being a contradiction, as the argument of chapter II of the *Proslogion* had implied. In order to answer this criticism, Murdoch joins recent interpreters who have sought to rehabilitate the proof and to bypass Kant's criticism by revising the standard view on which it is based. Chapter II of the *Proslogion* cannot be treated as a self-contained logical proof. Rather, any analysis of the ontological argument cannot be complete without a consideration of chapter III as well as Anselm's reply to his fellow monk Gaunilo presenting arguments not merely for God's existence but also for God's necessary existence. The conclusion is that there are not one but two versions of the logical argument. The second version shifts the grounds of the proof from the question of whether the idea of God entails God's existence to the issue of whether the idea of God entails *necessary* rather than contingent existence.[28] This form of the logical argument escapes Kant's charge that existence is not a predicate. Since a thing is greater if it *necessarily* exists than if it does not necessarily exist, Anselm proves that a being "a greater than which cannot be conceived" must be one whose *non*existence is logically impossible.

Murdoch contends that this second form of the logical argument is the real crux of the proof. In her usage, the so-called logical argument is expanded to include Anselm's initial formulation of the proof in chapter II, which he "corrects" in chapter III and his reply to Gaunilo by stressing God's necessary existence. Against Gaunilo's objection that the proof as originally stated could be used to argue anything into existence from the idea of a perfect instance of that thing (e.g., a most perfect island), Anselm insists that the proof refers uniquely to God. "In this case alone," Murdoch writes, "if you can conceive of this entity you are *ipso facto* certain that what you are thinking of is real."[29] She argues that Anselm is not speaking of something that *happens* to be greater than all other beings, "but of something than which a greater cannot be conceived, and whose *non-existence is impossible*. This is the respect in which God is unique."[30] On this stronger reading of the logical argument, then, the idea of God entails its reality in such a way that its *un*reality is impossible.

Murdoch takes this argument to mean that God cannot be considered one empirical *object* among others existing in the world. Rather, God's existence is distinctive from that of things because God exists in such a way that God cannot be "thought away" from human life. "God cannot be a particular, a contingent thing, one thing among others. . . . God's necessary existence is connected with his not being an object."[31] Unlike empirical objects, God exists in a manner that is beyond the power of thought to deny; God is the condition of thought itself. On this point, Murdoch agrees with the theologian Paul Tillich that the ontological proof is misstated if the reality to which it points is understood as a highest *being* called God.[32] The true meaning of the proof is its acknowledgment of what Tillich calls "the unconditional element in the structure of reason and reality."[33]

As this discussion indicates, Murdoch reads Anselm's proof along much the same lines as Charles Taylor. God's existence is grasped as necessarily real in and through the structures of human knowing. The reality of God is keyed to or correlative with the structure of human reason. In the very act by which reason grasps the meaning of the logical form of the proof, it is understood that God—as "that than which no greater can be thought"—is necessarily real. In this way, the proof establishes a fundamental correlation between human consciousness and a principle that both presupposes it and surpasses it. Murdoch preserves this essential reflexivity of the proof in her own constructive reinterpretation. She replaces the notion of God in Anselm's proof with the idea of the Platonic Good as the structuring principle of human consciousness. In the first stage of her argument, she transforms the logical argument into a transcendental argument for the necessary existence of the Good. "[Those] who feel that perhaps the Proof proves something, but not any sort of God," she writes, "might return to Plato and claim some uniquely necessary status for moral value as something (uniquely) impossible to be thought away from human experience."[34] Thus in Murdoch's revised version, the ontological proof proves that the good is the condition for human moral existence. Murdoch expresses this by saying that the good "adheres essentially to the conception of being human, and cannot be detached."[35]

This transcendental conception of the good is evident throughout Murdoch's writings in her repeated appeal to the Platonic image of the Good as the light of the sun, as we saw in Chapter 2. The Form of the Good is "the light which reveals to us all things as they really are."[36] As the ground or source of being and value, there can be no human experience apart from the good. All of reality appears to consciousness as "value-laden" in the light of the transcendental good. Because of this, we cannot know the good as we know other things; the transcendental status of this idea goes with it being an indefinable or imageless concept. In sum, just as Anselm argued that God's reality is grasped through the apprehension that God is the condition for thought itself, Murdoch's transcendental argument establishes the reality of the good as the condition for the possibility of moral knowledge. Further, the reality of the good establishes the reality of consciousness in a correlative way: if goodness is real, self-consciousness must also be real since it is that which grasps the reality of the good in the act of thinking.

The second argument that Murdoch identifies in Anselm's proof becomes the basis for her metaphysical or perfectionist argument for the good. While Anselm's logical argument analyzes the peculiar logic or grammar of the idea of God as the most perfect conceivable being, his metaphysical argument appeals to our actual *experience* of God's perfection through the things of nature. The metaphysical argument appears in chapter VIII of Anselm's reply to Gaunilo, and is intended to support the logical argument for necessary existence. Addressing Gaunilo's question of how we are to form the notion of a greatest conceivable being if such a being is indeed unique as Anselm claims, Anselm replies that we can conceive of God from our experience of greater and lesser goods in the world. "[E]verything that is less good, in so far as it is good, is like the greater good," Anselm writes. "It is therefore evident to any rational mind, that by ascending from the lesser good to the greater, we can form a considerable notion of a being than which a greater is inconceivable."[37] This argument should be accessible even to the "fool" who denies sacred authority, Anselm says, since it rests on the notion of gradations of value familiar to anyone. We gain an increasing understanding of God's unique reality and moral perfection by ascending through lesser goods to the most perfect good.

Murdoch traces a similar argument with reference to the Platonic Good in the second phase of her reconstruction of the proof. According to Plato's myth of the cave in the *Republic*, the universe comprises different levels of reality. Knowledge and morality (truth and value) are connected in such a way that the ascent from illusion to reality is at the same time an ascent toward goodness or virtue. We are led to believe in the supreme reality of what is perfect by discovering in lesser goods the shadow of higher degrees of goodness. Moral understanding, on this view, is linked to knowledge of the real. Murdoch uses this metaphysical argument as a support for her transcendental argument for the good. She argues that although we do not directly experience the good (since it is the condition and not the object of knowledge), we do experience images and shadows of perfect truth and goodness. In every sort of cognitive activity (e.g., intellectual studies, work, art, human relations), we intuitively learn to distinguish gradations of good and bad, better and worse. The whole of our experience thus furnishes us with evidence of the idea of perfection in the activity of truth-seeking. As Murdoch writes in *The Sovereignty of Good*:

> A deep understanding of any field of human activity (painting, for instance) involves an increasing revelation of degrees of excellence and often a revelation of there being in fact little that is very good and nothing that is perfect. . . . We come to perceive scales, distances, standards, and may incline to see as less than excellent what previously we were prepared to 'let by'. . . . The idea of perfection works thus within a field of study, producing an increasing sense of direction.[38]

This sense of "directedness" toward an ideal of excellence is the distinctive feature of Murdoch's second argument for the good. Consciousness is fundamentally *oriented* toward the good as its ideal. It discriminates among levels or degrees of goodness as it carries out its evaluative activity; it is led to seek true goodness through the gradual apprehension of lesser degrees of goodness in its surroundings. "We are always in motion toward or away from what is more real."[39] In this respect, the activity of consciousness is conceived as a pilgrimage from appearance toward perfected knowledge of reality, a pilgrimage that is carried on in every serious exercise of understanding.

Murdoch's proof clearly reinforces my claim that she is a reflexive realist in relation to Moore. With respect to Moore's question about the meaning of "good," Murdoch's transcendental argument shows that its meaning can only be understood in relation to a thinking, valuing consciousness. The good provides the condition for the possibility of moral knowledge because it is the "light" or the aspect under which moral consciousness regards anything as good. This argument bears out the reflexive character of Murdoch's realism because it shows that the reality of the good is validated in transcendental rather than perceptual terms. Goodness is not something that exists outside consciousness as a property of things or states of affairs; rather, goodness can only be apprehended through the reflexive activity of cognition. Thus the proof makes clear that the basis for Murdoch's realism is not an empiricist model of moral perception, but rather a transcendental model of the structure of human knowing. Further, with respect to Moore's question about "what things are good," Murdoch's metaphysical argument holds that the perfectionist character of the good is gradually revealed to conscious perception through specific practices of cognition. We find out what things are good, not through an immediate apprehension that certain things contain the "property" of goodness, as Moore held, but rather as we discern gradations of value through sustained acts of attention.

In light of these concluding points, we need to ask again whether Murdoch's theory of the good succeeds in defining an objective standard of moral knowledge that can avoid the charge of subjectivism. The transcendental argument does succeed in establishing the reality of the good on firmer grounds than Moore's view because it defines the good not in terms of an empirical reality dependent on intuition but in terms of "the unconditional element in the structure of reason and reality." Further, her metaphysical argument also makes some progress in this direction because it attempts to articulate a standard of perfected knowledge of reality that is not dependent on conceiving goodness as an empirical property of things. However, the problem remaining for this chapter is that in the case of both the transcendental and the metaphysical arguments, the good remains a formal idea whose content is as yet unspecified. We do not yet know the content of the good as transcendental idea, nor do we know what "perfected knowledge of reality" actually is in substantive terms. This requires us to move from metaethical considerations to Murdoch's normative thesis that the good is the principle of valid moral knowledge by which moral agency is transformed from illusion-ridden fantasy to perfected knowledge of reality.

Section II. A. Prelude to the Transformation of Agency

If we take seriously Murdoch's comment in *The Fire and the Sun* that "a portrayal of moral reflection and moral change (degeneration, improvement) is the most important part of any system of ethics,"[40] then her account of the transformation of agency is, by her own reckoning, the most crucial part of her moral theory. Seen in this light, Murdoch's retrieval of consciousness is the most important underpinning of her normative theory of the good, since it makes the human act of picturing reality through cognition and moral perception the medium of moral transformation. Before turning to her account of moral change, then, I want briefly to return to Murdoch's theory of consciousness as a transition to her normative theory of the good.

Recall that in Chapter 4, I attempted to articulate the outlines of Murdoch's view of moral agency by analyzing her account of consciousness or "self-being" as the fundamental mode of moral being. We saw that consciousness is already formally structured by an idea of the good. The activity of consciousness in moral vision is not merely a neutral "prelude" to choice and action, as the linguistic behaviorists held; rather, consciousness is the "value-bearing base . . . from which actions spring."[41] Moral vision thus becomes the necessary condition for moral choice and action. Further, as the example of M and D demonstrated, moral vision is "progressive" or "perfectionist" in nature. Its activity is guided by an implicit standard that helps it discriminate among degrees of value and truth. Since moral understanding moves in the direction of an increasing grasp of particulars, the perfectionist aspect of morality is linked in Murdoch's thought with the affirmation of the concrete individual as the privileged object of moral attention. My conclusion was that Murdoch's account of moral vision specifies the formal demand of morality as a perfectionist demand to "love individuals" (or, in her liberal political formulation, to "tolerate the diverse existence of others"). This is the ideal *telos* to which moral thinking and moral vision ought to be directed; it is the principle that converts self-consciousness into moral consciousness, strictly speaking.

However, this analysis gave us only the formal outlines, and not the substantive core, of Murdoch's ethic of vision. We need a substantive principle of valid moral knowledge that would allow us to determine the precise character of perfected vision, love, or knowledge. In addition, we need a substantive account of moral freedom that shows how freedom is related to knowledge and love rather than to choice. This is precisely what Murdoch's normative theory of the good must provide. Without it, it is hard to see how her position can answer the charge of subjectivism that she directs at both analytic and Sartrean ethics.

The most significant problem we face in this task is how to define the objectivity of a norm that is understood to be internal to consciousness. The reflexivity of Murdoch's realist position means that the idea of the good cannot depend for its objectivity on being conceptually located "outside" consciousness. Rather, the only kind of objectivity that is possible in the realm of ethics is one that is also "indexed to a personal vision." Access to the good is never direct or unmediated but must pass through the ambiguous and conflicting energies of human subjectivity. Thus if the good is to serve as the critical norm of consciousness, it must both reorganize and transcend the selfish energies of the psyche. This means that Murdoch's account of moral change can only be adequately understood in the context of her account of egoism as the central dilemma of the moral life. By insisting on the primacy of the inner life of consciousness in morality, Murdoch ensures that the normative problem is to prevent consciousness from collapsing in on itself. Thus the problem of egoism represents the major obstacle in her attempt to formulate an idea of the good as the realist norm of her ethics.

II. B. The Ethics of Vision:
Morality as Spiritual Change

Murdoch's account of the problem of egoism in *The Sovereignty of Good* is one of the most influential aspects of her moral thought and has been interpreted by many as the centerpiece of an ethic of vision that tends toward a religious or mystical ideal of "unselfing" in light of the good. This account is intended to challenge what Murdoch regards as the "unambitious optimism"[42] of modern analytic and existentialist ethics, both of which rely upon "an isolated principle of will"[43] and a facile understanding of the complexity of human motivation. "Briefly put," Murdoch writes, "our picture of ourselves has become too grand, we have isolated, and identified ourselves with, an unrealistic conception of will, we have lost the vision of a reality separate from ourselves, and we have no adequate conception of original sin."[44] In response, she seeks a rival psychology or "soul-picture" that takes a "darker, less fully conscious, less steadily rational image of the dynamics of human personality"[45] and represents morality as a disciplined achievement of purified vision or consciousness.

In posing this challenge to modern moral theory, Murdoch emphasizes the religious resonances of the alternative view she is proposing. Traditional theology and philosophy, in her view, have always been concerned with recognizing and countering the intractable selfishness of human beings and providing techniques for the transformation of agency. "Moral philosophy is properly, and in the past has sometimes been, the discussion of this ego and of the techniques (if any) for its defeat. In this respect moral philosophy has shared some aims with religion."[46] While modern moral theory represents "an authentic mode of existence . . . as attainable by intelligence and force of will,"[47] Murdoch appeals to "the vanishing images of Christian theology which represented goodness as almost impossibly difficult, and sin as almost insuperable and certainly as a universal condition."[48] Yet in spite of her clear sympathies with Christianity in this regard, Murdoch does not fully embrace a Christian diagnosis of the human moral fault or its correction. Rather than identifying the problem of egoism as the perversity of a will unable to will the good, her moral psychology locates egoism directly at the heart of the image-creating processes of human consciousness. As the literary critic David Gordon has argued, "Murdoch's position on this matter can appear contradictory, and has been misunderstood, because it is so emphatic about the rootedness of selfishness as to imply a doctrine like original sin, but our deepest fault lies not in our being but in our knowing or seeing."[49] He notes further that "the fundamental evil for her is always human vanity, not human will."[50] In this respect, the central shift I have repeatedly noted in Murdoch's moral thought from will to consciousness, from choice to vision, from outward conduct to inward knowledge, acquires normative force in her account of human egoism. The fundamental moral problem is acquiring clarity of vision as the condition for right action.

The significance of this point can be clarified by placing Murdoch's position in relation to the two thinkers who have most deeply influenced her moral psychology, Plato and Freud. They provide the critical conceptual resources from which Murdoch constructs her account of how vision effects moral change. There are at least two related areas in which Murdoch takes Plato as the model for her vision-centered ethic. First, as a cognitivist thinker, Plato's affirmation of the relation between knowledge and goodness serves as an important model for Murdoch's view. She repeatedly appeals to Plato's understanding of "the necessity of the concept of consciousness"[51] to challenge the will-centered psychologies of modern moral theory. For both Murdoch and Plato, morality is not solely about conduct; rather, it is about "the continual activity of our own minds and souls and with our own possibilities of being truthful and good."[52] In this respect, both thinkers draw a close connection between knowledge as a search for truth and knowledge as an apprehension of value. Murdoch expresses this by saying that consciousness is a "value-bearing continuum"[53] in which levels of intellectual awareness coincide with levels of moral awareness: "We are moving through a continuum within which we are aware of truth and falsehood, illusion and reality, good and evil. We are continuously striving and learning, discovering and discarding images."[54]

This conception of consciousness is directly related to the second point of contact between Murdoch and Plato. Both thinkers conceive the moral life as a pilgrimage or process of "unselfing" that binds knowledge together with vision. Moral change is a function of "progressively changing quality of consciousness"[55] that is at the same time a reeducation of moral vision. This inextricable connection between knowledge and vision is captured in Murdoch's constant reference to Plato's myth of the cave in both *The Sovereignty of Good* and *Metaphysics as a Guide to Morals*. Subjects in the cave who begin to turn from the deceptive fire to the transcendent sun

> begin to see different objects; they have a deeper and wider and wiser understanding of the world. The pilgrim will not only produce a better series of acts, he will have (down to last details) a better series of mental states. He can literally see better, see people's faces and leaves on trees, he will more rapidly and easily expel an unworthy thought or improper image . . . and the largely explicable ambiguity of the word 'see' here conveys the essence of the concept of the moral.[56]

Progress in moral understanding thus takes place through the agency of vision, which progressively learns to discriminate the false world of appearances and shadows from the real world lit by the sun outside the cave.

This brief account of Murdoch's dependence on Plato supports Gordon's reading that the problem of egoism is linked in her thought to vision rather than will. He writes, "Plato's myth of the cave, as Murdoch used it, implied that the human distance from truth results from a lack of clarity rather than from original sin. . . . It is not the will itself that is corrupt: 'no one errs willingly' (FS 81). Rather, when the ego is swollen by fantasies, either grandiose or consolatory, we do not *see* clearly."[57] What is not yet clear either from Gordon's commentary or Murdoch's own account, however, is how knowledge and vision can bring about moral change at the practical level. That is, we need to understand how vision is connected with the fundamental motive energy of human beings, eros or desire. In order to make this connection, Murdoch supplements her Platonic ethic of vision with a Freudian account of the psyche that she believes clarifies Plato's own intent. Using the religious terminology which Gordon finds misleading, Murdoch argues that Freudian psychology "has provided us with what might be called a doctrine of original sin. . . . One may say that what he presents us with is a realistic and detailed picture of the fallen man."[58] According to Freud, the human fault lies in the fact that "objectivity and unselfishness are not natural to human beings."[59] This is so because the basic energies of the human psyche are organized around the ego as their central focus. The Freudian psyche, Murdoch writes, is "an egocentric system of quasi-mechanical energy, largely determined by its own individual history, whose natural attachments are sexual, ambiguous, and hard for the subject to understand or control. Introspection reveals only the deep tissue of ambivalent motive, and fantasy is a stronger force than reason."[60]

The two most important elements to emphasize in this description are the language of "energy," which is described as sexual, ambiguous, and resistant to both reason and will; and the language of "mechanism," which likewise suggests a system of forces that are impersonal and thus impervious to human control or understanding. This language adds considerable force to the Platonic account of vision just noted and suggests a reason for Murdoch's references to "original sin" and "fallenness." Egoism is for her a natural feature of human consciousness that is not subject to solution by sheer "intelligence and force of will."

But Murdoch believes that these Freudian insights about the human psyche are not wholly original to Freud, since "partially similar views have been expressed before in philosophy, as far back as Plato."[61] In fact, Freud has only clarified in modern terms the central Platonic concept of eros, without which Plato's notion of vision is incomplete. Murdoch finds in the Freudian libido a direct descendant of the Platonic doctrine of eros. "Eros is sexual energy as spiritual energy. Freud's libido is also a concept of the energy of the *Seele* or *Psyche* which can make or mar the life of the individual."[62]

> Plato uses this concept of energy [Eros] to explain the nature of moral change. . . . He essentially accompanies the image of energy (magnetic attraction) by that of light and vision. The sun gives warmth and vital force, and also the light by which to see. We must transform base egoistic energy and vision (low Eros) into high spiritual energy and vision (high Eros). . . . The moral life in the Platonic understanding of it is a slow shift of attachments wherein *looking* (concentrating, attending, attentive discipline) is a source of divine (purified) energy. This is a progressive redemption of desire.[63]

It is clear from this passage that Murdoch understands Plato's account of vision as inseparably connected with the motive energy of human beings— that is, love, eros, or desire. For both Plato and Freud, in Murdoch's view, " 'cure' lies in redeployment of energy."[64]

Freud's account helps Murdoch to clarify the way in which the images and fantasies of consciousness function to direct both vision and psychic energy toward various objects of attention. On Murdoch's Platonic-Freudian view, images provide the focal point around which the undifferentiated force of psychic eros is organized. As a reflexive realist, Murdoch regards images as *mediating* the psychic energy of consciousness in such a way that the quality of the images to which we attend is "profoundly connected with our energies and our ability to choose and act."[65] Therefore, the problem of egoism in Murdoch's view is not merely a problem of the redirection of vision, but also of the transformation of psychic energy; these are in fact one and the same problem. Thus the central question of moral philosophy can be formulated as follows: "Are there any techniques for the purification and reorientation of an energy which is naturally selfish, in such a way that when moments of choice arrive we shall be sure of acting rightly?"[66] This question brings us to the threshold of Murdoch's normative theory of the good.

In spite of her reliance on Freud's diagnosis of human selfishness, Murdoch follows Plato rather than Freud in her understanding of the techniques for its cure. She does so for an important reason: Freud's account of the psyche, she believes, belongs "in the context of a scientific therapy which aims not at making people good but at making them workable."[67] In contrast, Murdoch conceives "therapy" to be an explicitly moral undertaking aimed at "[making] ourselves morally better."[68] Accordingly, the kind of "cure" that she imagines is not a psychoanalytic scrutiny of the psyche, but rather cultivating modes of attention intended to *break* the hold of the psyche. "It is an attachment to what lies outside the fantasy mechanism, and not a scrutiny of the mechanism itself, that liberates. Close scrutiny of the mechanism often merely strengthens its power."[69] The relentlessly "machine-like" nature of the psyche makes self-scrutiny dangerous because the psyche is in effect "programmed" to look after itself: "it is predisposed to certain patterns of activity. . . . Its consciousness is not normally a transparent glass through which it views the world, but a cloud of more or less fantastic reverie designed to protect the psyche from pain."[70] So relentless is this psychic machinery in Murdoch's view that even a negative judgment of oneself may perpetuate a consoling self-absorption: "One's self is interesting, so one's motives are interesting, and the unworthiness of one's motives is interesting."[71] The danger of the Freudian model of therapy, in brief, is that the reflexive nature of self-scrutiny allows the psyche to double back on itself and produce "plausible imitations of what is good"[72] under the guise of sado-masochism. This leads Murdoch to conclude that " 'self-knowledge', in the sense of a minute understanding of one's own machinery, seems to me, except at a fairly simple level, usually a delusion."[73]

It is not surprising, then, that Murdoch seeks a source of psychic transformation *outside* what she frequently calls the "mess" or "swamp" of the naturally selfish consciousness. She recognizes that reflexivity infects consciousness in such a way that looking inward may only heighten the psyche's tendency to console and deceive itself. "Self is such a dazzling object," she writes, "that if one looks *there* one may see nothing else."[74] This is why Murdoch believes that anything that alters vision "in the direction of unselfishness, objectivity and realism is to be connected with virtue."[75] The purification or transformation of consciousness requires finding objects of attention that will refocus and redirect vision and psychic energy *away* from the self. This is what makes her reflexive position *realist* in its fundamental orientation. But if moral change requires an object of attention *outside* consciousness, does this not contradict my central claim in this chapter that Murdoch understands the norm of the good to be *internal* to human consciousness? How are we to reconcile Murdoch's intense suspicion of the self-serving machinations of the human psyche with her reflexive posture towards the good established by her ontological proof?

In the following analysis I show that the various "techniques of unselfing" described in *The Sovereignty of Good* (e.g., the apprehension of beauty in nature and art, the practice of learning a language, and most important, attention to others) demonstrate Murdoch's acute awareness of both the necessity and the pitfalls of reflexivity. She responds to this conundrum by imagining the good as a "pure moral source" that lies outside consciousness, yet works *through* the energies of consciousness to effect moral change from within. I discuss these techniques in the order of their increasing reflexive complexity.

II. C. Techniques of "Unselfing": Cultivating Realistic Vision

The experience of "unselfing" occasioned by natural beauty is the clearest and most obvious example of the way in which consciousness may be altered by the perception of a reality outside the mechanism of selfish fantasy. Beauty, Murdoch argues, is "perhaps the most obvious thing in our surroundings which is an occasion for 'unselfing' ";[76] more important, beauty "appears as the visible and accessible aspect of the Good."[77] She describes the change effected by an experience of natural beauty as follows:

> I am looking out of my window in an anxious and resentful state of mind, oblivious of my surroundings, brooding perhaps on some damage done to my prestige. Then suddenly I observe a hovering kestrel. In a moment everything is altered. The brooding self with its hurt vanity has disappeared. There is nothing now but kestrel. And when I return to thinking of the other matter it seems less important.[78]

There are two basic movements described in this experience of unselfing that demonstrate the close connection between vision and psychic energy in Murdoch's thought. The first movement is *away* from self: in the precise moment that one attends to the kestrel, "self" (i.e., brooding, self-absorbed, hurt vanity) vanishes from consciousness. This movement is "automatic": attention to the new object is at one and the same time an extinction or suppression of self, since "seeing" redirects psychic energy from self to kestrel. The second movement is a *return* to self, in which the self's previous concerns now seem less important because they have been placed in a larger perceptual and psychic field: "when clear vision has been achieved, self is a correspondingly smaller and less interesting object."[79] The redirection of attention to the kestrel's "sheer alien pointless independent existence"[80] has become a new source of energy; consciousness has been altered by attention to an object outside its previous range.

The experience of natural beauty is the least reflexive of the techniques that Murdoch discusses. This is because nature, in its sheer "facticity," is most obviously an object that is external to us, and therefore is least vulnerable to the "grasping tentacles" of human egoism. Although we might be tempted (as Murdoch believes Kant and some romantic thinkers were) to *use* nature for a more intense experience of self,[81] on the whole we find it easy to recognize that nature is impervious to the demands of the psyche and frequently thwarts human purpose and expectation. This is why Murdoch believes that nature is both the most accessible, but also the *least important* place of moral change;[82] it does not fully engage the (potentially) devious reflexivity of the psyche.

Similarly, Murdoch's discussion of intellectual studies (adapted from Plato's discussion of the *techne*) as a technique of unselfing also displays only a limited degree of reflexive complexity. While Plato chose mathematics as the *techne* that might provide a route to change of consciousness, Murdoch chooses an example from her own experience—that is, learning a language—to show "the sense in which intellectual disciplines are moral disciplines."[83] A language confronts one with "an authoritative structure which commands my respect."[84] Thus the task of learning a language requires disciplined attention to an object that stands outside the usual limits of consciousness. "My work is a progressive revelation of something which exists independently of me. Attention is rewarded by a knowledge of reality. Love of Russian leads me away from myself towards something alien to me, something which my consciousness cannot take over, swallow up, deny or make unreal."[85]

Like the apprehension of natural beauty, an intellectual discipline enables the mind to perceive a reality that lies outside the selfish pathways of consciousness. Such an experience can teach both honesty and humility because it forces the student to evaluate his or her own limited knowledge in light of a new standard provided by unfamiliar subject matter.[86] In this respect, intellectual studies effect the same "double movement" we saw in the case of natural beauty. Learning a language initially directs attention and psychic energy away from self because it represents an authoritative object that cannot be absorbed into the selfish consciousness. Then, in the movement of return, the mind is able to "perceive a reality of a new kind,"[87] one that lies beyond one's previous limits and that helps to "stretch the imagination, enlarge the vision and strengthen the judgment."[88]

In contrast to these two examples, the practices associated with the creation and enjoyment of artistic beauty and those associated with human relations involve more complicated and reflexive occasions of unselfing. This is perhaps one reason why Murdoch frequently discusses art and morals as "aspects of a single struggle."[89] The beauty of good art is similar to natural beauty in that it "affords us a pure delight in the independent existence of what is excellent."[90] Yet because art is a product of human subjectivity, it is more vulnerable to the distortions of human egoism than is nature. "The experience of art is more easily degraded than the experience of nature. A great deal of art, perhaps most art, actually is self-consoling fantasy, and even great art cannot guarantee the quality of its consumer's consciousness."[91] Precisely for this reason, art is more "edifying" than nature in Murdoch's view "since it is actually a human product, and certain arts are actually 'about' human affairs in a direct sense."[92] Thus the creation and contemplation of art provides a more fitting but also a more difficult arena in which to practice the expulsion of self required for realistic vision. Indeed, Murdoch goes so far as to say that art is "the most educational of all human activities and a place in which the nature of morality can be *seen*."[93]

Art provides an occasion for unselfing in both its creation and its enjoyment. In its creation, it requires from the artist a moral discipline because it requires her or him to put aside "personal fantasy: the tissue of self-aggrandizing and consoling wishes and dreams which prevents one from seeing what is there outside one."[94] Similarly, "the consumer of art has an analogous task to its producer: to be disciplined enough to see as much reality in the work as the artist has succeeded in putting into it, and not to 'use it as magic.' "[95] In both cases, the apprehension of beauty in art requires a more deliberate effort of unselfing than that required by natural beauty. "To silence and expel self, to contemplate and delineate nature with a clear eye, is not easy and demands a moral discipline."[96] This is all the more difficult given the fact that the creation of art requires the artist to capture beauty in forms that are a product of his or her own imagination. "Of course, too, artists are pattern-makers. The claims of form and the question of 'how much form' to elicit constitutes one of the chief problems of art."[97] Thus any grasp of the real in art is necessarily mediated not only by the naturally selfish psyches of both artist and consumer but also by the media of artistic form, which may be used to conceal reality as much as to reveal it.

Given Murdoch's recognition of the explicitly reflexive considerations that come into play in the arena of art, and given the close connection that she draws between art and ethics throughout her writings, art may provide the best place to approach a normative understanding of what she means by "realistic vision" (i.e., the vision of the good) in both art and ethics. The reflexivity of this vision has not been sufficiently noted by critics of Murdoch's work, partly because it is not always made sufficiently clear by Murdoch herself. For example, in a famous passage describing the kind of vision that good art achieves, Murdoch seems to conceive the "reality" sought by the artist in the most *unreflexive* of terms. She writes: "Rilke said of Cézanne that he did not paint 'I like it', he painted 'There it is.' "[98] The sharp contrast drawn in this passage between the artist's personal or subjective desire on the one hand ("I like it"), and the clear vision he achieves on the other ("There it is"), suggests that "reality" stands apart from the self as something wholly "impersonal."[99] It is something that can be grasped only through the withdrawal of subjectivity—that is, through a complete renunciation of desire and an extinction of self. As Murdoch puts it, the artist must "cease to be in order to attend to the existence of something else."[100]

Further, Murdoch often implies that the kind of vision necessary to see the real is a form of "detachment"; that it requires a certain distancing of the self from the object of vision and its own desires and an assumption of an observer's standpoint:

> This exercise of *detachment* is difficult and valuable whether the thing contemplated is a human being or the root of a tree or the vibration of a colour or a sound. Unsentimental contemplation of nature exhibits the same quality of detachment: selfish concerns vanish, nothing exists except the things which are seen. . . . It is obvious here what is the role, for the artist or spectator, of exactness and good vision: unsentimental, detached, unselfish, objective attention. It is also clear that in moral situations a similar exactness is called for.[101]

The language Murdoch uses to describe "good vision" in this passage might lead one to conclude that she understands moral realism on the analogy of scientific observation. In both cases, what is required of the observer is "exactness" of vision, "unsentimental," "detached," "unselfish," and "objective" attention to the object under scrutiny.

Such passages have led critics such as the late Elizabeth Dipple to neglect the reflexive aspect of Murdoch's realism. In her study of Murdoch's novels, *Iris Murdoch: Work for the Spirit*, Dipple detects a "Platonic reality" lying in the background of Murdoch's fiction. She interprets this reality as "the sense of the world as existing objectively and powerfully outside us and our control" and one that "the twentieth century has been trying very hard to obliterate."[102] Analyzing the character of Murdoch's literary and ethical realism against this Platonic background, Dipple observes a tension between Murdoch's Platonic vision of an external reality (i.e., her ethical realism) and what she calls the "tricksterish" frame of Murdoch's fiction (i.e., her literary realism), which uses all the imaginative and magical devices of art to portray this reality. "Murdoch's work," she writes, "is plagued by contradiction and her best fiction reflects it: on the one hand her *oeuvre* illustrates her commitment to reality and her practice of a firm defensible realism; on the other hand her games, tricks and ironies indicate her reluctant acquiescence to the artifice and unreality of the form."[103]

This alleged contradiction between realism and artifice in Murdoch's thought might be resolved, however, by recognizing that Murdoch's realism (both literary and ethical) is reflexive in nature. Contrary to Dipple, Murdoch does not "reluctantly acquiesce to the artifice of form"; rather, she recognizes that the problems of "form" associated with art also pervade ethics and must be addressed not through an idea of radical "unselfing," but through an acknowledgment of the reflexivity of moral vision and artistic vision alike. In other words, Murdoch acknowledges the necessary mediation of our vision of reality by the structures of language and imaginative form not only in the practice of literary realism but also in the practice of moral realism. The point of understanding Murdoch as a reflexive realist is that she understands "reality" as existing not only outside us, as Dipple assumes, but mediated through consciousness and moral vision. Far from equating realism with the empiricist assumptions of the scientific gaze, Murdoch makes it clear that realism is always keyed to a personal vision. The force of her analogy between art and ethics is precisely to substitute an aesthetic analogy for the scientific analogy that undergirds much of modern moral theory as a suitable model for objective moral thinking. The idea of goodness that is implicit in these spiritual exercises of unselfing is objective in the sense that it represents a "reality principle" that contrasts with the illusions of the psyche: "The self, the place where we live, is a place of illusion. Goodness is connected with the attempt to see the unself, to see and to respond to the real world in the light of a virtuous consciousness."[104] Yet moral objectivity or realism is not divorced from the perceiving subject; rather, these terms only make sense *within* the deeply personal field of human moral vision. Thus Murdoch writes that art "exhibits to us the connection, in *human* beings, of clear realistic vision with compassion. The realism of a great artist is not a 'photographic' realism, it is essentially both pity and justice."[105] Good vision, in other words, is not "neutral," like the eye of a camera; it is *human* vision that has been purified of selfish desire.

The reflexive nature of realistic vision in Murdoch's ethics becomes most apparent when we turn to the techniques of unselfing that she associates directly with morality and human love. These particular fields of human practice represent the most valuable but also the most difficult approach to the good as an experience of moral change.

> Human beings are far more complicated and enigmatic and ambiguous than languages or mathematical concepts, and selfishness operates in a much more devious and frenzied manner in our relations with them. . . .

Our attachments tend to be selfish and strong, and the transformation of our loves from selfishness to unselfishness is sometimes hard even to conceive of.[106]

Murdoch's example of M and D in *The Sovereignty of Good* is perhaps the best example of how moral change comes about in the area of human relations. In her discussion, she introduces the notion of "attention," as opposed to the more neutral term "looking,"[107] to specify the normative or realistic kind of vision that transforms consciousness. Like the artist seeking a clear view of her subject, M makes a conscious effort to expel her own jealousy regarding D by "giving careful and just *attention*"[108] to D in order to see her in a clear light. Murdoch borrows this term from Simone Weil "to express the idea of a just and loving gaze directed upon an individual reality."[109] The adjective "loving" in this definition indicates that attention is a type of vision that does not merely seek neutral "accuracy" or "photographic realism" in relation to its object. Rather, "what M is *ex hypothesi* attempting to do is not just to see D accurately but to see her justly or lovingly."[110] In contrast to the "detachment" and near "extinction of self" noted earlier, these passages suggest on the contrary that good vision has its own *eros*. Goodness cannot be grasped apart from the evaluative and desire-laden gaze of a perceiving consciousness. By expelling selfish concern, attention purifies desire to yield both justice and rightly directed love.

Further, M's effort of attention is not "impersonal," as the earlier passages suggested; it is thoroughly personal and individual. It involves redescribing D with secondary moral words that provide alternative images of D and thereby refocus M's psychic energies. M's redescription of D as "refreshingly simple" rather than "vulgar," "spontaneous" rather than "undignified," and so on,[111] is something that she does in the privacy of her own consciousness, with the resources of own her moral temperament and imagination. In this respect, "M's activity is peculiarly *her own*. Its details are the details of *this* personality."[112] Yet these "subjective" aspects of M's moral vision do not prevent her from achieving clear vision; rather, they are the necessary condition for clear vision. As Murdoch puts it,

> We use our imagination not to escape the world but to join it. . . . The value concepts are here patently tied on to the world, they are stretched as it were between the truth-seeking mind and the world. . . . We can see the length, the extension, of these concepts as patient attention transforms accuracy without interval into just discernment. Here too we can see it as natural to the particular kind of creatures that we are that love should be inseparable from justice, and clear vision from respect for the real.[113]

Thus an individual's use of moral language plays a central mediating role in the refocusing of psychic energy. Realistic vision is not merely a simple empiricist apprehension of "the facts"; it is the product of an interpretive interaction or engagement between mind and world mediated by moral language and individual perception.

This analysis of the reflexive nature of Murdoch's ethic of vision helps to clarify, if not resolve, a persistent tension in her thought. On the one hand, some passages in her writings suggest that good vision requires the extinction of the self and its desire, leading some critics to comment on the quasi-mystical nature of the "unselfing" she advocates.[114] At other points in her writings, however, good vision seems to involve a redemption rather than an extinction of desire, as the passages above on "just and loving" attention indicate. A similar tension has been noted in Murdoch's novels. For example, both Elizabeth Dipple and Peter Conradi identify a tension in the novels between an essentially religious or Platonic ethic of "unselfing" and a more cheerful and ego-affirming hedonism. Dipple notes a double frame of reference in Murdoch's fiction. On the one hand, she reads Murdoch as an exacting moralist in the Platonic tradition whose "characters of the good" attempt to embody a religious ideal; on the other, she argues that the novels contain an equally vivid appreciation that human life is full of "comedy, replete with pleasure, enjoyment and fun in spite of its pain and failure."[115] Similarly, Peter Conradi structures his reading of Murdoch's novels according to the contrasting typology of "the saint and the artist," which also serves as the title of his book. This contrast identifies what he judges to be the tension in Murdoch's thought "between a spiritual and a secular or worldly view of the moral agent."[116] The novels demonstrate this tension by adopting a "brilliant but essentially tolerant double focus."[117] On the one hand, they appear to support an "other-worldly" ideal of unselfing represented by puritanical characters who aspire to a saintly mode of existence; on the other, they also seem to endorse a "worldly" aestheticism represented by characters who are "pagan innocents" or hedonists—that is, who embrace ordinary life and the pursuit of pleasure and happiness. Conradi traces this tension primarily in the fiction rather than seeing it as a tension that might also exist within the moral theory. He reads Murdoch's ethics mainly as a theoretical articulation of the "saintly" ideal of a radical unselfing. For example, he notes that in *The Sovereignty of Good*,

> Murdoch spoke eloquently for the unconsoled love of Good, and emerged as a puritan moralist in a tradition sanctioned by Plato, arguing for unselfing, and for the difficult task of ascesis. The austere project of the book is to rescue a religious picture of man from the collapse of dogma, to attack all forms of consolation, romanticism and self-consciousness, and to study the necessary degeneration of Good in morals.[118]

Although Conradi notes briefly that Murdoch qualifies this ethic of unselfing elsewhere in her ethics (he cites one unidentified Gifford Lecture and a radio interview),[119] his main preoccupation is to show that the "otherworldly asceticism" of Murdoch's philosophical ethic is undercut in the novels by the countervailing ideal of the artist.

Without denying that such a tension exists in Murdoch's fiction, my claim is that a similar tension between competing ideals exists within her moral philosophy. The ideal associated with Murdoch's Platonic ethic of vision in *The Sovereignty of Good* does not unambiguously support a saintly idea of unselfing, as Conradi and others suggest, but may allow for an affirmation of the moral agent as creative individual (i.e., as "artist" rather than saint). As a reflexive realist, Murdoch acknowledges that every act of human knowing must pass through the structures of human consciousness, imagination, and language. This undercuts the ideal of a total "unselfing" in her ethic, since what reflexivity presupposes is precisely a notion of the self. Thus the Platonic ethic of unselfing that both Conradi and Dipple associate with Murdoch's philosophical vision is not unambiguously present in her philosophy. Rather, a similar ambiguity pervades both her fiction and her philosophy as a result of the inescapable reflexivity of human moral being.[120]

In sum, Murdoch argues that through the work of attention, love is purified and becomes psychic energy in the service of Good: "Love . . . is capable of infinite degradation and is the source our greatest errors; but when it is even partially refined it is the energy and passion of the soul in its search for Good."[121] This, in my judgment, is the meaning of the phrase "the sovereignty of good" in Murdoch's ethics: the good is finally sovereign over love and indeed supersedes all other concepts that might rival it as the norm of morality. Since the deep and intractable problem of the moral life on this account is the proper character and direction of our loves (in the form of psychic energy or eros), then love cannot be the final norm of this ethic. Rather, Murdoch conceives goodness as the critical norm that guides perfected vision or love as knowledge of the individual. Attention is an imaginative and normative use of moral vision that burns away the selfishness of natural human desire (i.e., what Murdoch calls "low Eros"), leaving behind the purified desire of just and compassionate love (i.e., "high Eros"). Goodness may thus be understood as "the perfection of desire,"[122] rather than its negation. On Murdoch's reflexive reading of moral change, our grasp of the good is mediated not only by consciousness and language but also by desire or eros as the motive energy of human life. The vision of the good is only available through subjective resonance.[123]

We can conclude from this discussion that the idea of the good implicit in Murdoch's account of realistic vision is a reflexive principle whose objectivity is not conceived independently of a thinking, valuing consciousness. The good as criterion of truthful moral vision is not purely external to consciousness but is located *between* mind and world. As Murdoch notes in *Metaphysics as a Guide to Morals*:

Consciousness *au fond* and *ab initio* must contain an element of truth-seeking through which it is also evaluated. In this sense, some cognitions are purer than others; but we cannot descend by any unitary "scientific" or systematic method below the levels at which, in various ways, we test truth and reflect upon moral understanding.[124]

In other words, given the reflexive nature of human moral understanding, it is impossible to test the truth of human consciousness by a purely external standard. Rather, the standard by which consciousness is to be evaluated is internal to the structure of consciousness itself. This standard makes it possible for us to distinguish which of our cognitions are "purer" (i.e., more "perfect" in conforming to reality) than others, but there is no purely "scientific" notion of truth to be grasped apart from the reflexive limits of consciousness itself. This point allows us to see that the two aspects of the good in Murdoch's ontological proof are finally one. The good is at once transcendental (providing the conditions for moral consciousness) and perfectionist (providing the standard for the evaluation of consciousness) because its reflexivity allows it to assume the character of both an internal subjective ground and an objective norm.

This reading of the transformation of the self and its desire through realistic vision has important consequences for two aspects of Murdoch's moral psychology that have so far been missing from my analysis: (1) her understanding of freedom; and (2) her theory of moral motivation. In the following section, I show that freedom and moral motivation must also be understood in reflexive terms.

Section III. A. Freedom as Reflexive Knowledge of the Real

Since realistic vision brings about the purification of desire rather than its extinction, moral freedom on Murdoch's account must be understood *within* the conflictual realm of human desires rather than in abstraction from it. In this respect, Murdoch embraces what William Schweiker terms an "evaluative" rather than a "voluntarist" model of moral freedom.[125] I have already argued in Chapter 4 that Murdoch shifts the ground of moral freedom from a voluntarist emphasis on choice to a cognitivist emphasis on knowledge or vision. Freedom is not a matter of the will "leaping" out of any situation that threatens to constrain its choices; rather, freedom is a matter of perfecting one's knowledge of reality. This includes knowledge of others and of the moral world that precedes and conditions our choices. Schweiker's discussion of moral freedom in his *Responsibility and Christian Ethics* makes essentially the same distinction between conceptions of freedom but with important nuances that help to clarify Murdoch's cognitivism.

Schweiker defines the voluntarist model as the view that "an agent must be able to act on a principle of choice, and, furthermore, that this choice must not be determined by the situation to which an agent responds or by her or his inclinations and interests."[126] This is precisely the notion of freedom that Murdoch was combating in her critique of Sartre. On this view, the enemy of freedom is determinism, those forces which subject the agent to causality and thereby constrain the will as the principle of choice. The evaluative model of freedom, by contrast, holds that "the fact that what we value might be shaped by social roles, conventional beliefs, natural desires, and needs does not negate moral freedom if we come to endorse those values."[127] This model recognizes that the self is not "reducible to a principle of pure choice, a being stripped of relations, commitments, and desires" and denies that we are "really most free when we exist outside of relations with others, isolated in a domain of pure, unfettered choice."[128] In this respect, the evaluative model coheres with Murdoch's Natural Law view of morality to the extent that it situates freedom within an encompassing moral world.

However, Schweiker's evaluative model goes beyond Murdoch's cognitivist or Natural Law account of freedom by emphasizing the role of desire in moral knowledge. On the evaluative theory, "it is not the capacity for choice but the evaluation and formation of wants that is central."[129] Moral freedom on this view cannot be understood apart from human desires and inclinations but only in and through their proper direction. Further, the evaluative model recognizes that "human beings have distinct and diverse sources of motivation, and what is more, these sources can conflict."[130] Thus freedom on Schweiker's view can only be acquired by revising and interpreting one's values and desires through a reflexive act of radical interpretation which distinguishes basic values from mere desires:[131] "An evaluative theory argues that an agent is free if and only if she or he acts on what is most basically valued, what really matters to her or him, and not simply what is desired or wanted."[132] This reflexive act of self-understanding provides the possibility for moral change: "Granting the difficulty of change in the moral life, persons can interpret their lives and make revisions in their self-understanding. This process is basic to how we live in the world as moral beings and indicates the meaning of moral freedom."[133]

The evaluative model of freedom represents a more precise conceptual tool for understanding Murdoch's cognitivism in two respects. First, its recognition of the crucial role of desires and inclinations coheres with my reading of Murdoch's ethic of vision as a purification rather than an extinction of desire. The enemy of freedom on Murdoch's view is not a determinism that constrains the will, but rather fantasy, which improperly directs desire or psychic energy toward the self. Freedom for her is not freedom *from* desire, but is rather experienced as accurate vision that *re-orders* desire in relation to a new object of attention.[134] Realistic vision has its own eros, but it is an eros purified of selfishness, also known as love or compassion: "It is in the capacity to love, that is to *see*, that the liberation of the soul from fantasy consists. The freedom which is a proper human goal is the freedom from fantasy, that is the realism of compassion."[135] Thus the evaluative model makes sense of the claim that goodness is sovereign over love in Murdoch's ethics by demonstrating that the norm for valid moral knowledge is at the same time the norm for the purification of desire.

Second, Schweiker's description of moral change as a process of self-revision or radical interpretation indicates that the evaluative model of freedom is explicitly reflexive in nature. That is, freedom is not only a matter of the self *conforming* itself to an antecedent order of existing values, as Murdoch's Natural Law view had suggested. Rather, freedom involves the self's active and critical interpretation of itself and its desires in relation to these values. This insight into the reflexive nature of freedom helps to answer the charge of "bad faith" that a voluntarist like Sartre might level at Murdoch's position. On a purely cognitivist reading of the Natural Law view, it is not clear how the moral agent could ever criticize, transcend, or decide against the values of his or her own circumstances. The limits of moral freedom seem to be wholly determined by convention. On the evaluative view, however, freedom includes "the ability to do otherwise,"[136] to act against social roles, conventional beliefs, or natural desires by virtue of the critical interpretive work of attention. The evaluative theory takes what Murdoch calls "the continual strife in the deep patterns of desire"[137] as the material or datum of moral freedom. Desire is then purified through the work of consciousness in the act of attention. This reading of Murdoch's theory of moral freedom coheres with her reflexive account of moral change because it demonstrates that her realism contains the resources for a critical evaluation of the moral world through the work of attention. What this analysis does not address, however, is whether there is any place for the notion of will in Murdoch's theory of freedom, or indeed in her moral psychology as a whole. In the following section, I examine this issue through an analysis of Murdoch's theory of moral motivation, which concerns the relation between vision and will in moral agency.

III. B. Seeing and Doing the Good: Vision, Will, and Moral Motivation

Murdoch's persistent critique of voluntarism might suggest that the concept of the will is virtually absorbed into her notion of consciousness or moral vision. But I contend that the will plays a significant and sometimes surprising role in Murdoch's theory of moral change that is not always readily apparent given her critique of voluntarism. In order to redress this problem and to cast her theory of the will in a new light, I want to place Murdoch's theory of moral motivation in the context of two other ideal typical options, the Socratic model and the Christian model, which explicitly treat the relation between vision and will in an account of moral change.[138] Murdoch's view represents a mediating position between these two models, revealing the complex interaction between vision and will in her ethics.

Given the technical nature of theories of moral motivation, a brief introductory discussion is in order.[139] A theory of moral motivation attempts to articulate the relationship between moral attitudes and action. The basic question that this poses for any ethical system is the following: Is knowledge sufficient for moral conduct, or is something more needed to compel right action? According to Jonathan Dancy, there are two basic approaches to this issue in contemporary moral theory: internalism and externalism. Both of these approaches assume a distinction between desires and beliefs in defining what a moral attitude is like.[140] Internalists, as the name implies, hold that since moral attitudes are more like desires than beliefs, there is an *internal* relation between moral attitudes and practical moral action. On this view, moral attitudes are understood to contain a motive force (i.e., desire) that compels action. Externalists, on the other hand, hold that since moral attitudes are more like beliefs than desires, some *external* desire is required to motivate moral action; beliefs by themselves cannot compel action on this view. Cognitivist thinkers (such as Murdoch) are thought to be externalists on this question, since cognitivists presumably hold that moral attitudes are essentially beliefs about the world.

The distinction between beliefs and desires on which this typology of internalism and externalism is based may be disputed, however. One might argue, for example, that since certain desires are themselves *based* on beliefs, then changing the belief will affect the desire. If this is the case, then the distinction between belief and desire, and hence between internalism and externalism, falls apart or must be made on different grounds. Murdoch's account of how vision organizes psychic eros directly challenges the separation of belief from desire. On her view, vision (as a form of knowledge or belief) itself contains the desire that motivates the will in moral action. Holding a moral belief automatically compels the will to act. Murdoch's position may be summed up in her phrase, "true vision occasions right conduct,"[141] which clearly indicates an internalist posture toward the relation of moral attitudes and action. Thus if moral attitudes are understood as a complex of belief and desire, Murdoch may be classified as an internalist in her theory of moral motivation.

This reading of Murdoch's theory of moral motivation coheres with her evaluative theory of freedom because it confirms that the activity of the will is always conditioned by the limits of moral knowledge or vision. The will can no longer be understood as an isolated, independent principle of self-assertion that is detached from its conditioning background in moral vision. Rather, the will is embedded in the entire complex of consciousness[142], which mediates and organizes the psychic energy available to the will through various images and objects of attention. Thus the efficacy of the will is a direct function of moral vision. As Murdoch puts it, "I can only choose within the world I can *see*, in the moral sense of 'see' which implies that clear vision is a result of moral imagination and moral effort. . . . One is often compelled almost automatically by what one *can* see."[143] This notion of the world as "*compulsively* present to the will"[144] indicates that the quality of human moral vision is directly related to the range of our freedom to act: "we are not free in the sense of being able suddenly to alter ourselves since we cannot suddenly alter what we can see and ergo what we desire and are compelled by."[145] Thus moral change is not first and foremost a matter of choice or action, but rather of revising the beliefs and desires which compel action: "In a way, explicit choice seems now less important: less decisive (since much of the 'decision' lies elsewhere). . . . If I attend properly I will have no choices and this is the ultimate condition to be aimed at."[146]

Given this internalist reading of the relation between vision and will in Murdoch's theory of moral motivation, one might assume that she holds a "Socratic" theory of moral motivation (i.e., the view which Plato attributes to Socrates),[147] which is also internalist in the revised sense noted above. The Socratic view holds that the relation between moral knowledge and moral action is such that one cannot act contrary to one's knowledge of the good. No one does wrong willingly or deliberately, since one can only act on one's current state of knowledge or insight: "we always act on the good we see."[148] Wrong action is thus the result of ignorance or lack of insight rather than the fault of a will gone astray. In fact, the will on this view cannot stray from knowledge because it is not an independent principle of movement, but is rather dependent on the knowledge which compels it to act. Murdoch seems to endorse such a view when she notes that "will is obedience not resolution,"[149] and "Will cannot run very far ahead of knowledge, and attention is our daily bread."[150]

This denial of the independence of the will from knowledge or moral vision is the essential feature that distinguishes the Socratic model from a Christian theory of moral motivation. Charles Taylor has called the Socratic model a "linear" theory of moral motivation because it posits a direct or linear relation between seeing (knowing) the Good and willing (doing) the Good.[151] The Christian model, by contrast, is "circular" because it assumes that the will is not merely the "dependent" variable, "shaped by what we see," but also "the independent variable, determining what we can know."[152] The contrast between the two models can be exemplified through a comparison of Plato and Augustine, following Taylor's discussion in *Sources of the Self*. This comparison provides the basis for my claim that Murdoch articulates a mediating position between these two models of moral motivation that provokes a reevaluation of her notion of the will.

Both Plato and Augustine agree that the soul's attention may be directed in either of two directions: toward the good or away from it. The direction of attention determines the direction of desire. In this respect, both thinkers appear to affirm the intrinsic relation between vision and desire, and thus both appear to have the potential for embracing the Socratic model of moral motivation. However, there are two relevant features of Augustine's account that distinguish him from Plato and from the Socratic model. First, Augustine has a more developed notion of the will than Plato. "Where for Plato," Taylor writes, "our desire for the good is a function of how much we see it, for Augustine the will is not simply dependent on knowledge."[153] This relative independence of the will from moral vision on the Augustinian account introduces "a potential conflict between vision and desire,"[154] because the will (as the motive energy of desire) may act against the good it knows. In contrast to Plato's view, where wrong action is explained by lack of vision or insight, on Augustine's view "the perversity in the will can never be sufficiently explained by our lack of insight into the good; on the contrary, it makes us act below and against our insight."[155] This is why the phenomenon of *akrasia*, the problem of the weakness, bondage, or perversity of the will, is an intellectual conundrum on the Platonic view but becomes "the central crisis of moral experience"[156] for Christian thinkers such as Augustine.[157]

The second relevant difference that Taylor notes between Augustine and Plato is that Augustine embraces a more "radical" notion of reflexivity in his understanding of the relation between the soul and the Good. In contrast to Plato, "Augustine takes our focus off the objects reason knows, the field of the Ideas, and directs it onto the activity of striving to know which each of us carries on; and he makes us aware of this in a first-person perspective."[158] This radical reflexivity, when combined with Augustine's more developed notion of the will, complicates and deepens the problem of *akrasia* and thus widens the gap between Augustine and Plato. It means that the will doubles back on itself as "both cause and consequence of a kind of slavery."[159] In other words, the will on Augustine's view is not only perverse because it is dependent on and therefore enslaved by the soul's misdirected vision; rather, the will is also "the independent variable, determining what [vision] can know."[160] The perversity of the will, which is the consequence of distorted vision, in turn causes vision to be chained to the will's own perversity. As Taylor notes, "the causality [between will and vision] is circular and not linear."[161]

On the basis of this discussion, it seems obvious at first that Murdoch would count herself a Platonist in her denial of the independence of the will from knowledge and of desire from moral vision. In fact, she seems to collapse her notion of the will into vision or consciousness. However, the reflexivity of Murdoch's account of realistic vision makes any simple comparison with Plato problematic and suggests a closer look at her relation to Augustine, as Taylor reads him. The "circularity" between vision and will that is a function of the radical reflexivity of Augustine's position has an analogue in Murdoch's thought. Contrary to first appearances, Murdoch acknowledges what I will call a "reciprocal," if not a "circular," relation between will and vision or knowledge. That is, the influence between vision and will may be pictured as mutual rather than strictly linear. Several passages from *The Sovereignty of Good* support this claim. For example, Murdoch states that "will and reason then are not entirely separate faculties in the moral agent. Will continually influences beliefs, for better or worse, and is ideally able to influence it through a sustained attention to reality."[162] She also suggests that the will is in some measure capable of "leaping ahead of what we know" rather than completely dependent on what we know: "[W]e may sometimes decide . . . to ignore vision and the compulsive energy derived from it; and we may find that as a result both energy and vision are unexpectedly given."[163] Finally, she acknowledges that will may exert some direction over vision, and not only the reverse: "[Man] is a unified being who sees, and who desires in accordance with what he sees, and who has some continual slight control over the direction and focus of his vision."[164]

All of these passages suggest that the relation between vision and will in Murdoch's theory is not as purely linear (i.e., Socratic) as it first appeared. Not only does vision condition the will but the will may also influence vision. The causality seems to be reciprocal, and thus more Augustinian than Platonic. This suggests that the problem of *akrasia* or weakness of will should pose a dilemma for Murdoch, as it does for Augustine. In other words, if will and vision mutually condition each other, it is not clear that right vision will necessarily compel the will; the will may also influence vision. Therefore, the will too must be transformed in order for right action to be possible. However, two related observations would seem to invite caution before reading Murdoch as an Augustinian. First, it is clear that in spite of her sporadic acknowledgment of the ability of the will to influence moral vision, her position as a whole clearly affirms the primacy of vision as the dominant mode of moral being. On this point at least, she remains more Platonic than Augustinian in her lack of a fully developed doctrine of the will. Second, if we accept Gordon's claim (noted earlier) that Murdoch's ambiguous terminology of "original sin" refers not to the perversity of the will but to the distortion of vision by egoism, then she cannot wholly endorse the Augustinian account of *akrasia*.

Yet I believe it is still possible to claim Murdoch as Augustinian with respect to the second crucial point that Taylor believes separates Augustine from Plato—namely, the radical nature of the reflexivity she embraces. For in spite of her consistent reliance on Plato's myth of the cave throughout her work, Murdoch does not clearly embrace a Platonic theory of external moral sources or an "ontic logos"[165] any more than Augustine does. The good, as I have tried to show in this chapter, is not to be found in an objective moral order (i.e., a world of Forms) that exists for all purposes outside and beyond us; rather, the good on Murdoch's view is a reflexive principle that is "stretched between the truth-seeking mind and the world."[166] This is not to say that there is no difference between Murdoch and Augustine on the nature and location of moral sources (Murdoch affirms the Good, but not God); it is only to point out that both thinkers appear to embrace a more radical reflexivity than Plato.

The force of this insight is to show that radical reflexivity deepens the predicament of the self for Murdoch as it does for Augustine because of the mutual relation between vision and will on both accounts. For Augustine, radical reflexivity intensifies the bondage of the will because our perverse drive "to relate everything to ourselves, to dominate and possess the things which surround us" results in our being "dominated, captured by our own obsessions" in turn.[167] This is the force of the circular relation between vision and will on the Christian model. For Murdoch, radical reflexivity intensifies the dilemma of egoism in a slightly different way. Since vision not only conditions the will but is also in turn influenced by the will, "the world we see already contains our values";[168] values have been "placed" in the world by the activity of the will in the building up of moral vision. If the will is active in moral vision, then "the good and evil that we dream of may be more incarnate than we realise in the world within which we choose."[169]

The mutual or reciprocal relation between will and vision in Murdoch's thought can be clarified if we look again at the notion of attention. Attention can be understood as a form of moral vision that seems to have a direct linear relation to the will. That is, what the self attends to and loves conditions the will and determines the nature of its actions; vision compels the will. This is why Murdoch can say that "at crucial moments of choice most of the business of choosing is already over."[170] On the more complex reading I am proposing here, however, attention must now also be understood as influenced by the will: the relation is not simply linear; it is reciprocal in two directions rather than one. In *The Sovereignty of Good*, Murdoch describes attention not merely as a passive or neutral kind of moral vision; rather, attention actively and imperceptibly "builds up structures of value round about us."[171] That is, the work of attention not only *discovers* values in the world, it *constructs* them or builds them up.

In developing this more constructive or "willful" aspect of attention, Murdoch sometimes likens attention to the activity of imagination. In a review essay on Stuart Hampshire's *Freedom and the Individual*, for example, she describes imagination in terms very reminiscent of the notion of attention:

I should like to use the word [imagination] . . . to describe something which we all do a great deal of the time. This activity, which may be characterised by a contrast with "strict" or "scientific" thinking . . . might [be described] as follows: a type of reflection on people, events, etc., which builds detail, adds colour, conjures up possibilities in ways which go beyond what could be said to be strictly factual. When this activity is thought to be bad it is sometimes called "fantasy" or "wishful thinking."[172]

In another passage she again links attention to imagination by speaking of the "constant quiet work of attention and imagination."[173] In contrast to Hampshire, who she thinks relegates the imagination to a passive, isolated, and "non-responsible faculty,"[174] Murdoch describes imagination as active, even as a form of willing: "But if we admit active imagination as an important faculty it is difficult not to see this as an exercise of will. Imagining is *doing*, it is a sort of personal exploring."[175] From this perspective, attention must now be understood as a concept that signals the confluence of vision and will in the imagination of an evaluating moral agent. As a form of vision or belief, attention conditions the will by directing psychic energy toward certain perceived aspects of the moral world. As an exercise of will, attention (or imagination) influences moral vision by building up structures of value in the world. This double-sided character of attention as having both a "vision" aspect and a "willing" aspect means that it is impossible on Murdoch's view to separate the activity of willing from the activity of moral perception. There is a mutual or reciprocal relation between vision and will at work in attention. For better and for worse, "The world which we confront is not just a world of 'facts' but a world upon which our imagination has, at any given moment, already worked."[176]

The conclusion to be drawn from this analysis is that the problem of *akrasia* or weakness of will is a problem for Murdoch in a somewhat different sense than it is for Augustine. This reflects the difference between Augustine's "circular" view and what I am calling Murdoch's "reciprocal" view of the relation between vision and will. *Akrasia* is the central crisis in the moral life for Augustine because his notion of the will is strong enough to assume a relative independence from moral vision that becomes extremely problematic in the context of radical reflexivity. Vision turns away from the good it sees, thereby ensnaring the will in false goods, which then misdirect vision all over again, forming a circle without clear beginning or end.[177] In Murdoch's case, however, the relation between vision and will should be understood as reciprocal or mutual, but not circular. This is because Murdoch does not fully share Augustine's developed notion of the will as a principle that can assume a troubling independence from moral vision. The problem of *akrasia* is situated more centrally within the domain of moral vision for Murdoch. It concerns the way in which attention, as a mode of both attending and imagining, creates structures of value in the moral world that then influence action. Murdoch writes:

Akrasia is only a paradox if we assume (with Aristotle) that we really desire the good, or (with Hampshire) that we are really rational, that is readily able to become detached. . . . But the good and evil that we dream of may be more incarnate than we realise in the world within which we choose. . . . We are obscure to ourselves because the world we see already contains our values and we may not be aware of the slow delicate processes of imagination and will which have put those values there.[178]

Thus *akrasia* for Murdoch has less to do with the perversity of the will and more with what she calls "the darkness of practical reason."[179] Vision may be distorted by the building up of false structures of value by the willful work of imagination in the guise of fantasy, making psychic energy flow in the direction of the self rather than toward the real. This means that moral change requires a transformation of both vision and will through a normative use of imagination as attention or realistic vision.

For both Murdoch and Augustine, radical reflexivity not only complicates the self's predicament but may also contribute to its liberating solution. As Taylor writes of Augustine's view, "Evil is when this reflexivity is enclosed on itself. Healing comes when it is broken open."[180] Both Murdoch and Augustine believe that the remedy for the curving in of the soul on itself involves transforming the relation between vision and will in such a way that both are directed to the service of good rather than self. For Augustine, the work of divine grace disrupts the circular enslavement between vision and will by restoring the capacity of the eye to see the good, thereby transforming reflexivity into the knowledge of God within. As Taylor writes, "[T]he discovery which dissipates the perversity of the will, and which the rectifying of this perversity makes possible, is that of our dependence on God in the very intimacy of our own presence to ourselves, at the roots of those powers which are most our own."[181] In this transformation, vision and desire continue to relate in circular fashion, but grace has turned vision and desire toward the love of God: "[J]ust as in our perverse condition of sin, our desire for the good was so much less than our insight; in being turned towards God, our love for him goes beyond the measure of any order, however good. . . . So both for better and for worse, the will leaps beyond the desire appropriate to a cosmos ordered for the Good."[182] The ability of desire both to fall short of moral vision (in sin) and to surpass moral vision (in grace) testifies, in Taylor's view, to the gratuitousness of the Christian concept of love, a gratuity that signals the sovereignty of (God's) love over goodness.

For Murdoch, too, moral transformation involves a "breaking open" of reflexivity. But in Murdoch's case, the discovery that brings the cure for egoism is not an effect of divine grace, but rather of an innately human power, the imagination. The reflexivity that formerly enclosed consciousness in its own fantasies is now opened to the real through imaginative vision. The work of attention purifies selfish vision and builds up just and compassionate images in the moral world so that psychic energy may flow toward the good rather than away from it. When vision and desire are thus purified by attention, the will functions as "obedience not resolution;"[183] it conforms itself to realistic vision, rather than constructing false pictures that inform moral choice and action. In contrast to Augustine's circular account, in which the infusion of divine grace replaces the deficit in our desire for the good with a surplus that surpasses the order of the good, on Murdoch's reciprocal account of moral change, vision and desire work together reciprocally, in obedience to reality or the good. Vision does not leap ahead of desire, nor desire ahead of vision. In the absence of a divine principle of transformation, the good remains sovereign over love in Murdoch's ethics.

The foregoing analysis of the reciprocal relation between vision and will in Murdoch's theory of moral motivation suggests that her notion of the will functions primarily *within* the realm of moral vision rather than as an independent principle that may oppose vision. Attention and imagination, after all, are associated more readily with vision than with the kind of activity we normally associate with the will. However, the question of the status of the will in Murdoch's ethics is not completely resolved by this discussion. Rather, the will continues to exert a certain pressure on Murdoch's ethics of vision that becomes evident in her account of moral obligation. In the following section, I consider the question of whether the emergence of the will as a factor in Murdoch's ethic of vision helps to expose some of the limitations of her account of moral change as a form of vision or insight.

Section IV. A. The Limits of Vision

Since Murdoch's emphasis on vision and the primacy of consciousness in the moral life indicates that she understands morality primarily as a matter of insight rather than as adherence to impersonal rules and principles, it is important to consider whether she avoids intuitionism and subjectivism in her account of the good. Murdoch herself takes on the charge of intuitionism by offering a number of important qualifications to her ethic of vision. These qualifications suggest that she understands the limitations and possible dangers of her reflexive view of moral change.

She insists, first, that her account of moral vision is not to be understood as a universal "formula" for morality: "I have several times indicated that the image which I am offering should be thought of as a general metaphysical background to morals and not as a formula which can be illuminatingly introduced into any and every moral act. There exists, so far as I know, no formula of the latter kind."[184] The role of vision in moral change should not, Murdoch argues, be taken as a new "method" of ethics that can be universalized (like the categorical imperative) to cover every moral situation. Nor is an ethic of vision supposed to produce insights into the same fixed value or property of goodness inherent in certain objects or states of mind (as in Moore's intuitionism). Rather, Murdoch regards the idea of vision as a necessary background concept to other aspects of morality (e.g., will, choice, action, duty) that she believes have dominated modern ethical thinking to its detriment. In this respect, she intends the idea of vision to be a necessary corrective to, but not a substitute for, a morality centered on will, choice, and actions. This is consistent with Murdoch's attempt to retrieve a notion of consciousness as the fundamental mode of moral being.

In a second but related point, Murdoch recognizes that her account of morality as spiritual change may have the unintended effect of presenting morality as an esoteric pursuit rather than an integral part of ordinary human life and action: "I am well aware of the *moral* dangers of the idea of morality as something which engages the whole person and which may lead to specialized and esoteric vision and language."[185] In other words, the contemplative, intuitive, or quasi-mystical aspects of her account of "unselfing" may be perceived as separating morality from the ordinary lived experience of most moral agents. But vision, Murdoch insists, is not the sum total of the moral life: "Often, for instance when we pay our bills or perform other small everyday acts, we are just 'anybody' doing what is proper or making simple choices for ordinary public reasons."[186] Consequently, Murdoch acknowledges that the inner life of consciousness must be understood in the context of the public world of morality that requires outward acts of choice and decision. "Give and take between the private and the public levels of morality is often of advantage to both and indeed is normally unavoidable."[187]

Third and most significantly, Murdoch distances herself from an intuitionist reading of her own ethic by explicitly denying that a morality of vision should be understood as superior to a morality of will or duty.

> I would not be understood, either, as suggesting that insight or pureness of heart are more important than action: the thing which philosophers feared Moore for implying. Overt actions are perfectly obviously important in themselves, and important too because they are the indispensable pivot and spur of the inner scene. The inner, in this sense, cannot do without the outer.[188]

This last point in particular supports the conclusion that Murdoch did not intend her account of morality as spiritual change, vision, or insight to represent a comprehensive theory of the moral life. Rather, she was aware that the price of reflexivity is that her normative theory of consciousness is in danger of collapsing in on itself. For this reason, I believe, Murdoch increasingly sought to balance her ethic of vision with an ethic of duty centered in acts of the will. This move is nascent in *The Sovereignty of Good* (as the above passages imply), and in her theory of the imagination, where the will assumes an important role in attention. But by the time she wrote *Metaphysics as a Guide to Morals*, she had supplemented her account of morality as spiritual change with a parallel account of morality as obligation. This account represents a crucial turn from the "inner" to the "outer" life and finds an important place for a rule-based morality of will *within* Murdoch's general theory of consciousness.

IV. B. The Ethics of Duty: Morality as Obligation

Murdoch recognized that neither vision nor the idea of consciousness can account for the whole of morality. She acknowledged that the outer or public realm of behavior, choice, and action is crucial to the moral life and cannot be swallowed up in an account of morality as "inwardness." From this perspective, her concern to develop an account of duty and obligation in her later work may be seen simply as an attempt to redress this deficiency by providing an account of "public morality" to balance her account of the inner life. However, given Murdoch's concern to avoid intuitionism, this turn toward duty and obligation may also raise a more basic question about the integrity of her reflexive approach. It may suggest, in fact, that reflexivity continually threatens to devolve into an intuitionism that is not stable enough to provide objective knowledge of the real. In spite of the intuitive certainty about the good connected with the ontological proof, Murdoch was compelled to supplement her reflexive account of morality with a more stable morality of principles and axioms to guide conduct in the public realm. On this reading, Murdoch's theory of obligation would represent not merely a useful counterpart to her emphasis on the inner life, but a necessary corrective against the subjectivism implicit in her starting point in consciousness.

The question that lies in the background of these considerations is whether Murdoch's theory of obligation should be understood as *competing* with her reflexive account of consciousness, or whether it should be understood as an *integral part* of her ethical system. Inner and outer, vision and duty, public and private clearly constitute important conceptual dyads in her thought. How are these to be related? Does Murdoch end up articulating a "two-level" ethic, one related to personal morality and the other to politics?[189] Or does she succeed in synthesizing these two dimensions, one public and one private, in a comprehensive account of the moral life? There is evidence to support both views. On the one hand, Murdoch intends her theory of obligation to represent aspects of the moral life that are "not easily assimilated into inwardness,"[190] and are relatively autonomous from her account of consciousness. On the other hand, there is also evidence to suggest that Murdoch is attempting to integrate an account of public morality into her general theory of consciousness.

There is in fact a complex interaction between private and public dimensions of morality in Murdoch's ethic, one that resists systematic formulation and requires what she calls "a give and take between an axiomatic and abstract level, and the deeper more densely cognitive personal level of my consciousness and my world."[191] We need to clarify what this "give and take" involves. While Murdoch does want to retain a distinction between morals and politics, she also finds a way to relate them through the activity of imagination and moral cognition. In this respect, the demand of reflexivity required by her ethics of vision seems to have an analogue in her theory of obligation, as the demand for an interpretive engagement between personal consciousness and abstract principles operative in the public realm. Morality, in her view, encompasses both an internal and an external dimension held in "continual volatile dynamic relationship."[192]

I turn first to a text that provides an important clue to this new direction in her thought and helps frame the issues discussed above. The text is a brief passage from her Platonic dialogue on "Art and Eros" in *Acastos*, written in the years between the publication of *The Sovereignty of Good* and *Metaphysics as a Guide to Morals*. In the context of a debate over the nature and function of art in society, Murdoch's fictional Socrates offers a definition of morality that conceives its public dimension as integral. He argues that the role of art is "to explore the relation between the public and the private," and he continues: "Art turns us inside out, it exhibits what is secret. What goes on inwardly in the soul is the essence of each man, it's what makes us individual people, the relation between that inwardness and public conduct *is morality*. How can art ignore it?"[193] What is notable about this passage is the character Socrates' claim that although the inner life of consciousness or the soul is the individuating principle of human moral identity ("what makes us individual people"), it is not the only locus of morality. Rather, morality resides in the *relation between* that inwardness and an agent's public conduct. This suggests that it would be a mistake to read Murdoch as defending the view that morality is solely a matter of the inner life of consciousness.[194] Rather, morality encompasses the relation between inner and outer, or between private and public aspects of human life, and it is the role of the artist (and by analogy the moralist) to clarify or exhibit the nature of that relation.

This brief excerpt from *Acastos* is suggestive of the concern to address the public aspect of morality that is a feature of Murdoch's mature thought, but it does not answer the question of *how* the inner and outer realms are to be related. A more fully developed account of the public dimension of morality and its relation to the inner life does not appear in Murdoch's work until the publication of *Metaphysics as a Guide to Morals*.

In that text, she supplements her account of morality as spiritual change (the ethics of vision) with an account of morality as obligation (the ethics of duty) based on a theory of moral principles and axiomatic values that does not depend so exclusively on the inner life of consciousness.

Certain structural features of the text of *Metaphysics* are relevant to my claim that Murdoch is attempting in this work to integrate a rule-based morality of duty into her ethical system. Starting from its implicit organizational principles, the text can be read as divided into roughly three main parts. The first third of the book is devoted to the theme of art (chapters 1–5), the second third to the idea of the self or consciousness (chapters 6–12), and the final third is devoted to religion and the idea of the good (chapters 13–18).[195] Not surprisingly, the chapters on consciousness occupy the center of the book, testifying to the essential role this concept plays in Murdoch's ethics. Two chapters are devoted to the theme of "Consciousness and Thought" (chapters 6 and 8) defending the moral status of the idea of consciousness from diverse threats in the history of thought. Two other chapters take up specific challenges to the idea of consciousness or the inner life from thinkers in the Continental and analytic traditions, respectively: Derrida (chapter 7) and Wittgenstein (chapter 9). Taken together, these chapters exemplify Murdoch's insistence—against the anti-Cartesian trend of moral philosophy in this century—that consciousness is the fundamental mode of moral being.

What is noteworthy, however, is that Murdoch chooses to treat her theory of obligation in the context of this defense of consciousness. She includes chapters on will and duty (chapter 10), morals and politics (chapter 12), and significantly, the imagination (chapter 11) in this section of the book. This placement suggests that Murdoch considers matters of obligation and public conduct to be integral to an account of consciousness, rather than mere side issues. The structure of her exposition thus lends support to the claim of her character Socrates in *Acastos* that morality has to do not only with inwardness (i.e., consciousness) but also with the *relation between* inwardness and public conduct. The question is how such a relation between these two seemingly contrasting aspects of morality is to be articulated.

Murdoch's theory of obligation does not, in my judgment, threaten the centrality of consciousness in her ethics. Rather, she sees the claim of duty as *embedded within* her understanding of morality as spiritual change. This is evident in her chapter on will and duty, where she begins by reaffirming the primacy of morality as a matter of inward spiritual change. "I would regard the (daily, hourly, minutely) attempted purification of consciousness as the central and fundamental 'arena' of morality."[196] Elsewhere, she notes: "I certainly want to suggest that the spiritual pilgrimage (transformation—renewal—salvation) is the centre and essence of morality, upon whose success and well-being the health of other kinds of moral reaction and thinking is likely to depend."[197] In other words, Murdoch understands consciousness and the demand of moral change to be the continuous background of the moral life. It is, after all, through the medium of consciousness that we apprehend the claim of the good, and this claim requires the constant purification of consciousness in relation to the real.

Having said that, however, Murdoch insists that duty has an essential role to play in morality that is not reducible to this general background of consciousness. Duty has a more "external" aspect. "Certainly the idea of duty must be not be analysed or 'reduced' away, though it must also be seen in a wider landscape. . . . Duty is not to be absorbed into, or dissolved in, the vast complexities of moral feeling and sensibility."[198] The idea of duty captures a different but no less important aspect of human moral experience than inward feeling and sensibility. It is a more piecemeal concept, frequently expressed as a list of particular demands, maxims, or moral rules, and it seems to enter consciousness as if from "outside." For example, as Murdoch notes in *The Sovereignty of Good*, duty is not always connected with a deep struggle to purify our own consciousness: "Often, for instance when we pay our bills or perform other small everyday acts, we are just 'anybody' doing what is proper or making simple choices for ordinary public reasons."[199] Similarly, children learn the notion of duty in the form of maxims that are intended to form moral sensibility in a relatively straightforward and nearly unconscious way (e.g., be kind, be generous, don't lie). In these respects, duty seems to have a fundamentally different character than the complexities associated with moral feeling and sensibility.

But the concepts of consciousness and duty do not merely represent two contrasting aspects of moral experience unrelated to one another. Rather, Murdoch wants to claim that they are mutually dependent. For example, if the idea of duty is completely severed from the more general notion of consciousness, it may encourage heteronomy or undermine the absoluteness of morals: "If thought of without the enclosing background of general and changing quality of consciousness, of moral experience, of acquired moral fabric, [the idea of duty] may seem stark, inexplicable except as arbitrary orders given by God, or be considered as mere historically determined social rules."[200] A separated idea of duty may also undermine the sense in which the claim of morality on human life is continuous, as Murdoch intends her image of the good as "a light which always shines" to express. It may suggest that "morality is an occasional part-time activity of switching on the ethical faculty on separate occasions of moral choice."[201] In this respect, duty without its background in consciousness may give rise to existentialist conceptions of choice as an unconditioned "leap" of the will.[202]

From the opposite direction, however, the idea of consciousness without duty has its own dangers. Specifically, it might lead to what Murdoch calls a possible "aestheticization of the moral"—a form of intuitionism. As Murdoch conceives it, the idea of duty functions as a defense against the charge that "the sort of neo-Platonic moral view on which I have been reflecting is really a sort of aesthetic view, a kind of wander through pleasant groves of quasi-religious experience."[203] Echoing earlier criticisms of G. E. Moore, she worries that a morality centered purely in a notion of insight or perception "could degenerate into a relaxed surrender to an aesthetic attitude, an ethic of 'beautiful thoughts.' "[204] In contrast, the idea of "plain stark duty" represents "something alien, the outer not the inner, the command whose authority may be recognised as running against the stream of the inner life."[205]

In this context, the idea of duty functions as a check against the dangers associated with an intuitive understanding of morality. As Murdoch sometimes puts it (quoting Wittgenstein), duty "cuts off any road to an explanation."[206] Given the strength of human desire and inclination, duty represents a fixed point "outside" consciousness that cannot be compromised or evaded by the infinitely varied self-regarding consolations of egoism.

> The concept of duty is *sui generis*, its separateness is an aspect of its efficacy. It is not the whole of morals, but is an essential rigidly enduring part. . . . Duty can appear when moral instinct and habit fail, when we lack any clarifying mode of reflection, and seek for a rule felt as external. Most often perhaps we become aware of duty when it collides head-on with inclination.[207]

In this respect, duty functions as "a bridle placed on egoism."[208] It forces a confrontation between consciousness and an alien or external demand to abide by a moral rule that thwarts selfish desire. This confrontation comes to a focal point in the will, which is the instrument of duty. Murdoch carefully distinguishes her view of the will from "an inflated monistic view of moral will"[209] that she believes emerged in existentialism after Kant's notion of rational will was stripped of its metaphysical background. In contrast, Murdoch restricts her notion of the will to the experience of an "immediate straining. . . . against a large part of preformed consciousness" provoked by the clash between duty and desire.[210] In this context, the idea of the will functions, as duty does, as a barrier against inclination.[211]

This exposition of the role of duty and will in Murdoch's ethics indicates that she recognizes important aspects of moral experience that cannot and should not be absorbed into consciousness. The idea of duty acts as a counterforce to a morality of vision or insight by establishing certain barriers that cannot be abridged by the ego. In a similar way, Murdoch develops an account of what she calls "axioms" that function in the realm of political morality in a manner not unlike the operation of duty in the realm of private morality. Like the idea of duty, axioms are *sui generis* and unsystematic.[212] They represent isolated statements of values rather than a general moral sensibility: "The term 'axiom' points to piecemeal moral insights or principles which are active in political contexts."[213] Further,

"'Duty' is like 'axioms' in that it can operate as a battle flag or as a barrier."[214] For example, in a political context axiomatic values are expressed in rights claims that protect the well-being of individuals or prohibit certain actions toward them.

Yet in spite of these similarities, the idea of duty and the idea of axioms are also importantly distinct in Murdoch's view. This is in part because she wants to retain an important distinction between morals and politics. Murdoch believes duty belongs essentially in the private realm of morals, whereas axioms belong in the public realm of politics. For example, even though the idea of duty is initially experienced as acting on the psyche from without, it is also capable of extending "into a personal sphere of potentially minute and not publicly explicable detail. Here, where it loses its automatic or semi-public character, it becomes a part of what seems more like personal moral desire or aspiration, of experience and consciousness and the continuous work of Eros."[215] In other words, duty can be assimilated into consciousness through the work of moral cognition. This is in fact how moral education occurs: "we learn 'external rules' as a child and then internalise them as values."[216] Thus for Murdoch, the idea of duty might eventually "shade" into the inner life through the reflexive activity of consciousness and thereby modify the direction and quality of our psychic energy. In this respect, Murdoch qualifies her original description of duty as "external rules."

The idea of axioms, by contrast, cannot be so assimilated. Axioms belong more intransigently to the domain of political morality. Their function lies in the public sphere rather than the private.

> A difference between what I have called . . . "axioms," and the ordinary idea of duty (as "rules"), is that duty merges into, is organically connected with, the hurly-burly of reason-feeling, rule-desire, whereas "axioms" do not and are not. One could also say that duty recedes into the most private part of personal morality, whereas axioms are instruments of the public scene.[217]

Axioms thus have an important role to play in the distinction between morals and politics. Murdoch relates axioms to the idea of "natural law," "a sort of human and humane standard which accompanies the detail of ordinary (positive) law and provides a critique of the uses of political power."[218] For example, the declaration of truths that are "self-evident" in America's founding political document represents a statement of axiomatic values. So does the language of natural rights, toleration, the rights of man, and human rights, all of which are a legacy of the Enlightenment tradition of natural law.[219] This kind of axiomatic thinking is directly concerned with establishing certain barriers of principle related to the treatment of human individuals based on an implicit idea of human nature.

In fact, Murdoch argues that a conception of the individual may itself serve as an influential axiomatic check and ideal.[220] Axioms "arise out of and refer to a general conception of human nature such as civilised societies have gradually generated."[221] This function of axioms is one of the primary reasons that Murdoch insists on a distinction between morals and politics: she wants to render the value of the individual inviolable in the context of public morality. When a conception of human nature becomes axiomatic in a political context—as the idea of the unique and valuable individual has become in western democratic societies—it exerts what she calls a "negativising appeal," the appeal of " 'Stop. You can't do that to a person.' "[222] The axiomatic value of the individual must remain "inflexible" and "isolated," "outside the main moral spectrum,"[223] so that it may resist any attempt to absorb it into a general system of morality.[224] Thus for example Murdoch argues that "the claim to a human right is designed to remain in place whatever the situation. . . . We 'cut off the road to an explanation' in order to safeguard the purity of the value, and remove it from vulnerability to certain kinds of argument."[225]

The unassimilable nature of political axioms into a general view of morality points to a certain "refusal of system" that is essential to liberal political procedures, in Murdoch's view. This lack of system disrupts the threat of tyranny and preserves the possibility of argument among citizens in a democracy about the relative values of freedom, happiness, equality, goodness, and so forth. "The lack of internal relations [among such values] acts as a defence of the citizen as Hobbesian individual. That we, politically, 'are' such individuals is axiomatic."[226] In this respect, Murdoch defends what she calls "the rough-and-ready unavoidably clumsy and pragmatic nature"[227] of political liberalism, which guards against totalitarian attempts (including utopian ones) to raise a single social ideal to the level of a political program.[228]

In spite of her avowed concern to affirm the difference between morals and politics, Murdoch nevertheless seeks to avoid a strictly "segregated" ethic. She does so by identifying two important connecting points between morals and politics. First, although Murdoch acknowledges a distinction between two conceptual "persona"—"the (moral) ego which retires into privacy" and "the (political) individual who is irreducible and has inalienable rights,"[229] or between "the person as moral-spiritual individual," and "the person as citizen"[230]—she does not believe human beings are *essentially* divided in this fashion. Rather, she suggests that the moral-spiritual individual (and thus the idea of consciousness) retains a certain primacy even in the political context. "Innumerable moral problems and moral passions touch on and emerge into political situations, and private feeling and reasoning may provide the 'heat' of the forging of political policy. . . . The 'politics' of the individual has a background in his consciousness and his world."[231]

This reaffirmation of the moral-spiritual individual means, second, that private morals and political axioms can be connected through the constructive work of consciousness (i.e., as moral cognition and the internalization of duties) and imagination. Even in the political context human beings remain in Murdoch's view *unified* individuals who must constantly weigh abstract principles against their intuitions. "The realm of axioms and the realm of densely textured moral cognitive consciousness are (morally) connected through the (limited) operation of abstract rules in private life."[232] This suggests that although duty and axioms are not the product of "insight" and are not easily assimilable into "inwardness," moral agents are bound to reflect on these axioms against the general background of their own private morality, and to sift them in relation to both their convictions and their self-interest. Thus Murdoch sees a role for the imagination not only in private morals but in politics as well. Imagination combines "an ordering activity . . . with an ability to picture what is quite other; especially of course to picture and realise, make real to oneself, the existence and being of other people."[233] We recognize the truth of political axioms and rights claims and "make [them] 'our own'" through the work of "sympathy and imagination (compassion)."[234]

However, the question of the relation between morals and politics in Murdoch's thought is not entirely resolved by these points of connection. In fact, it is important to her position that they remain in unresolved tension with one another. Attempts completely to integrate private and public morality in a general system (like most attempts at systematic unity in Murdoch's judgment) threaten to efface the freedom of individuals to exercise creative imagination in particular contexts. In this respect, Murdoch affirms the "clumsy" nature of liberal political procedures, which provide a necessary space for individuals (rather than the state) to relate the private and public aspects of morality. "[O]ne does not have to choose between activism and inwardness," she writes. "A morality of axioms needs the intuitive control of a more widely reflective and general morality. In a good society these ways of thinking, while always in tension, know their roles and places, and when they have rights against each other. This procedure belongs with political liberalism."[235]

I want to conclude this discussion of Murdoch's theory of obligation with two insights, one of which points backward and the other forward in her thought. First, it is important to recognize that Murdoch's theory of obligation represents her political answer to Sartre. We saw in Chapter 3 that Murdoch was sympathetic to Sartre's concern to preserve the value of the individual, which she identifies as the key to his thought. But she criticizes Sartre's reductionistic ontology as being unable to provide adequate support for this value because it severs consciousness both from a realm of value and from the existence of others. Without a supporting moral ontology, Sartre relies on the notion of the will as the creator of its values and as engaged in a perpetual (and ultimately futile) struggle to realize value in its projects without losing its freedom. Murdoch's theory of obligation answers this problem in Sartre's thought by reaffirming the importance of consciousness as the background for her theory of duty. This allows her to contextualize the claim of the other as a claim of duty against the background of consciousness, thus preventing duty from becoming an arbitrary leap of the will. And further, it allows her to assume a moral ontology that can account for the individual's striving toward perfection (i.e., the realization of value) without sacrificing its freedom. In these respects, Murdoch affirms the centrality of the individual as both the subject and the object of her theory of obligation, without risking the subjectivism she found in Sartre's account.

The second insight points forward. Murdoch's attention to questions of the public dimensions of morality in her later work contains important clues as to how we might trace the trajectory of her thought for the future. Her treatment of the "outward" aspects of morality within her theory of consciousness indicates that her moral psychology is not narrowly constrained by questions of egoism and spiritual change, but invites engagement with broader public and cultural questions. In the final chapter, I contend that the way in which Murdoch reflexively mediates conceptual oppositions—such as private and public, inner and outer, and so forth—suggests a possible model or pattern of interpretation that can be used to extend her position into the areas of cultural analysis and critique. This represents the next frontier for a continued defense of consciousness and moral realism along Murdochian lines.

6

PROSPECTS FOR MURDOCHIAN ETHICS

The previous chapter completed my exposition of the central themes of Murdoch's moral thought. Specifically, the chapter drew together the themes of morality, the self, and the good through an interpretation of Murdoch as a "reflexive realist." I showed that Murdoch's realist and metaphysical ethic correlates her account of consciousness with an idea of the good through the reflexive structure of the ontological proof. So understood, the proof reveals that the good is an objective principle of perfected moral knowledge that is only accessible through the medium of "personal resonance." This account complicates standard readings of Murdoch's rhetoric of vision and unselfing by exposing the constructive role of the imagination in moral vision and the role of the will in moral motivation. It also led to a consideration of the limits of Murdoch's account of morality as spiritual change, limits which compel her to formulate a morality of rules and axioms in a theory of obligation.

This chapter fulfills two remaining tasks set out in Chapter 1. In Section I, I review the main outlines of the argument in order to assess the validity of Murdoch's reflexive position both internally and in responding to contemporary debates in ethics. In the remainder of the chapter, I unfold the broader implications of reflexive realism for thinking about personal and social life in late modern culture. My central contention is that Murdoch's reflexive realism has implications that reach far beyond debates in academic ethics to address the cultural condition of late modernity. In a culture increasingly characterized by rationalized systems of knowledge and power, the question is whether we retain any longer the capacity to conceive or imagine a reality "outside" abstract systems. This capacity is crucial to the task of a realistic ethics as Murdoch conceives it, and is necessary in order to avoid certain dangers that attend contemporary constructions of subjectivity.

In order to extend Murdoch's position in this direction, I employ my own conceptual hermeneutic to work through the dyadic or oppositional structures of Murdoch's thought and interpret them reflexively to produce a moral position capable of responding to the current cultural condition. After completing the task of assessment in Section I, my argument proceeds as follows. I begin with the claim that Murdoch's recovery of the idea of consciousness in ethics seems to fly in the face of the overwhelming turn to language and critique of subjectivity that characterize current thought. Yet I show in Section II that Murdoch retrieves consciousness *beyond* the turn to language in order to avoid the loss of the idea of the individual person in neurosis or convention. The latter are dangers that have only intensified with the cultural dynamics of late modernity. In Section III, I contend that contemporary attempts to escape the dominance of subjectivity by appeals to language that reject the idea of consciousness fall into dangers analogous to that of neurosis and convention. Expanding on Murdoch's analysis, I show that a reflexive realist position retains the notion of consciousness while articulating the idea of a good that lies beyond the dominance of subjectivity. In doing so, it provides critical resources for interpreting the forces exerted on human existence by abstract systems. I conclude the chapter in Section IV by returning to two core issues in Murdoch's moral thought—freedom and moral change—and recasting their significance in the context of late modern culture.

The direction of my analysis in this chapter may strike some readers as a surprising way to conclude a book on Murdoch's ethics. Given the influence that her thought has exerted on such areas as moral psychology and virtue ethics, the relation of philosophy and literature, the critique of liberalism and voluntarism, the retrieval of a Platonic ethic centered on the good rather than God, and so forth, any of these issues might seem a more likely way to conclude a study of her thought.[1] But I believe that the direction I take can be justified in terms of central impulses in Murdoch's own thought. First, an analysis of contemporary culture in terms of the control of increasingly rationalized and abstract systems is an extension of Murdoch's longstanding concern for the status of individual persons in relation to totalizing forms of thought. The theme of the "refusal of system" in her work is constant, beginning with her early references to the dangers of monism in *The Sovereignty of Good*[2] and continuing through her frequent criticisms of Hegel, who emerges in *Metaphysics as a Guide to Morals* as a paradigm case of the way in which holistic forms of thinking can render the idea of the individual "unreal." Hegel is in fact emblematic of the problem against which Murdoch recasts her defense of consciousness in her later work—the problem of totality, which she regards as a threat to the idea of value and the individual. On this point, the conceptual contrast between Hegel and Kierkegaard plays as central a role in Murdoch's thought as the contrast between Plato and Kant.

Second, Murdoch consistently battled what she regarded as behaviorist and deterministic forms of thinking that deny the reality of the inner life of consciousness. Contemporary appeals to language that deny the role of individual users and speakers of language are, in her view, simply new forms of linguistic behaviorism. Likewise, she detects a recurrence of determinism in forms of thought that have replaced the notion of consciousness with impersonal systemic processes within the human body as well as culture. Linguistic structures and information processes, rather than individuals, become the primary locus of reality and value. Murdoch's persistent concern with the idea of freedom is thus reconfigured in an intellectual and cultural context in which language has become a "prime philosophical concept,"[3] and the battleground on which the question of the individual and the status of the human is being fought.

The third and final reason for extending Murdoch's thought into areas of cultural analysis has to do with how we decide to interpret her philosophical legacy. It would be possible to identify Murdoch's central philosophical contribution with any number of insights documented in previous chapters: her retrieval of metaphysics in a postmetaphysical age; her challenge to existentialism at the height of its popularity; her attack on the fact-value distinction when it was considered a received article of faith in the analytic tradition; her retrieval of moral psychology, and so forth. But to do so would be to suggest that her thought was best suited to the problems and philosophies cast up by post-World War II Europe, thus confining her impact to the century that is passing rather than the one that is just beginning. My contention, on the contrary, is that the resources of her thought are powerful and resilient enough to provide new places for reflection in an age that has only intensified many of her original concerns. This is what I hope to demonstrate in what follows, beginning with an assessment of reflexive realism.

Section I. Assessing Reflexive Realism

Previous chapters have shown that Murdoch occupies a mediating position in relation to two lines of thought in contemporary ethics. The first, descending from Kant, identifies the defining situation of human moral identity as a self-determining or autonomous mode of existence. The second, descending from Hegel, identifies this defining situation in terms of the formation of moral identity with respect to particular communities and social practices. This basic division of positions, noted in Chapter 1, characterizes the current debate between liberals and communitarians over the status of the self, as well as the debate in religious ethics between agential and social theories of moral identity. Also noted in Chapter 1 was a third line of thought, represented by poststructuralism, which radically questions the notion of subjectivity itself and presents an even sharper challenge to Murdoch's position than either of the other two alternatives.

How, then, are we to assess the validity of Murdoch's position? The first task is to show that Murdoch's argument for a correlation between consciousness and the good is internally consistent. The second is to ask if it represents a "cognitive gain" over the options just noted by virtue of its argumentative and explanatory power; in other words, whether it answers questions left unresolved by the other positions.[4] I treat each of these tasks of validation in turn.

Murdoch's attempt to articulate a metaphysical framework for ethics (Chapter 2) was the first step in establishing a correlation between selfhood and the good. In contrast to both linguistic analysis and existentialism, which center morality on the individual agent and deny any overarching structure of value, Murdoch appeals to a metaphysical conception of ethics in order to identify a more encompassing framework for morality and moral agency. Her descriptive contrast between Natural Law and Liberal morality was intended to picture the way in which a metaphysical ethic conceptualizes the relation between the individual agent and an evaluative framework. In contrast to Liberal moralities, which conceive the agent as the solitary originator of its own values, the Natural Law view pictures human beings as immersed in a reality that transcends them and as striving to conform to its purposes. This argument provided the condition for Murdoch's claim that ethics is a form of realism, that the norm of morality cannot be reduced to subjective terms but is connected to objective conditions such as truth, perfection, and reality.

The second step in Murdoch's effort to correlate selfhood with an idea of the good was to show that consciousness is the fundamental mode of human moral being and, furthermore, that it is internally structured according to a realist notion of the good. After retrieving the moral significance of consciousness against both existentialist and linguistic behaviorist critiques (Chapter 3), Murdoch argues that the idea of the good is implied in the activity of thinking itself, as both its transcendental condition and its ideal standard of perfection (Chapter 4). As a transcendental notion, the idea of the good renders all of our perceptions "moral" by showing that thinking occurs against an evaluative background. As an ideal of perfection, the idea of the good guides the progressive nature of moral deliberation by serving as the standard by which we make qualitative distinctions with respect to persons, actions, and our own states of mind.

The third step in Murdoch's correlational argument was to specify the content of this perfectionist ideal in the context of a normative account of human moral transformation and political existence (Chapter 5). This was necessary in order to show that her account of the good as internal to consciousness avoids a charge of subjectivism or "bad faith." She does so, I argued, by conceiving the idea of the good reflexively. This means that the good is discovered through the medium of consciousness, but surpasses consciousness by representing a form of perfected knowledge of the real that transcends human egoism. Murdoch justifies this reflexive argument with a version of the ontological proof. The transcendental aspect of the proof demonstrates the good as the necessarily real condition for the possibility of moral knowledge, while the metaphysical aspect proves the idea of perfection from our perception of gradations of value in the exercise of cognition.

The proof for the good represents the most condensed expression of Murdoch's argument for a correlation between moral identity and the good. The validity of this argument must be assessed both internally and in relation to other positions. With respect to its internal validity, the proof is self-validating because it provokes an intuitive certainty about the reality of both selfhood and the good through the very structure of its argumentation. In the very act by which consciousness grasps the transcendental meaning of the good (i.e., as "the unconditional element in the structure of reason and reality"), the good is understood as necessarily real. To understand the meaning of the idea of the good is thus to affirm it in every conscious act. Conversely, if goodness is understood as real, then that which grasps the good in the act of thinking must also be real. Thus the idea of the good and the idea of the self as a thinking consciousness are grasped in one and the same act of understanding. The intuitive certainty provided by the proof is grounded in its reflexive understanding of consciousness.

The task of assessing this argument in relation to other positions is more complex. How does Murdoch's understanding of the correlation between self and good, validated in terms of the proof, answer problems or questions left unresolved in the other positions noted above? In order to answer this question, I start from the premise that an adequate model of moral subjectivity must take into account both the human capacity for autonomy and self-determination, as well as the social mediation of identity through communities, linguistic practices, and traditions.[5] Any account that neglects one or the other of these aspects of human identity is not comprehensive enough to do justice to our experience both as self-determining agents who define their own ends and purposes, and as "situated" agents whose identities are formed and maintained in communities.

When evaluated against this standard, Murdoch's position can be shown to represent a more comprehensive account of moral identity than the alternatives noted above. This argument requires taking each of these positions seriously, since my claim is that Murdoch's position answers the deficiencies in these accounts with a more adequate ethical position. First, with respect to liberal ethics in the Kantian tradition, it is clear that Murdoch remains in many respects a liberal thinker in her concern to preserve as irreducible the value of the individual and its freedom from a deterministic mode of existence. On this crucial point, as I argued in Chapter 4, Murdoch cannot in the end be classified purely as a Natural Law type of moralist even though her retrieval of a metaphysical framework for ethics seems to point in that direction. Rather, she resists (as Sartre does) any attempt to reduce the value and significance of the individual by assimilating it without remainder into a social whole. Moreover, Murdoch's account of liberal politics in *Metaphysics as a Guide to Morals* indicates that she affirms some aspects of a liberal proceduralist ethic in her recent thought. Although I argued that her distinction between morals and politics is not absolute, Murdoch does acknowledge the need in the context of political theory to differentiate two "conceptual persona"—the moral agent and the citizen—for certain purposes, and to set aside the moral aspiration to perfection when theorizing about the principles of a good society.[6] In this respect, Murdoch "brackets" her normative ethic of morality as spiritual change and seems to qualify her general conviction about the primacy of the good over the right to some extent in order to draw attention to the axiomatic character of political thinking.[7]

On the other hand, Murdoch's critique of liberal ethics is considerable. She exposes the limitations of liberal ethics to account for the way in which moral identity is not only self-constituted but also conditioned by institutions, communities, and traditions that precede the act of choice and inform the agent's values. Theories that attempt to preserve the agent's freedom from determinism by positing a rupture between consciousness and value (Sartre), or by affirming a distinction between noumenal and phenomenal existence (Kant), fail in Murdoch's judgment to account for the unity of consciousness in relation to transcendental value and the mediated nature of moral agency and freedom. In response to these deficiencies, Murdoch depicts the individual within a moral ontology that recognizes the claim of the good and the other as constitutive of moral identity. This ontology pictures consciousness in relation to a transcendental background and as oriented toward perfected knowledge of individuals. Moral identity is mediated by the activity of consciousness in relation to a moral world of others that exists in a space of questions about the good.

This reading of Murdoch's position in relation to liberal ethics suggests that her account would find at least some points of contact with social theories of the constitution of moral identity—for example, narrative ethics and communitarian ethics. Murdoch acknowledges the way in which moral identity is socially formed and linguistically mediated. If this were not the case, Stanley Hauerwas could never have used Murdoch's thought in the service of a Christian ethic of character, as he did earlier in his career.[8] He found in the example of M and D from *The Sovereignty of Good* a clear recognition in Murdoch's thought of how moral identity is formed in narrative contexts and mediated through specific linguistic practices. Further, Murdoch's insistence on the role of narratives in moral education, her emphasis on the value of particularity, her recognition of the historical nature of moral language, and her attempt to picture different types of human moral existence all make her position congenial to some forms of narrative and communitarian ethics.

Nevertheless, there are at least two related problems with narrative ethics that Murdoch's position seeks to overcome. First, it offers no standard outside a community's narratives by which to criticize the validity of the social practices that form moral identity; and second, it recognizes the community rather than the individual agent as morally central. In fact, on this view there can be no account of the moral self outside of the community and its practices. Murdoch has registered her opposition to both of these points in her critique of the conceptual dyad of convention and neurosis. While neurosis threatens to enclose the individual in a solipsistic world that effaces the reality of others (as in existentialist ethics), convention denies the autonomy of the individual by allowing a social whole uncritically to determine our moral reactions to ourselves and others. In response to this danger, Murdoch grounds moral identity and the cognitive status of moral claims transcendentally in the structure of reason and reality, rather than in a communal standard that cannot be critically validated beyond the community's own resources. This is the point of her claim that the authority of morals is the authority of truth (i.e., reality), and not the authority of social convention. Ethics requires a metaphysical and realist framework in order to validate its cognitive claims.

Further, Murdoch's account of the way in which moral identity is socially and linguistically mediated does not efface the centrality of the individual and the individual's freedom, but rather presupposes them. In fact, her reflexive account of moral knowledge and vision indicates that she actually holds a more complex understanding of the mediated character of social identity than narrative ethics does. As I noted in Chapter 5, Murdoch's reflexive position requires the agent critically to evaluate his or her own values in relation to natural desires, social roles, and conventional beliefs. This view coheres with an evaluative theory of moral freedom that allows the agent to act *against* social roles or beliefs if the act of evaluation uncovers reasons for doing so. The demand of reflexivity is to evaluate the claims of the social whole through consciousness in relation to the good. In this respect, Murdoch's reflexive realism acknowledges both the self-transcending nature of moral identity and also its mediated character.

Murdoch thus answers the deficiencies of both liberal ethics and narrative ethics by defining a position that attempts to mediate between them. Her constant oscillation between the thought of Kant and Hegel (and other such philosophical pairings); her concern to find a middle way between the dyadic structure of the Liberal view and the Natural Law view; her effort to avoid the twin dangers of neurosis and convention—all suggest that she is seeking to acknowledge both the autonomous and self-transcending nature of human moral identity, and its inevitable embeddedness in natural, social, historical, and linguistic systems. The primary instrument of this effort is the reflexivity of her position as she works through these binary oppositions, which may be counted an important gain over both narrative and liberal ethics. Neither liberal ethics nor narrative ethics can escape the demand of reflexivity that Murdoch's position represents. Liberal ethics, as its critics note, cannot assert the self-determining character of the human agent and bracket the substantive aspects of moral subjectivity in its theory of justice without eventually being forced to acknowledge what is left out of this account. Similarly, narrative ethics cannot circumvent the self simply by appealing to the primacy of social mediation and the role of narratives in the formation of identity. In both cases, Murdoch's position requires that the individual agent, whether in the political or the moral context, must critically evaluate the claims of abstract principles (or traditions, religious narratives, and so forth) against the moral intuitions and imaginative perception of his or her own consciousness.

The final position in contemporary ethics in relation to which Murdoch's position must be assessed is poststructuralism. In relation to the two options summarized above, poststructuralism may be seen as a radical challenge to the idea of the self-constituting or autonomous agent that takes the fact of mediation to its conceptual extreme. In other words, poststructuralists take the point about the socially and linguistically mediated character of human subjectivity to mean that there can be no account of a discrete "individual" apart from various discursive practices. The self becomes a cipher, functionary, or effect of linguistic systems without remainder.[9] Seyla Benhabib summarizes the general shift associated with poststructuralist and other contemporary challenges to subjectivity in terms with which I began this study: "*the paradigm of language has replaced the paradigm of consciousness.* This shift has meant that the focus is no longer on the epistemic subject or on the private contents of its consciousness but on the public, signifying activities of a collection of subjects."[10]

This characterization of poststructuralism articulates the essential point that Murdoch seeks to contest in this form of thought, its denial of the primacy of consciousness. The retrieval and defense of the notion of consciousness is the consistent strand running through Murdoch's philosophy, from her earliest critiques of analytic philosophy of mind and linguistic behaviorism, to her more recent critiques of Wittgensteinian philosophy of language and of structuralism and poststructuralism in *Metaphysics as a Guide to Morals*. I will explore the implications of this crucial aspect of Murdoch's thought in greater detail later in the chapter. But for now, Murdoch identifies at least three related problems in poststructuralism in her recent work, each of which can be traced to the shift Benhabib describes.

First, although Murdoch clearly grants the point that moral subjectivity is mediated by linguistic and other forces beyond our control, she rejects the stronger thesis about the primacy of language over consciousness that poststructuralism defends. The problem with any position that threatens the notion of individual consciousness, in her view, is that it threatens to reduce the being and value of the individual to a mere functionary in a larger whole that is seen as authoritative—whether that is a social whole (Hegel), the network of ordinary language (Hampshire), the *lebensform* (Wittgenstein), or the play of signifiers in a linguistic system (Derrida).[11] In response to this point, Murdoch defends human individuality and autonomy by insisting that individuals are *users* of language and not only used *by* language. In other words, Murdoch affirms a reflexive relation between the individual and language that preserves the creative language use of individuals within the linguistic system. The story of M and D, for example, clearly demonstrates that an individual's use of language is uniquely personal, creative, and irreducible to publicly shared meanings or linguistic codes. What is left out of the poststructuralist picture, she believes, is that "statements are made, propositions are uttered, by individual incarnate persons in particular extra-linguistic situations, and it is in the whole of this larger context that our familiar and essential concepts of truth and truthfulness live and work."[12]

The second point that Murdoch contests in the poststructuralist account is its rejection of the ontological status of value. This is directly related to her concern to preserve the reality of individual consciousness. As we have seen, Murdoch's ontological proof for the idea of the good holds that the idea of transcendental value requires the idea of consciousness as its reflexive medium. Both poststructuralism and Wittgensteinian philosophy attempt to circumvent this reflexivity by denying the notion of the Cartesian self as a being with hidden, inward depths. "The denial of any *philosophical* role to 'experience' or 'mental contents' has left no place for a consideration of consciousness. 'Value' is placed outside philosophy or else is accommodated by . . . a form of behaviorism based on will and rules."[13] In losing the idea of consciousness as the bearer of moral substance, we are left with philosophies that deny the inner life and conceive value as a function of public or collective meanings and actions.

The third aspect of poststructuralism that Murdoch criticizes is implicit in all the others but deserves separate mention: its rejection of the referential or realistic function of language in relation to a notion of truth. On this view, Murdoch writes, "what is 'transcendent' is not the world, but the great sea of language itself which cannot be dominated by the individuals who move or play in it, and who do not speak or use language, but are spoken or used by it."[14] As a reflexive thinker, Murdoch does not hold a simple realist theory of truth according to which language transparently refers to nonlinguistic reality. Rather, she recognizes the mediated nature of all knowledge through the structures of language and consciousness. The truth-value of language depends not on simple conformity to "the way things are," but on "the struggle of individuals creatively to adjust language to contingent conditions outside it."[15] This appreciation for the constructive dimension of the human apprehension of truth only strengthens rather than diminishes the demands of Murdoch's reflexive realism. "[W]e all, not only can but *have* to, experience and deal with a transcendent reality, the resistant otherness of other persons, other things, history, the natural world, the cosmos, and this involves perpetual effort. . . . Most of this effort is moral effort."[16] Thus Murdoch believes that an affirmation of human agency is consistent with an acknowledgment of the constructive nature of language; in fact it is required by it.

Murdoch's position thus represents a cognitive gain over its rivals. Reflexive realism is able to account for both the self-determining and the mediated nature of moral identity by showing that the individual must engage in a critical assessment of moral claims through the work of moral cognition guided by an idea of perfection. Without a recognition of reflexivity as central to human moral being, liberal ethics neglects the fact of linguistic and social mediation, while narrative ethics neglects human autonomy. This point about reflexivity also holds with respect to poststructuralist thought. In the face of poststructuralism's apparent capitulation to linguistic mediation at the cost of autonomy and agency, Murdoch insists that individuals exist both within language and outside of it. We are creative and individual *users* of language even as language mediates and informs our identity. This means that we have the capacity both to evaluate this process of formation and, potentially, to transform it. Given this fact, poststructuralism's denial of agency in the face of the linguistic "system" fails to be convincing.

The central conclusion that emerges from these considerations is that Murdoch's acknowledgment of the reflexive power of moral cognition and imagination affirms the burden of our freedom as individual and creative moral agents. In other words, reflexivity is a form of responsibility. As Murdoch says, "we all, not only can, but *have to*" deal with and encounter a reality that is other than ourselves." And further, "Truth' is inseparable from individual contextual human *responsibilities*."[17] The authority of morals, as Murdoch notes repeatedly, is the authority of truth (i.e., reality), and truth requires an interpretive engagement between an evaluating agent and the reality that the agent encounters. From this perspective, the denial of reflexivity weakens the responsibility that is proper to us as creative moral beings. Murdoch acknowledges this responsibility in her reflexive account of consciousness.

From this argument showing the greater merit of Murdoch's position in relation to other options in ethics, it is now possible to chart some of the constructive implications of her thought for moral inquiry. In the remainder of this chapter, I elaborate the significance of Murdoch's recovery of the notion of personal consciousness in the face of intellectual and cultural trends that seem determined to efface it. In the process, I use my conceptual hermeneutical method to extend the substance of Murdoch's reflexive position into areas of cultural analysis and critique.

Section II. A. Moral Subjectivity Beyond the Turn to Language

If there is one feature of contemporary thought that emerges most forcefully as a challenge to Murdoch's position, it is Benhabib's insight about the ascendancy of language over consciousness. Many thinkers have noted the importance that the notion of language has assumed in an account of human being. For example, Charles Taylor has observed that "language has become central to our understanding of man";[18] "we are constantly forced to the conception of man as a language animal, one who is constituted by language."[19] To a large extent, Murdoch's thought supports this recognition of the centrality of language. Her reflexive account of consciousness demonstrates that even for thinkers like herself who consider themselves realists or cognitivists about moral truth, the question of moral subjectivity—of who we are and what is binding on us—must now pass through the question of language.

Yet what is distinctive about Murdoch's position is that she challenges the tendency of contemporary thought to recast the meaning of subjectivity in linguistic terms that exclude the notion of consciousness. I contend that her defense of consciousness is significant for contemporary thought at two related levels of reflection. At the first level, Murdoch's position demonstrates that the so-called critique of subjectivity, to which so much energy has been devoted in modern and postmodern thought, may not necessarily require jettisoning the idea of consciousness. Although it may seem counterintuitive, the critique of subjectivity and the issue of consciousness can be separated in the following respect: what is really at stake in the critique of subjectivity is not the problem of consciousness per se, but a particular form of consciousness associated with the idea of subjective dominance or "totalization"—the absorption of the world into consciousness. The import of Murdoch's position at this level is to suggest that a critique of subjective dominance may be possible without rejecting the idea of consciousness.

Second, Murdoch's defense of consciousness addresses an important feature of the current cultural situation: the extent to which late modernity is increasingly characterized by internally referential systems of knowledge and power that resist reflective criticism. An analysis of reflexive realism in this context suggests that an effective critique of the cultural effects of subjective dominance might be better served by retaining the notion of consciousness rather than jettisoning it in favor of a wholesale turn to language. This represents the cultural potential of a reflexive account of consciousness.

II. B. The Problem of Subjective Dominance

The idea of subjective dominance, a term I am borrowing from Charles Winquist, is not new; it surfaces frequently in contemporary critiques of modernity and Enlightenment rationality. Winquist traces its origins to the thought of Descartes, whose strategy of radical doubt produced a notion of subjectivity that became "the dominant currency of the Enlightenment and the culture developed from it."[20] According to this notion, "the inner reality of the subject and the privileging of consciousness became the truth of the self. . . . Reality was construed not just as what is present but as what is present to consciousness. Subjectivity was the source and arbiter of reality."[21] Like other contemporary thinkers, Winquist describes the formation of this type of subjectivity as a process of "totalization" whereby the world shrinks to the dimensions of consciousness: "A reversal into modernity occurred in this move. Inner reality was valued over the external world."[22] This process of totalization took place when "the self, in order to be completely identified with subjectivity," attempted to "control the domain of its discourse so that its order remains intact."[23] By transforming the world into "a substitute system of subjective signification" (i.e., clear and distinct ideas in the mind) and identifying the self with the active production of this substitute world, what is lost is "the *other* of both the world and the self. It is the loss of a pluralistic world and a variegated self."[24] In the end, "the subject is the measure of all things and the subject knows itself in the production of a signifying system that ideally is universalized and closed. This is a process of totalization."[25]

The turn to language in contemporary thought has played a key role in efforts to counter this notion of subjective dominance and its cultural effects.[26] In fact, we can isolate two basic strategies that have been used in recent thought to challenge the notion of subjective dominance. These strategies represent my own conceptual pair, roughly analogous to Murdoch's pairing of convention and neurosis, but understood with respect to the problem of subjective dominance rather than the problem of solipsism. The first strategy attempts to "situate" the subject in relation to some larger order of meaning or value, such as a language community or a tradition. For example, contemporary narrativist and communitarian thinkers call into question the "unencumbered" modern self by insisting on its embeddedness in complex historical, social, and narrative contexts. For many such thinkers, as William Schweiker notes, the purpose of this turn to language is "to counter the axiology and theory of moral knowledge found in modern ethics," and more specifically, "to challenge the modern enthronement of the self" associated with what is often judged to be the destructive anthropocentrism of western ethics.[27] In this respect, Schweiker notes, the turn to language or narrative is one of several contemporary efforts to search for a nonanthropocentric value scheme—a good beyond subjective dominance—by situating the subject in relation to some "whole" such as tradition (in narrative ethics), the natural order (in biocentric or ecological ethics), a notion of the divine (in theocentric ethics), or in relation to the concrete other (in the ethics of alterity).

The roots of the "situating" strategy of narrative or communitarian ethics can be found in the expressive theory of language traceable to Romantic thought. The expressive view, as Charles Taylor notes, holds that "language does not only serve to *depict* ourselves and the world, it also helps *constitute* our lives."[28] Language is not merely an instrument of the subject's purposes; it is a medium of self-understanding that "articulates and makes things manifest, and in so doing helps shape our form of life."[29] Human beings are understood as partly constituted by their self-understanding through language. This means that "certain ways of being, of feeling, of relating to each other are only possible given certain linguistic resources."[30] The expressive view challenges subjective dominance by conceiving the human agent as enmeshed in a social and linguistic order beyond his or her control. It emphasizes "the way in which an individual is constituted by the language and culture which can only be maintained and renewed in the communities he is part of."[31] Language becomes "a pattern of activity, by which we express/realize a certain way of being in the world . . . against a background which we can never fully dominate."[32] Language is thus "always more than we can encompass; it is in a sense inexhaustible."[33]

The strategy of situating subjectivity presents certain dilemmas for contemporary thought. If, in an important sense, one only becomes a subject by virtue of one's membership in a linguistic community, the question left unanswered by this account is whether subjectivity becomes wholly reducible to the linguistic community.[34] The issue is "whether the *subject* of speech is not always in some sense, and on some level, a speech *community.*"[35] Given this, the dilemma posed by the strategy of "situating" subjectivity, from a Murdochian perspective, is that it seems to lead to a loss or diminution of the idea of the individual and the inner life.[36] What is sacrificed is an idea that seems, at the very least, intuitively important: the sense of being a private self in a world of other selves whose inner being remains mysterious or unknowable. Moreover, this view makes it difficult to account for the idea that individuals use and appropriate language in their own unique ways, a capacity which, for reflexive realism, is indispensable to the notion of freedom as well as moral change.

The second strategy that has been used to challenge the notion of subjective dominance also proceeds by an appeal to language, but language conceived as a self-enclosed system of signs, as in poststructuralism. This view does not simply *situate* the human subject in a larger order but rather signals the *erasure* of the subject in the face of the dominance of the linguistic system. This leads not only to "a dethroning of the human subject, but the expulsion of any concern for consciousness and inwardness."[37] The roots of this strategy lie partly in the same expressive tradition noted earlier. Poststructuralism may be seen as a form of radical expressivism in the sense that it rejects the depictive or referential function of language by "refus[ing] to allow any relation to a reality outside the text to serve as our key to understanding it."[38] The crucial unit of meaning is no longer the word, or even the sentence, but "the text as an indissociable whole."[39] Further, poststructuralism denies that language is a "medium" of either representation or self-understanding. As Murdoch notes, poststructuralism sees language as "a vast system or sign structure whereby meaning is determined by a mutual relationship of signs which transcends the localized talk of individual speakers."[40] This strategy attempts to solve the problem of subjective dominance by effacing the subject altogether. In the process, Benhabib comments, "the subject is replaced by a system of structures, oppositions and differances [*sic*] which, to be intelligible, need not be viewed as products of a living subjectivity at all."[41]

This solution to the problem of subjective dominance also poses certain dilemmas for contemporary thought. In particular, it raises the question of whether the language system may become a "totalizing" force similar to the totalization attributed to consciousness. That is, poststructuralism seems to shift the problem of subjective dominance from the autonomous subject to language. Language expands to fill the dimensions of the world or reality;[42] or, viewed from the opposite perspective, the world shrinks to the dimensions of language. Either way, the result is the same: nothing remains "outside" language, including the speaking subject. Reality has become "linguistic." The problem of subjective dominance is now duplicated at the level of culture as the structures of language—and the cultural spheres delimited by various forms of discourse—come to dominate personal and social life.

The cultural import of this phenomenon is not be underestimated. It is part and parcel of what Anthony Giddens refers to as the "reflexivity" of knowledge systems in late modernity.[43] This concept describes the way in which human action and self-reflection are increasingly filtered through abstract and rationalized knowledge systems that then become impervious to external criteria. Reflexivity sets in motion a process whereby "nature" becomes a social product, utterly subordinated to human purposes and transmuted into a field of human action. As Schweiker describes it, "the world of reflexive modernization is one in which persons, nature, and traditions are increasingly embedded in rationalized systems."[44] Giddens explains that this process looks at first like "an extension of 'instrumental reason,'" the application of science and technology to the mastery of the natural world.[45] But it is more than that; it signals the emergence of nature as *"an internally referential system of knowledge and power."*[46] As such, the reflexivity of modernity signals "the end of nature," in the sense that "the natural world has become in large part a 'created environment', consisting of humanly structured systems whose motive power and dynamics derive from socially organised knowledge-claims rather than from influences exogenous to human activity."[47] Existentially, this means that we are now confronted everywhere with the products of the human mind and human action; the world is drained of otherness, emptied of criteria external to the abstract systems that constitute it.[48] "External 'disturbances' to such reflexively organised systems become minimised."[49] This phenomenon may require a fundamentally different response to the problem of totalization than either of the strategies discussed so far.

Before considering that possibility, we can draw some preliminary conclusions from the foregoing analysis. I have tried to show that the strategies of "situating" and "effacing" the modern subject are attempts to combat subjective dominance and to locate a good beyond dominance through a turn to language. The situating strategy addresses the problem by exposing the complex social, material, and linguistic forces that help to constitute personal identity, thus rendering any account of the supposedly unencumbered or disengaged subject inadequate and even destructive. However, by compromising the notion of individual consciousness in relation to the linguistic community or some other "whole," this strategy seems hard pressed to account for the possibility of freedom in the form of rational dissent from the whole on the part of individuals.[50] The second strategy, exemplified in the poststructuralist turn to language, pursues a more radical solution to the problem of subjective dominance by effacing the idea of the subject in the linguistic system. But this strategy may only succeed in repeating the problem of totalization at the level of language, as language threatens to become an abstract system that contributes to the pervasive rationalization of personal life. This inflation of language merely repeats at the level of culture the problem of subjective dominance or totalization that appears at the level of consciousness.

This analysis suggests that in pursuing the two strategies just noted, current thought has conflated two issues—the critique of subjectivity and the problem of subjective dominance—and in doing so repeats the very problem it set out to avoid. The problem that sets into motion the modern critique of subjectivity is not the problem of consciousness per se, but rather the tendency of consciousness toward "totalization." If this is so, it leaves open the possibility that consciousness might be conceived or reconstituted in a way that is *non*totalizing. Neither of the two strategies above investigates this possibility: both treat the problem of subjective dominance through a turn to language that excludes or at least radically compromises the idea of individual consciousness. But the phenomenon of reflexive modernization suggests that such a response may no longer be sufficient. The complexity of the ways in which language operates in late modern culture, particularly with respect to the development of sophisticated electronic media, suggests that efforts to combat the problem of subjective dominance through an "expulsion" of consciousness or "inflation" of language may be misguided. Since language itself may become totalizing, a different remedy is needed than appeals to language alone. The resources for such a view may be found in a reflexive account of moral realism.

II. C. The Return to Consciousness: Neurosis and Convention Revisited

Murdoch's thought exemplifies a third strategy involving the turn to language that responds to the problem of subjective dominance in and through the notion of consciousness. Unlike the first two strategies, this model unambiguously retains the notion of consciousness in ethics, but it does so on grounds that attempt to avoid the dynamics of totalization. In other words, instead of either "situating" subjectivity in relation to some larger value scheme, or "effacing" subjectivity in relation to the linguistic code, this strategy attempts to "reconstitute" subjectivity by conceiving it reflexively in relation to language and to an idea of the good that lies beyond subjective dominance. The success of this strategy will be measured by its ability to avoid the deficiencies of the other two approaches to the critique of subjectivity. It must address both aspects of the problem of totalization: the absorption of the world into consciousness and the expansion of language to encompass reality. Remarkably, Murdoch anticipated both sides of this dilemma in her analysis of the dangers of neurosis and convention. A brief review of this contrast will allow me to articulate a reflexive position beyond it.

As discussed in Chapter 4, neurosis refers to the human tendency to construct self-absorbed myths or fantasies that inflate the self's importance and obscure the reality of others. In this respect, neurosis is another term for the relentless and obliterating egoism that Murdoch insisted is the primary characteristic of consciousness and human moral existence in general. As Martha Nussbaum comments, "Murdoch, more than any other contemporary ethical thinker, has made us vividly aware of the many stratagems by which the ego wraps itself in a cozy self-serving fog that prevents egress to the reality of the other."[51] Neurosis is Murdoch's term for the way in which egoistic perception functions as a form of totalizing vision that subordinates the reality of the world and others to its own self-consciousness. The neurotic self is so enclosed in its own solipsistic fantasy that it never confronts anything real outside itself. Others appear as either "menacing extensions" of its own consciousness or "wish fulfillments" keyed to its own fantasies. This represents a triumph of subjective dominance. Murdoch herself noted the "totalizing" tendencies of neurotic self-consciousness when she represented this view of the moral self with the conceptual persona of Totalitarian Man found in the philosophy of Hegel and of Romanticism.

While neurosis inflates the self to the point of obliterating any sense that the real may lie outside or beyond the self-serving consciousness of the ego, convention represents the opposite tendency. The self becomes absorbed in a social whole that determines its perceptions and reactions and obscures the separateness and autonomy of others. Convention thus diminishes the reality of persons in relation to a more authoritative social reality. Yet although utterly surrounded by social reality, the conventional self does not really interact with concrete others; that would presume a notion of "separate individuals" that this view cannot thematize. Instead, what is dominant is the socio-linguistic whole, the network of relations and linguistic practices in which the self is immersed and that determines its being in relation to others. In effect, the conventional self is not simply immersed but dominated by the conventional structures of society and its language. Murdoch emphasized this feature of convention when she represented its view of the moral agent with the conceptual persona of Ordinary Language Man, as portrayed in the philosophy of Wittgenstein and others.

Murdoch's analysis of the dilemma of neurosis and convention provides the conceptual resources for a response to the problem of subjective dominance. To begin with, she isolates the problem of neurosis or egoism from the more general issue of consciousness by attempting to articulate a *non*-egoistic form of consciousness. That is, she seeks to escape the totalizing neurotic ego not by expunging the notion of consciousness from her ethics, but rather by *reconstituting* consciousness in relation to an idea of the good and the reality of the other. In this respect, Murdoch's work articulates a notion of consciousness beyond the idea of totality, and on grounds other than self-relation. What breaks the drive of consciousness to totality is not an appeal to an abstract social or linguistic whole, but an encounter with the concrete other person.[52]

From this basic starting point, Murdoch's "reconstituting" strategy moves in basically two steps that parallel the two aspects of her idea of the good. First, she pursues what might at first look like a "situating" strategy in that she attempts to position the moral self in relation to a larger metaphysical framework. This is the import of the Natural Law view of morality as she describes it. Like other situating strategies, this is intended to expose the way in which the self's values are not completely generated by its own voluntaristic activity, but also originate from a prior framework of value in which the self is already set. However, for Murdoch this framework is not delimited by a linguistic community or tradition; rather, it is metaphysical and transcendentally constituted. The idea of the good in its transcendental aspect sets the boundaries for her moral ontology in the sense that it is the condition for consciousness and moral agency.

It grounds self-consciousness in an objective principle that is part of the structure of consciousness and yet, in its perfectionist aspect, also surpasses consciousness. The idea of the good blocks the totalizing drive of consciousness because it is in an important respect "outside the range" of the ego.

This leads to the second step in Murdoch's response to subjective dominance, which is accomplished through her specification of the normative content of the good. In its perfectionist aspect, the good is defined as perfected moral vision or illusionless knowledge of reality. This is the inner meaning of the concept of love. Love is a form of conscious attention to the other that has been purified of egoistic illusion. As a perfectionist ideal, love under the aspect of the good (i.e., "high" rather than "low" eros) sets a limit to the totalizing, egoistic energies of consciousness. The fantasy-driven ego is broken by its encounter with what cannot be wholly absorbed into fantasy. This is the crucial moral import of Murdoch's techniques of "unselfing" noted in Chapter 5. These techniques are not intended as a quasi-mystical expulsion or annihilation of consciousness; rather, they are intended progressively to transform and purify consciousness in relation to an ideal that lies beyond the ego's grasp.

This analysis shows that Murdoch's return to consciousness succeeds in avoiding the deficiencies in the other two approaches to the critique of subjective dominance. First, her account of the correlative structure of consciousness with an idea of the good shows that a critique of subjective dominance does not necessarily have to do away with consciousness. Rather, Murdoch reconstitutes consciousness beyond egoism via a principle of goodness that is both the transcendental condition for consciousness and the perfected goal of its successful moral pilgrimage. In this respect, Murdoch's remedy for neurosis comes from a principle that does not simply originate outside consciousness (as in appeals to language or tradition), but is also found within the very structure of consciousness. Consciousness can thus limit its own totalizing energies by imagining its own "outside."

We must now consider Murdoch's response to the other side of the dilemma of subjective dominance, represented by the problem of convention. This problem is partially answered by her account of the correlation between consciousness and the good. By situating the self within a metaphysical framework of the good, and not solely within a linguistic community or tradition, Murdoch attributes to consciousness the reflexive capacity to evaluate its own desires, social relations, and commitments. It can resist convention by virtue of its correlation with an objective good. But a more complete answer to the problem of convention must be sought in Murdoch's account of the individual and the role of language in moral vision. Although Murdoch would agree with narrativist thinkers that moral vision always depends on "convention" insofar as it depends on the acquisition of linguistic skills in a community of others, it is always mediated through the consciousness of an individual and an individual's unique grasp of language.[53] Murdoch therefore defends the possibility that language may become in part the "property" of individual speakers, rather than remaining irreducibly bound to its communal context.

An important implication of this view is that language remains a reflexive *medium* between consciousness and reality. This indicates the primary source of Murdoch's disagreement with poststructuralist thought. She regards the poststructuralist tendency to inflate language to the dimensions of reality as a form of linguistic monism or determinism that effaces the reality of persons in impersonal systems.[54] In contrast, Murdoch resists the totalization of language in her contention that language does not exhaust the meaning of the real; reality must be understood in an important sense as existing "outside" language. This is not to say, as I have tried to stress, that Murdoch falls into a naive realism that denies the mediation of language in the mind's grasping of truth. On the contrary, her thought provides ample evidence of the formative power of language with respect to the grasp of consciousness on the real.[55]

Yet in granting this point, Murdoch nevertheless denies that all we ever have is linguistic mediation. As Patricia Werhane puts this point, "meanings are linguistically constituted, although reality is not merely linguistically constructed."[56] In this respect, Murdoch articulates a position with respect to language midway between two trajectories of the expressive tradition noted by Charles Taylor. These positions can be distinguished by their response to the question: What comes to expression in language?[57] The first position, which might be called "subjectivist," holds that what comes to expression is essentially the self. Through language "we are mainly responding to our way of feeling/experiencing the world, and bringing this to expression."[58] This view of language is exemplified in Romanticism. The second position, at the opposite end of the spectrum, holds that what comes to expression in language is not the self, but the power of language. In this case, as in some forms of poststructuralism, expressivism devolves into the exact opposite of subjectivism: the self as speaking subject is effaced in relation to the language system. These two positions thus recapitulate the two sides of the problem of subjective dominance.

The third response attempts to mediate between the other two by seeing the expressive power of language as a response "to the reality in which we are set, in which we are included of course, but which is not reducible to our experience of it."[59] This view represents an attempt "to go beyond subjectivism in discovering and articulating what is expressed."[60] Hermeneutical thinkers such as Martin Heidegger and Hans-Georg Gadamer, for example, understood language as articulating the relation between the expressive power of human beings and the world. "In this kind of expression, we are responding to the way things are, rather than just exteriorizing feelings."[61] Expressivism of this variety is thus "radically anti-subjectivist"[62] because it is "striving rather to be faithful to something beyond us, not explicable simply in terms of human response."[63] Language is thus the medium for the perception of the real; it expresses something irreducible to either language or self-expression.

By insisting that language is a reflexive medium between consciousness and reality, Murdoch limits the drive of consciousness to reduce all linguistic expression to self-expression, while also avoiding the inflation of linguistic structures to the point of effacing consciousness. The ethical import of this view is that it makes possible "the search for moral sources outside the self which nevertheless resonate within the self" through the expressive power of language. This is the core insight of a reflexive account of consciousness in relation to the good. In light of this, I now want to explore the cultural dimensions of Murdoch's recovery of consciousness for ethics.

Section III. A. Reflexivity and the Cultural Conditions of Late Modernity

Any contemporary analysis of the problem of totalization in late modern culture must come to grips with the dynamics of institutional reflexivity and the internal referentiality of knowledge systems—the severing of abstract knowledge systems from influences and criteria external to human action. This phenomenon, as described by Giddens and others, may be seen as the cultural manifestation of the idea that "the paradigm of language has replaced the paradigm of consciousness." The dynamics of reflexivity mean, first, that the institutions of modernity tend to organize human experience into self-enclosed institutions and systems defined by their own internal logic. Although there are exceptions to this process, "day-to-day social life tends to become separated from 'original' nature and from a variety of experiences bearing on existential questions and dilemmas."[64] For example, by organizing the experiences of madness, criminality, illness, death, and even sexuality (i.e., as "eroticism") into institutions that remove them from the ordinary life of the general population, modernity "sequesters" these experiences from personal life.[65] Contact with such experiences are minimized by a process of institutional totalization that removes them from consciousness. As Giddens puts it, "The sequestration of experience means that, for many people, direct contact with events and situations which link the individual lifespan to broad issues of morality and finitude are rare and fleeting."[66]

There is a second respect in which reflexivity signals the triumph of the paradigm of language over that of consciousness. It has to do with the increasingly complex mediation of experience through information technologies. The growth of printed and especially electronic media contribute to reflexivity by actively shaping and forming the realities they represent as well as altering the experience of time-space relations.[67] Although Giddens insists that we should not therefore "draw the conclusion that the media have created an autonomous realm of 'hyperreality' where the sign or image is everything,"[68] thinkers such as Jean Baudrillard and others have drawn precisely this conclusion. The pervasiveness of information technologies signals that language is no longer strictly speaking a medium *between* consciousness and reality, but an autonomous system whose impact "does not depend primarily on the content or the 'messages' it carries, but on its form and reproducibility."[69]

The two features of reflexivity just noted suggest that the problem of totalization, previously described in terms of subjective dominance and the inflation of language, has intensified under conditions of late modernity. As such, it requires a different kind of ethical response than the ones offered by either narrative or poststructuralist thought. I can clarify this point by noting that the construal of the cultural situation in terms of reflexivity represents an important shift from the one that inspired the turn to language in communitarian and narrative ethics. Those forms of ethics understand totalization primarily in terms of the dominance of instrumental reason and the Enlightenment ideal of the autonomous subject. This ideal is regarded by many as sponsoring a disturbing series of historical and cultural consequences such as the destruction of the environment, the legacy of colonialism, the oppression of women and other marginalized peoples, the dominance of utilitarian and scientific values in the public and economic spheres, and so forth. The basic insight underlying this critique is that advances of technical reason and the emphatic individualism of modern thought have brought about the "disembedding" of traditional institutions and values.[70] Modernity is essentially a "post-traditional" order, whose chief ethical feature, to use Hegelian terminology, is the loss of *sittlichkeit* (i.e., the shared ethical practices of particular traditions and communities) and a correlative turn to rationalist, universalizing theories of morality. From this perspective, it should not be surprising that current forms of ethics have been preoccupied with countering the moral and cultural consequences of totalization by appealing to notions of tradition and community—as well as to ideas of "nature" or the concrete "other"— to decenter the autonomous subject. The cure for the disembedding mechanisms of modernity is to *resituate* the subject in relation to some shared order of value, and to reclaim voices that have been marginalized by the dominant ideal of so-called universal reason.

Although this form of the critique of totalization is still prevalent in contemporary ethics and has inspired many incisive analyses of modernity, it may be insufficient as a response to the problem of reflexive totalization. The problem of late modernity is not simply the mastery of nature through technical reason; it is the loss of the concept of "nature" altogether. Further, modernity confronts us not simply with the loss of *sittlichkeit*; it confronts us also with a pluralization of worlds made possible by global processes that allow social relations to take place across wide spans of time and space.[71] And while it has long been recognized that "virtually all human experience is mediated—through socialisation and in particular the acquisition of language,"[72] the forms of mediation available in late modernity may not simply shape the "message" to the "medium," but collapse medium and message altogether. In short, reflexivity represents an intensification of human control over nature through abstract systems to such an extent that it appears to signal a change in the very conditions of thinking. One feature of this transformation is that certain dimensions of human experience are increasingly sequestered from consciousness through the dominance of internally referential systems over personal and social life.

In the face of the cultural transformations wrought by reflexivity, the strategies used by both narrative and poststructuralist thinkers to combat totalization are inadequate. With respect to narrative ethics, any attempt to escape reflexive totalization through an appeal to the linguistic resources of particular communities is a response primarily to a loss of *sittlichkeit* rather than to the dynamics of reflexivity. In fact, the turn to tradition may signify an effort to ignore or resist the reflexivity of modern culture by withdrawing into a particular community of discourse. But the phenomenon of reflexivity is so pervasive that it touches even renewed appeals to tradition, as Giddens notes: "appeals to traditional symbols or practices can themselves be reflexively organised and are then part of the internally referential set of social relations rather than standing opposed to it. The question of whether tradition can be 'reinvented' in settings which have become thoroughly post-traditional has to be understood in these terms."[73]

Poststructuralism's response to reflexive totalization is even more ambiguous. On the one hand, poststructuralism often casts itself as the critic of *all* forms of totalization. This is largely because, like narrative ethics, poststructuralism arose as a response to particular historical and cultural conditions. As Mark C. Taylor has noted,

At the time poststructuralism emerged, the sociopolitical situation in postwar Europe made its critique not only understandable but necessary. Faced with totalitarianism on the Right (i.e., fascism) and the Left (i.e., Stalinism), there was a compelling need to resist every principle of totality. . . . By soliciting the return of repressed differences and outcast others, poststructuralist criticism calls into question the integrity of every intellectual, social, political, and cultural system that claims to be all-encompassing.[74]

Despite its sustained critique of the idea of totality, however, poststructuralism appears to have capitulated to the mechanism of reflexive modernization insofar as it accepts the internal referentiality of knowledge systems as inescapable. The type of reflexivity it affirms has less to do with the "sequestering" of experience from consciousness than with reconfiguring experience altogether in terms of the basic trope of the "information network." For example, recent work by Taylor and other poststructuralists on the philosophical significance of virtual reality and the complex homologies between data processes and biological systems suggests that "information" has replaced consciousness as the central interpretive category for understanding both living and nonliving reality.[75] This form of poststructuralism has shifted its focus from the critique of totality and the recovery of difference to articulating a nontotalizing form of wholism[76] whose basic template is the information network. Whether this response avoids totality, as it is intended to, or simply reinstates a more insidious form of totalization through the all-encompassing trope of information remains an open question.

Reflexive totalization thus poses serious questions for contemporary ethical thought. Most immediately, it raises the question of whether the concept of personal consciousness can have any relevance in a culture dominated by internally referential systems. This question gains ethical force from its connection to the status of persons and the issue of how persons are to be valued in relation to communities or systems of thought. Although this question is itself not new, it has intensified with the phenomenon of reflexive modernization. Where is the locus of reality and value in a culture dominated by internally referential systems? As we have seen, the basic impulse of contemporary thought has been to avoid subjective dominance and hence the reduction of all value to human value through the critique of subjectivity. But in seeking a good beyond subjective dominance, poststructuralism and narrative ethics threaten to repeat the dynamics of reflexive totalization by appealing to social wholes or impersonal processes. The question we must now address is whether it is possible to affirm an idea of the good beyond subjective dominance while still retaining the notion of consciousness and the worth of persons.[77] This is precisely the question that a reflexive account of consciousness and moral realism helps to answer.

III. B. Reflexive Moral Realism and Contemporary Culture

The task of reflexive moral realism, as I construe it in the current context, is to imagine a limit to the drive of subjective dominance at both the personal and cultural levels while acknowledging the internal reflexivity of knowledge systems. Such an approach to ethics, as we have seen, starts with the idea that consciousness exists in correlation with an idea of the good. The structure of this correlation provides a pattern or analogy for how reflexive realism might respond to the problem of totalization. Recall that the transcendental aspect of the correlation shows that the good is part of the structure of consciousness and thus requires consciousness as its reflexive medium. The perfectionist aspect holds that consciousness is not identifiable with the good, but rather aspires to a good beyond the reach of subjective dominance or egoism. Translated into cultural terms, this correlation might provide us with the conceptual resources to conceive a normative idea of reality "outside" internally referential systems while acknowledging the pervasive, and perhaps inescapable, dynamics of institutional reflexivity.

At the first level of this analogy, the idea of a good implicit in the structure of consciousness finds a parallel in the fact that abstract systems do not entirely succeed in sequestering certain depth experiences (such as morality or finitude) from consciousness. On the contrary, as Giddens notes in discussing this phenomenon, "external anchorings in aesthetic and moral experience refuse to disappear completely."[78] A "return of the repressed," he contends, may occur at the very heart of modern institutions under certain social conditions. For example:

> At fateful moments, individuals may be forced to confront concerns which the smooth working of reflexively ordered abstract systems normally keep well away from consciousness. . . . Fateful moments perhaps quite often can be dealt with within the confines of internally referential systems. But just as frequently they pose difficulties for the individual . . . which push through to extrinsic considerations . . . [M]any such moments do more than bring the individual up short: they cannot easily be dealt with without reference to moral/existential criteria. . . . Most of the main transitions of life represent moments at which external criteria force themselves back into play.[79]

The intrusion of deeply existential concerns into "the smooth working of reflexively ordered abstract systems" suggests that such systems cannot (any more than consciousness can) entirely relegate the notion of value outside their own boundaries. Abstract systems are in this respect neither "neutral" nor entirely impersonal; they are products of human thought and action that cannot completely escape the moral and existential dilemmas that first inspired their construction. A "gap" in the dynamics of reflexive totalization opens up at certain fateful moments from within the very experiences that abstract systems were originally designed to repress.[80]

This leads to the second level of my analogy. The idea that abstract systems contain an opening to their own "outside" is structurally similar to the notion of the good as an ideal standard that allows egoistic consciousness to be critically evaluated from a point within consciousness. This is what is signified in the phenomenon of the return of the repressed just noted. Issues related to the moral meaning of existence that have been repressed by abstract systems return and may even compel the restructuring of the system.[81] This process is not entirely alien to the dynamics of reflexivity, nor is it alien to consciousness. Rather, the fact that the totalizing dynamics of self-referential systems can be broken through by the eruption of a reality outside the system is part and parcel of the phenomenon of reflexivity. As Giddens notes, the dynamics of late modernity include a point when "the expansion of internally referential systems reaches its outer limits; on a collective level and in day-to-day life moral/existential questions thrust themselves back to centre-stage."[82]

There is a third level of the analogy to be noted that is closely related to the second. This concerns the specification of the content of the norm of reality or perfection and thus represents a move to the specifically moral level of my analysis. With respect to the correlational structure of consciousness, the good as ideal of perfection represents a form of moral knowledge that perceives the real apart from egoistic fantasy. The paradigmatic instance of this occurs when consciousness apprehends the reality of another person. As Murdoch puts it, "The central concept of morality is 'the individual' thought of as knowable by love."[83] The question is, how can this idea be translated to the cultural processes of reflexivity? In other words, can the idea of the individual be specified as the moral good of reflexive systems, as it is on a reflexive account of consciousness? If it can, then the idea of the individual could be said to limit the drive toward totalization in a culture of reflexivity, just as it limits the drive of subjective dominance or egoism in an account of consciousness. This conclusion would help establish the merits of a reflexive moral realism as an interpretive response to our cultural situation.

A partial answer to this question can already be found in Giddens's account of how totalization is disrupted by the intrusion of moral and existential concerns into self-referential systems. His analysis suggests that what abstract systems cannot absorb is precisely the reality and experience of individuals. This is partly because, as we have seen, reflexivity and the modern sequestering of experience are not homogenous but contain their own "faultlines."[84] The dynamics of reflexivity tend to generate both contradictions and possibilities of reappropriation.[85] This is what makes possible the return of repressed experiences. More pointedly, however, abstract systems can be disrupted because individuals are not "essentially passive in relation to overwhelming external social forces."[86] To think otherwise is "to hold an inadequate account of the human agent."[87]

> If we do not see that all human agents stand in a position of appropriation in relation to the social world, which they constitute and reconstitute in their actions, we fail on an empirical level to grasp the nature of human empowerment. Modern social life impoverishes individual action, yet furthers the appropriation of new possibilities; it is alienating, yet at the same time, characteristically, human beings react against social circumstances which they find oppressive. Late modern institutions create a world of mixed opportunity and high-consequence risk. But this world does not form an impermeable environment which resists intervention.[88]

In other words, Giddens believes that individuals in late modern culture retain the capacity for evaluative freedom. Even the process of capitalist commodification, which is "a driving force towards the emergence of internally referential systems,"[89] is not "all-triumphant" on either an individual or collective level. Rather, Giddens contends that "even the most oppressed of individuals—perhaps in some ways particularly the most oppressed—react creatively and interpretatively to processes of commodification which impinge on their lives. . . . [I]ndividuals actively discriminate among types of available information as well as interpreting it in their own terms."[90]

Contrary to what one might expect, then, this analysis suggests that in a culture dominated by self-referential systems, the locus of reality and value is not the system per se, but rather the ways in which individuals reflexively respond to and interact with abstract systems. We have already seen that fateful moments expose the limits of abstract systems to sequester experience from consciousness. But even apart from such moments, moral agents do not inhabit abstract systems passively, but with a complex set of interpretive and discriminating responses. This view suggests a picture of moral rationality and evaluative freedom consistent with that of reflexive realism. The individual's ability to resist, reconfigure, or reconstitute his or her experience with respect to these systems comes in and through an active engagement with the mediations they offer. The reflexivity of self-identity in late modernity, as Giddens notes, means that individuals do not seek to deny or escape abstract systems altogether, but rather use them actively to restructure new forms of personal and social life.[91]

This analysis shows that the idea of the individual functions conceptually to limit the drive of totalization in a culture of reflexivity; this idea becomes, in effect, a subversive force in a culture dominated by systemic processes.[92] But this does not yet answer the substantive question of how to define the specifically moral good in a culture of reflexivity. What is the moral good of abstract systems? And what norm or principle guides individuals in their evaluation of and interaction with reflexive systems? From the perspective of a reflexive moral realism, the solution to the problem of subjective dominance or totalization requires the idea of the individual or concrete person not only as a formal or conceptual limit to the very idea of system or totality, but also at an explicitly moral level—as the content of the norm by which systems are evaluated. This latter point would mean, first, that the moral good of abstract systems could only be fulfilled by acknowledging the value of persons (i.e., a value beyond reflexive totalization). And second, it would mean that although persons in late modernity inevitably continue to make use of and reappropriate the possibilities offered by reflexive systems, they would do so guided by a good that lies beyond the self and the forms of self-fulfillment offered by abstract systems.

To clarify this argument, I want to return to the resources of Murdoch's thought in order to complete my analogy between the correlational structure of consciousness and the dynamics of cultural reflexivity. The point of connection is the analogy between personal moral change represented in the idea of "unselfing" and the possibility of cultural transformation. Recall that for Murdoch, the psyche is, in effect, an internally referential system that perpetuates its own self-consolation at every available opportunity. As Murdoch puts it, "we are largely mechanical creatures, the slaves of relentlessly strong selfish forces the nature of which we scarcely comprehend."[93] Because of this reflexive structure, the psyche can convert even a seemingly honest scrutiny of its own motives into an excuse for further self-absorption and defensiveness. For this reason, the cure for psychic egoism lies not in direct forms of self-contemplation such as psychoanalytic therapy, but in disciplined modes of attention to what lies *outside* the fantasy-producing psyche. Unselfing is the process by which consciousness progressively sheds its egoism by attending to the reality of the world and others beyond egoistic fantasy.

Murdoch outlines several techniques of unselfing intended for this purpose, yet as we saw in Chapter 5, the efficacy of the simpler techniques is limited by the fact that they do not fully engage the deviousness of psychic self-regard. For example, contemplating beauty in nature can succeed in an initial redirection of selfish energy, but the natural world is too "factic," too "external" to self-consciousness fully to challenge the ego where it lives. So deep is psychic egoism in Murdoch's view that the cure must be reflexive enough to use the very form of the problem in its solution. This is why the process of purifying consciousness of subjective dominance requires attention to other persons to perfect itself. Techniques of unselfing that appeal to nature, and even art or intellectual truths, do not have a sufficient degree of internal reflexivity required to engage fully the reflexively structured egoism of the psyche. Only the reality of other persons can sufficiently break through the protective fog of egoism. In the light of realistic vision, the concrete other person confronts the psyche with the prospect of an ego that resists the projection of fantasies onto itself and thus can never be entirely dominated.

The idea of unselfing, I suggest, can be extended to the cultural level. It refers to the process by which a reflexively structured culture breaks through its own self-referential systems to attend to the reality of persons. Like consciousness, internally referential systems need a principle both internal to its own processes and external enough to break the drive toward totalization. In both cases, the process of defeating subjective dominance requires the idea of persons. First, as we saw, reflexive systems require the creative, appropriating activity of individuals to sustain their own dynamism (for example, in processes of commodification). Yet this very fact allows for the possibility that individuals may actively resist or reconfigure these forces even as they continue to participate in them. Further, consider again the phenomenon of fateful moments. Why is it that experiences related to morality and finitude break through the control of reflexive systems? Such moments are experienced as "fateful" not simply because they signal the sudden return of moral and existential concerns that have been sequestered from consciousness, but also because they represent the reassertion of the value of persons within reflexive systems. This analysis shows that reflexive moral realism provides a moral theory that preserves the relation between persons and abstract systems and thus is able to respond more adequately than other forms of ethics to the totalizing dynamics of late modern culture.

Section IV. Conclusion: Freedom and Moral Change

We can now draw together the strands of the analysis in this chapter. I have argued that Murdoch's reflexive moral realism demonstrates that a return to the notion of consciousness is possible beyond the dominance of language and subjectivity. My extension of Murdoch's reflexive position into areas of cultural analysis indicates the productive role that the notion of consciousness and the correlation of consciousness and the good can play in interpreting the cultural dynamics of late modernity. Moreover, I have pursued this analysis through the use of a conceptual hermeneutic that engages the substance of Murdoch's ethics—her conceptual oppositions and pictures of the human—and interprets them reflexively to advance her thought into new areas. In concluding, I want to note a final conceptual opposition—between freedom and moral change—in order to bring the present inquiry back to the originating concerns of Murdoch's moral thought.

As previous chapters have argued, freedom and moral change lie close to the heart of Murdoch's ethics. In fact they are the conceptual equivalent of her philosophical pairing of Kant and Plato. If "the dialogue between Plato and Kant underlies the whole of western philosophy,"[94] as she has said, the concepts of freedom and moral change in a sense underlie the whole of Murdoch's ethics. Yet although these two concepts are closely connected for her in the idea of the individual, contemporary forms of ethics often neglect one or the other of them insofar as they challenge the notion of consciousness. Liberal ethics, for example, emphasizes the freedom of the autonomous will from any determining moral context. The notion of moral change is absent, except insofar as it can be conceptualized in terms of choice and decision. The noncognitivist and voluntarist underpinnings of the liberal position make the idea of moral change in Murdochian terms virtually unthinkable, since change depends so centrally for her on the relation between cognition and morality. This is precisely what voluntarism denies.

Narrativist and communitarian ethics, on the other hand, neglect the concept of freedom in favor of an emphasis on the formation of moral subjectivity in community. Freedom, as on Murdoch's Natural Law construct, is a matter of conforming the self to the narratives of the social whole rather than a matter of autonomy or self-determination. But without a fully developed notion of evaluative freedom—which includes rational dissent, "the ability to do [and think] otherwise"—this position cannot adequately thematize the idea of moral change. The scope of change is limited by the possibilities inherent the community's narratives and ethos. The "situating" strategy of narrative ethics is thus correlative with a view of moral change as "habituation," the process of internalizing the traditions and socio-linguistic practices of the community.

Finally, poststructuralism radically questions the ideas of both moral change and freedom because it effaces the notion of self-consciousness most completely. These concepts can only be conceptualized, if at all, with respect to the linguistic structures and information networks that have replaced self-consciousness. Freedom, then, is not the freedom *of* a subject, but rather the freedom *from* subjectivity. The subject has been dissolved into the linguistic system or (as in Mark C. Taylor's poststructuralism) into the information processes that form the connective substratum between living and nonliving reality. But if there is no way for subjects to transcend these processes and networks, evaluative freedom as the reflexive activity of a thinking consciousness is inconceivable. Similarly, the relevant locus of moral change on this view is not the subject, but the system. Change is definitive of the system as "process." The real is recast as the play of linguistic differences, or as "the endless interplay of information that knows no depth."[95] In the absence of a notion of self-consciousness, interplay or process becomes the matrix of reality. The "erasing" strategy of poststructuralism is thus correlative with an idea of moral change as a radical "dispossession" of subjectivity. It signals the giving up of self-consciousness as the cause of subjective dominance.

In contrast to these positions, Murdoch holds freedom and moral change together as internally related concepts integral to the idea of the individual. Both concepts depend on a notion of distance or separation between the grasping, dominating ego and a reality that exceeds the ego. This distance is defined as the reflexive power of moral imagination, the ability of consciousness to escape its own totalizing energies by imagining a good beyond itself. Understood in these terms, freedom is the condition for moral change, since moral change cannot occur without a liberation from egoistic fantasy; conversely, moral change involves the exercise of freedom, the progressive discovery of a reality beyond subjective dominance through the process of unselfing.

The deep insight of Murdoch's account of the relation between freedom and moral change is that moral positions that lose one or the other of these concepts are not simply conceptually inadequate, but morally false. They are, in effect, forms of consolation that mask renewed attempts by the ego to protect itself from reality. "Almost anything that consoles us is a fake," Murdoch writes.[96] In liberal ethics the emphasis on freedom of choice and the neglect of a progressive notion of moral change can lead (as in the case of existentialism) to voluntaristic forms of self-assertion, which console with the illusion of total autonomy. Murdoch's moral theory constitutes a sustained attack against this most obvious form of consolation—the overestimation of what the will can accomplish without engaging in sustained acts of attention. The other two ethical positions, narrative and poststructuralist ethics, represent more complex and less obvious forms of consolation. If the "situating" and "erasing" strategies are intended to dethrone the autonomous liberal subject through a critique of subjectivity, what could possibly be consoling about *them*?

From a Murdochian perspective, these forms of ethics only repeat the dynamics of subjective dominance under the guise of an escape from subjectivity. What consoles most of all, in her view, is the idea that one can escape the struggle against egoism by giving up the concept of consciousness or the individual. In narrative or communitarian ethics, the neglect of the concept of freedom and the emphasis on "habituation" console with the thought that one can escape from egoism by conforming oneself to a larger whole. But this position obscures the demand critically to examine the values, social practices, and conventions of the community that forms one's subjectivity. Conventional values may be false or consoling in their own right. The "dispossession" of subjectivity, on the other hand, is perhaps most consoling of all because it signals the relinquishing of the self to impersonal structures or processes. Murdoch sees this as a surrender to a linguistic form of determinism, which consoles because it "satisfies a deep human wish: to give up, to get rid of freedom, responsibility, remorse, all sorts of personal individual unease, and surrender to fate and the relief of 'it could not be otherwise'."[97]

Murdoch's recovery of consciousness and the individual does not allow us these consoling ways out. "Moral progress (freedom, justice, love, truth) leads us to a new state of being. This higher state does not involve the ending but rather the transformation of the 'ordinary' person and the world."[98] Reflexive realism presents us with an ethical demand, the demand critically to assess the pictures and narratives we construct of ourselves, others, and the world. This demand, which is the demand of the good, is unconditional and allows "no time off."[99] This is the challenge of evaluative freedom and the imperative of perfection.

The task of this book has been to show the internal coherence of Murdoch's moral thought and its richness in providing conceptual schemes and explanatory pictures of human moral being in relation to the good. Remarkably, these pictures of the human have retained their explanatory force and evocative power over several decades and through cultural and philosophical shifts that might have rendered them obsolete. This testifies to the depth and insight of Iris Murdoch's moral imagination. With a systematic analysis of her thought now in hand, the resources of her thought can be engaged more fully in the considerable ethical challenges that lie ahead.

NOTES

Chapter 1: Iris Murdoch and Contemporary Moral Inquiry

1. Seyla Benhabib, *Situating the Self: Gender, Community and Postmodernism in Contemporary Ethics* (New York: Routledge, 1992), 208.

2. For a useful introduction to this debate, see Kate Soper, *Humanism and Anti-Humanism* (La Salle, Ill.: Open Court, 1986).

3. Charles Taylor, *Sources of the Self: The Making of the Modern Identity* (Cambridge: Harvard University Press, 1989), 3. Taylor has also acknowledged Murdoch's influence in his essay, "Iris Murdoch and Moral Philosophy," in *Iris Murdoch and the Search for Human Goodness*, ed. Maria Antonaccio and William Schweiker (Chicago: University of Chicago Press, 1996).

4. Iris Murdoch, "Against Dryness: A Polemical Sketch," in *Revisions: Changing Perspectives in Moral Philosophy*, ed. Stanley Hauerwas and Alasdair MacIntyre (Notre Dame: University of Notre Dame Press, 1983), 48.

5. Among those who have explicitly taken up aspects of Murdoch's moral thought in recent years are such prominent moral philosophers as Charles Taylor, Martha Nussbaum, and Cora Diamond, as well as theologians such as David Tracy and theological ethicists such as Stanley Hauerwas and William Schweiker. For recent essays on Murdoch's thought by these and other thinkers, see *Iris Murdoch and the Search for Human Goodness*. Other thinkers who have deeply engaged Murdoch's thought while formulating their own distinctive positions include Susan Wolf, *Freedom Within Reason* (New York: Oxford University Press, 1990); Hilary Putnam, *Realism with a Human Face* (Cambridge, Mass.: Harvard University Press, 1990); and Wendy Farley, *Eros for the Other: Retaining Truth in a Pluralistic World* (University Park, Penn.: Pennsylvania State University Press, 1996). See also Taylor, *Sources of the Self*; and Stanley Hauerwas, *Vision and Virtue: Essays in Christian Ethical Reflection* (Notre Dame, Ind.: University of Notre Dame Press, 1981).

6. Iris Murdoch, *The Sovereignty of Good* (London: Routledge & Kegan Paul, 1970).

7. *Existentialists and Mystics: Writings on Philosophy and Literature*, ed. Peter Conradi (New York: Allen Lane/The Penguin Press, 1997). This volume represents a much needed compilation of Murdoch's theoretical and philosophical

treatises which have until now been available mainly in widely scattered journals and periodicals.

8. For a moving account of Murdoch's life during her illness, see the remarkable "Elegy for Iris," by John Bayley, in *The New Yorker*, July 27, 1998, 44–61 and the longer memoir by the same title (New York: St. Martin's Press, 1998).

9. Jeffrey Stout, *The Flight from Authority: Religion, Morality, and the Quest for Autonomy* (Notre Dame, Ind.: University of Notre Dame Press, 1981), 2–3.

10. Taylor, *Sources of the Self*, 364.

11. See Isaiah Berlin, *Two Concepts of Liberty* (Oxford: Oxford University Press, 1958).

12. The terms of my discussion of freedom in this section owe much to Charles Taylor's concluding chapter in *Hegel* (Cambridge: Cambridge University Press, 1975). See 537–71, and esp. 560–64.

13. Ibid., 563.

14. Ibid.

15. For a classic statement of Rawls's position, see *A Theory of Justice* (Cambridge: The Belknap Press of Harvard University Press, 1971). For a critique and reconstruction of liberal proceduralist ethics from a perspective informed by communitarianism, feminism, and postmodernism, see Benhabib, *Situating the Self*.

16. This characterization of Tillich's position is William Schweiker's. See his account of agential theories of moral identity and responsibility in *Responsibility and Christian Ethics* (Cambridge: Cambridge University Press, 1995), 78–86.

17. For an early and concise statement of this view, see Michael Sandel, "The Procedural Republic and the Unencumbered Self," *Political Theory* 12, no. 1 (February 1984): 87. See also Sandel's critique of Rawls in *Liberalism and the Limits of Justice* (Cambridge: Cambridge University Press, 1982).

18. See Alasdair MacIntyre, *After Virtue: A Study in Moral Theory* (Notre Dame, Ind.: University of Notre Press, 2nd edition, 1984), 220.

19. For a discussion of social theories of moral identity and responsibility, including Hauerwas, see Schweiker, *Responsibility and Christian Ethics*, 86–94.

20. This is not to suggest that significant differences do not exist between Taylor's and Benhabib's positions, especially with respect to their critique of liberalism. Benhabib notes the differences between Taylor's "communitarian" critique of liberalism, and her own critique informed by the communicative ethics of Apel and Habermas. See Benhabib, *Situating the Self*, esp. chap. 2.

21. See Mette Hjort, "Literature: Romantic Expression or Strategic Interaction," in *Philosophy in an Age of Pluralism: The Philosophy of Charles Taylor in Question*, ed. James Tully (Cambridge: Cambridge University Press, 1994), 123.

22. Ibid.

23. For two recent accounts of the debate between theory and anti-theory in ethics, see *Anti-Theory in Ethics and Moral Conservatism*, eds., Stanley G. Clarke and Evan Simpson (Albany, N.Y.: State University of New York Press, 1989) and Dwight Furrow, *Against Theory: Continental and Analytic Challenges in Moral Philosophy* (New York and London: Routledge, 1995).

24. I take this to be MacIntyre's effort in *After Virtue*.

25. Iris Murdoch, *Sartre, Romantic Rationalist* (London: Bowes & Bowes, 1953), 13.

26. Specifically, Murdoch embraces a "reflexive" type of moral realism, as noted in the next section of this introduction and more fully in Chapter 5.

27. This is the argument of the essay "On 'God' and 'Good'" in *The Sovereignty of Good*, 55.

28. Iris Murdoch, "Metaphysics and Ethics," in *The Nature of Metaphysics*, ed. D. F. Pears (London: Macmillan & Co. Ltd., 1960), 77. This essay has been reprinted as an appendix in *Iris Murdoch and the Search for Human Goodness* and is also included in *Existentialists and Mystics*.

29. Ibid., 107.

30. Ibid., 121. I have retained Murdoch's use of noninclusive language in all direct quotations from her work. As she writes in *Metaphysics as a Guide to Morals*, 354: "By 'man' in such contexts throughout, I mean 'human person'."

31. Murdoch, "A House of Theory," 25, my emphasis.

32. Murdoch, "Metaphysics and Ethics," 112.

33. Ibid.

34. Ibid., 115. These contrasts between Kant and Hegel and between the Liberal and Natural Law views of morality function primarily as "types" in Murdoch's thought and are thus not presented in their full historical and philosophical complexity.

35. The term is William Schweiker's. See his *Responsibility and Christian Ethics*, 106–114 for an articulation and defense of this position in relation to current debates over realism and anti-realism in ethics. Schweiker's work on this subject has deeply informed my own thinking as the argument of this book will make clear. The reflexive nature of Murdoch's realism is presupposed by her view of metaphysics as a form of "imaginative construction."

36. The image is pervasive in Murdoch's thought; see for example, *Sovereignty of Good*, 70, 92, 98.

37. This transcendental conception of the good thus undergirds even those values we might judge "wrong" or "evil" when we adopt a specifically moral point of view.

38. Again, at this transcendental level, the notion of perfection does not yet have specifically moral content. Perfection as a condition of the human activity of evaluation applies even to values we might judge morally wrong from a moral point of view—e.g., "the perfect crime" or "the perfect murder." We apply qualitative distinctions of good and bad, better and worse even in cases we judge "immoral."

39. For a concise narrative of the major features of Murdoch's development as philosopher and writer, see the "Editor's Preface" by Peter Conradi in *Existentialists and Mystics*, xix–xxx. Conradi is currently writing a full-length biography of Murdoch.

40. See W. K. Rose, "An Interview with Iris Murdoch" in *Shenandoah*, vol. XIX, no. 2 (Winter 1968): 8.

41. See Murdoch's interview with Christopher Bigsby in *The Radical Imagination and the Liberal Tradition: Interviews with English and American Novelists*, eds. Heide Ziegler and Christopher Bigsby (London: Junction Books Ltd., 1982), 211.

42. See Rose, 8 and Bigsby, 211.

43. See Bigsby, 212, where Murdoch notes Wittgenstein as a continuing and major influence.

44. George Steiner reports in his foreword to *Existentialists and Mystics* (xiii) that in her later years Murdoch was working on a book on Heidegger that remains unfinished after her death. For a listing of Murdoch's works see the bibliography. For a more comprehensive and secondary bibliography, see John Fletcher and Cheryl Bove, *Iris Murdoch: A Descriptive Primary and Annotated Secondary Bibliography* (New York: Garland Publishing, 1994).

45. This is no less evident in her magnum opus, *Metaphysics as a Guide to Morals*, which one reviewer described as "the philosophical equivalent of Murdoch's devotion to the loose baggy monster of a novel." See Terry Eagleton, "The good, the true, the beautiful," in *The Guardian* (December 5, 1993): 29.

46. Murdoch was in fact trained in this philosophical method at Oxford and retained an immense appreciation for its clarity and analytic rigor in spite of her criticisms of it. See her interview with Rose, 10.

47. It is an interesting question whether Murdoch's early criticisms of Hampshire may have influenced the subsequent evolution in Hampshire's thinking, as an anonymous reviewer of this manuscript has suggested.

48. Murdoch, *The Sovereignty of Good*, 45.

49. The most recent major studies that attempt a comprehensive assessment of the fictional works are the following: Elizabeth Dipple, *Iris Murdoch: Work for the Spirit* (Chicago: University of Chicago Press, 1982); Peter Conradi, *Iris Murdoch: The Saint and the Artist* (New York: St. Martin's Press, 1986); and David J. Gordon, *Iris Murdoch's Fables of Unselfing* (Columbia: University of Missouri Press, 1995). A complete listing of the critical monographs may be found in the bibliography.

50. Several of the critical monographs do engage important aspects of Murdoch's philosophy as a means of assessing the context and achievements of her fiction. For example, Elizabeth Dipple, in *Iris Murdoch: Work for the Spirit*, concentrates on the relation between Murdoch's literary realism and her moral realism by examining the Platonic notion of reality underlying both her philosophy and her fiction. A. S. Byatt, in her early *Degrees of Freedom: The Novels of Iris Murdoch* (London: Chatto & Windus and New York: Barnes & Noble, 1965), and David Gordon, in his recent *Iris Murdoch's Fables of Unselfing*, identify Murdoch's relation to Sartre and the Sartrean notion of freedom as crucial to understanding the formative background of Murdoch's fiction. Both Gordon and Peter Conradi, in *Iris Murdoch: The Saint and the Artist*, focus on the role of eros in Murdoch's fiction and its background in the thought of Freud and Plato. All of these readings draw insightful connections between Murdoch's fiction and her philosophical preoccupations, but none purports to represent a systematic reading of the moral philosophy as a whole.

51. The work of Martha Nussbaum is the most prominent example of the trend, but see also Richard Eldridge, *On Moral Personhood: Philosophy, Literature, Criticism, and Self-Understanding* (Chicago: University of Chicago Press, 1989) and Samuel Goldberg, *Agents and Lives: Moral Thinking in Literature* (Cambridge: Cambridge University Press, 1993). Numerous other examples could be cited. An early collection of essays on this subject was published as a special issue of *New Literary History* titled "Literature and/as Moral Philosophy," vol. xv, no. 1 (Autumn 1983). It includes contributions by Nussbaum, Cora Diamond, Nathan Scott, D. D. Raphael, Richard Wollheim, and others. In religious ethics the turn to literature is evident in the work of narrative theologians such as Stanley Hauerwas, Katie Cannon, and many others. For a theoretical statement

of the method of narrative theology, see *Why Narrative? Readings in Narrative Theology*, eds. Stanley Hauerwas and L. Gregory Jones (Grand Rapids: William B. Eerdmans, 1989).

52. Murdoch once said that she preferred to be called a "reflective" novelist, a category she associates with Dostoevsky and Tolstoy. See her interview with Bigsby, 301.

53. See her interview with Simon Blow in *The Spectator* (25 September 1976), 24. "People think that because I'm a philosopher there's a philosophical view being put across, but this is not so. I've got a philosophical viewpoint but I certainly don't want to force it across in the novels, although a certain amount of one's metaphysics in a very general sense comes across as it would with any writer." See also Bigsby, 301.

54. "I don't think that an artist should worry about looking after society *in his art*. . . . A novelist working well and honestly, and only saying what he knows and what he understands, will in fact tell a lot of important truths about his society. This is why, of course, tyrannical societies are often frightened of novelists. . . . I think it's a novelist's job to be a good artist, and this will involve telling the truth, and not worrying about social commitment. I think social commitment, in so far as it interferes with art, is very often a mistake. It can make the novelist nervous and anxious and not able to open himself to the whole of reality as he understands it." See Rose, 5.

55. This interview, originally conducted in 1978, has been reprinted as "Literature and Philosophy: A Conversation with Bryan Magee" in *Existentialists and Mystics*. The quotation is from 4. Murdoch makes a similar point in her interview with Bigsby: "To my mind, philosophy is a completely different game, although the intuitive element enters into it. This is quite unlike writing stories. I play the game according to the rules. It's a separate operation and one's mind is working very differently in philosophy. . . . I find really no difficulty in separating these activities." Bigsby, 300.

56. Specifically, Nussbaum quotes Murdoch's comment to Magee that, "Philosophers vary and some are more 'literary' than others, but I am tempted to say that there is an ideal philosophical style which has a special unambiguous plainness and hardness about it, an austere unselfish candid style. A philosopher must try to explain exactly what he means and avoid rhetoric, and idle decoration. Of course this need not exclude with and occasional interludes; but when the philosopher is as it were in the front in relation to his problem I think he speaks with a certain old clear recognisable voice." See "Literature and Philosophy."

57. See Martha C. Nussbaum, *The Fragility of Goodness: Luck and Ethics in Greek Tragedy and Philosophy* (Cambridge: Cambridge University Press, 1986), 16.

58. Nussbaum herself would probably agree with this judgment. See her essay, "Love and Vision: Iris Murdoch on Eros and the Individual" in *Iris Murdoch and the Search for Human Goodness*, 29–53.

59. Murdoch, "Literature and Philosophy," 10–11.

60. Murdoch, *Sovereignty of Good*, 34. Among contemporary thinkers who interpret Murdoch in this light, see for example Geoffrey Harpham, *Getting It Right: Language, Literature, and Ethics* (Chicago: University of Chicago Press, 1992), 159.

61. I have explored these questions in detail in an essay titled "The Consolations of Literature," forthcoming in the *Journal of Religion*.

62. It is hoped that the appearance of her collected essays in *Existentialists and Mystics* will facilitate more sustained attention to Murdoch's philosophical works.

63. For two essays that analyze this avoidance of system and the relation between form and content in *Metaphysics as a Guide to Morals*, see Maria Antonaccio, "Form and Contingency in Iris Murdoch's Ethics" and David Tracy, "The Many Faces of Platonism" in *Iris Murdoch and the Search for Human Goodness*.

64. This analogy between the cave allegory and the M and D example was suggested to me by William Schweiker.

65. Conradi, *Iris Murdoch: The Saint and the Artist*, 73.

66. Ibid., 210. As the title of his study indicates, Conradi's own reading of Murdoch's thought focuses on the central opposition between the artist and the saint as two moral types who represent different conceptions of "the good life" in Murdoch's fiction.

67. I leave aside for the moment numerous other "types" of human individual in Murdoch's thought which are not framed in terms of conceptual oppositions. These include the demonic individual, the Kantian man-God, the authentic hero, the Romantic man, etc.

68. Murdoch, "Metaphysics and Ethics," 121. This point will be explored in detail in Chapter 2.

Chapter 2: Metaphysics and Ethics

1. See Gamwell's essay "On the Loss of Theism" in *Iris Murdoch and the Search for Human Goodness*, ed. Maria Antonaccio and William Schweiker (Chicago: University of Chicago Press, 1996), 171–189. This essay contains one of the most concisely accurate and elegant expositions of Murdoch's thought available on the subject of metaphysics as well as on what Gamwell characterizes as Murdoch's "emphatic moral realism."

2. Iris Murdoch, "The Sublime and the Beautiful Revisited," *Yale Review* 49 (December 1959), 255.

3. Ibid., 254.

4. In her most recent work, the idea of metaphysics is cut loose from this initial debate with analytic philosophy and becomes the locus for some of Murdoch's most fertile and thought-provoking reflections on the nature of theory, issues of philosophical method, the relation of art and philosophy, the dangers of "system" or totality, and a host of other issues. See *Metaphysics as a Guide to Morals* (New York: Allen Lane/The Penguin Press, 1992).

5. Iris Murdoch, interview by Christopher Bigsby, in *The Radical Imagination and the Liberal Tradition: Interviews with English and American Novelists*, ed. Heide Ziegler and Christopher Bigsby (London: Junction Books Ltd., 1982), 213.

6. Ibid., 22.

7. Iris Murdoch, "A House of Theory," *Partisan Review* 26 (Winter 1959): 19.

8. Ibid., 19.

9. Ibid., 22.

10. Ibid., 21

11. I discuss this metaethical theory in contrast to Murdoch's realism in section III of this chapter.

12. Ludwig Wittgenstein, *Tractatus Logico-Philosophicus* (London: Routledge & Kegan Paul, 1961); quoted in Iris Murdoch, "The Novelist as Metaphysician," *Listener* 43 (16 March 1950): 476.

13. Iris Murdoch, "Metaphysics and Ethics," in *The Nature of Metaphysics*, ed. D. F. Pears (London: Macmillan & Co. Ltd., 1960), 108.

14. Such a position is often associated with certain forms of antirealism in ethics.

15. Murdoch, "House of Theory," 19.

16. Ibid., 22.

17. Ibid., 23.

18. Ibid.

19. Ibid.

20. Ibid.

21. Ibid., 21.

22. Ibid., 22.

23. Ibid.

24. A. J. Ayer, "The Vienna Circle," in *The Revolution in Philosophy*, with an introduction by Gilbert Ryle (London: Macmillan & Co. Ltd., 1957), 74.

25. Ibid.

26. Murdoch, "House of Theory," 24.

27. Ibid., 23.

28. Ibid.

29. Emotivism plays a key role in Alasdair MacIntyre's diagnosis of modern moral theory in *After Virtue*: "Emotivism is the doctrine that all evaluative judgments and more specifically all moral judgments are nothing but expressions of preference, expressions of attitude or feeling, insofar as they are moral or evaluative in character . . . [M]oral judgments, beings expressions of attitude or feeling, are neither true nor false; and agreement in moral judgments is not to be secured by any rational method, for there are none." See *After Virtue: A Study in Moral Theory*, 2nd ed. (Notre Dame, Ind.: University of Notre Press, 1984), 11–12.

30. Murdoch, "A House of Theory," 24.

31. Anthony Quinton, "Philosophy and Beliefs," *The Twentieth Century* clvii, no. 940 (June 1955): 495–496.

32. Ibid., 495.

33. Murdoch, "Metaphysics and Ethics," 107.

34. Murdoch, "House of Theory," 21.

35. Paul Johnston, *Wittgenstein and Moral Philosophy* (London: Routledge, 1989), 127.

36. Stuart Hampshire, "Metaphysical Systems," in *The Nature of Metaphysics*, ed. D. F. Pears (London: Macmillan & Co. Ltd., 1960), 35–36.

37. Iris Murdoch, "Against Dryness: A Polemical Sketch," in *Revisions: Changing Perspectives in Moral Philosophy*, ed. Stanley Hauerwas and Alasdair MacIntyre (Notre Dame, Ind.: University of Notre Dame Press, 1983), 46.

38. See " 'We are Perpetually Moralists': Iris Murdoch, Fact, and Value" in *Iris Murdoch and the Search for Human Goodness*, 79–109. This quotation is from 79. Diamond provides an exceptionally clear and persuasive analysis of the issues surrounding Murdoch's critique of the fact-value distinction, placing them in the context of Murdoch's debate with R. M. Hare.

39. Ibid., 104. Diamond notes that *The Sovereignty of Good* is "often treated as groundbreaking in this regard," citing Hilary Putnam's treatment of it in

Realism with a Human Face (Cambridge: Harvard University Press, 1990). See 166.

40. Ibid., 105.

41. Murdoch treats these arguments along closely parallel lines in two key essays from which I have drawn freely in these pages, "Metaphysics and Ethics" and "Vision and Choice in Morality," *Proceedings of the Aristotelian Society* suppl. vol. 30 (1956): 32–58. I have followed her slightly more expansive analysis in "Vision and Choice" in explicitly identifying four rather than three components of the argument, but she makes it clear in both essays that the argument from meaning is an essential component of the general argument against naturalism.

42. Murdoch, "Vision and Choice," 52.

43. Ibid.

44. Ibid., 52–53.

45. Ibid., 52.

46. Ibid. In spite of her appreciation of Hegel's treatment of metaphysics noted earlier, Hegel does not play a role in Murdoch's reconstruction of metaphysical ethics. This may be because Murdoch classifies Hegel as a "romantic" thinker whose systematic pretensions, she judges, threaten the reality and value of the individual with absorption into the social whole. This critique of Hegel will emerge over the course of the coming chapters.

47. Ibid., 53.

48. Murdoch, "Metaphysics and Ethics," 106.

49. Murdoch, "House of Theory," 25.

50. Murdoch, "Metaphysics and Ethics," 107.

51. Murdoch, "House of Theory," 25. I will return to the idea of moral concepts when I treat the argument from meaning.

52. Murdoch, "Metaphysics and Ethics," 105.

53. Ibid.

54. Ibid., 107–108.

55. Gamwell argues that Murdoch rejects Kant's critique of theoretical reason precisely because it separates knowledge and morality, thus giving rise to the distinction between values and facts which she is contesting. In this respect, Gamwell notes, Murdoch would substantially agree with Alasdair MacIntyre's judgment that "the separation of fact and value is 'the epitaph' of the Kantian or Enlightenment project and . . . [that] the modern dissolution of moral theory derives from the dominance of this separation in thinking subsequent to Kant." See "On the Loss of Theism," 172.

56. "Vision and Choice," 53.

57. "Metaphysics and Ethics," 107.

58. Ibid., 106.

59. See Diamond, " 'We are Perpetually Moralists,' " 80 ff.

60. Murdoch, "Vision and Choice," 53.

61. Diamond, " 'We are Perpetually Moralists," 81.

62. Ibid., 81.

63. Ibid., 80.

64. Ibid., 80–81.

65. Ibid. Diamond notes that Murdoch's discussion of suppressed premises connects directly with Stanley Cavell's discussion of moral rationality in Part III of *The Claim of Reason* (New York: Oxford University Press, 1979).

66. Ibid., 83.

67. Murdoch, "Vision and Choice," 53.

68. Ibid., 34.

69. Ibid.

70. Ibid.

71. Ibid., 54.

72. Diamond, " 'We are Perpetually Moralists," 83.

73. Murdoch, "Vision and Choice," 35.

74. Ibid., 54.

75. Ibid., 41.

76. Ibid., 54.

77. Ibid., 44–45.

78. Ibid., 44.

79. Ibid., 40–41.

80. Ibid., 55.

81. Ibid.

82. Murdoch, "Metaphysics and Ethics," 106.

83. Ibid., 110.

84. Murdoch, "Vision and Choice," 52.

85. Murdoch, "Metaphysics and Ethics," 111.

86. Ibid., 110–111.

87. Murdoch, "Vision and Choice," 48.

88. Murdoch, "Metaphysics and Ethics," 111.

89. Murdoch, "Vision and Choice," 55.

90. Ibid., 47.

91. Murdoch, "Metaphysics and Ethics," 111.

92. Murdoch, "Vision and Choice," 46–47.

93. Murdoch, "Metaphysics and Ethics," 111.

94. Ibid., 56.

95. Ibid.

96. Ibid.

97. Diamond, " 'We Are Perpetually Moralists,' " 91.

98. Ibid., 82–83.

99. Ibid., 91.

100. Murdoch, "Vision and Choice," 56.

101. Ibid., 39.

102. Ibid.

103. "Metaphysics and Ethics," 123.

104. Ibid., 122.

105. Ibid., 121.

106. Diamond, " 'We Are Perpetually Moralists,' " 91.

107. Murdoch, "Metaphysics and Ethics," 118.

108. Murdoch, "Vision and Choice," 43.

109. Murdoch, "Metaphysics and Ethics," 118–119.

110. Ibid., 119.

111. Ibid.

112. Murdoch, "Vision and Choice," 49.

113. Murdoch, "Metaphysics and Ethics," 120. The clearest demonstration of Murdoch's views on this matter is the example of M and D in *The Sovereignty of Good*, which will be discussed in detail in Chapter 4.

114. Ibid.

115. Ibid.

116. Ibid.

117. Ibid., 122.

118. Ibid.

119. *Sovereignty of Good*, 52.

120. See Charles Taylor, "Self-Interpreting Animals," in *Human Agency and Language: Philosophical Papers* vol. 1 (Cambridge: Cambridge University Press, 1985), chap. 1.

121. This theme will be explored further in subsequent chapters.

122. Murdoch, "Metaphysics and Ethics," 112.

123. Ibid.

124. Ibid., 114.

125. Ibid., 115.

126. Ibid.

127. Ibid., 117.

128. Ibid., 116.

129. Ibid.

130. Ibid., 115.

131. Ibid.

132. Ibid.

133. Murdoch, *Sovereignty of Good*, 59.

134. Ibid.

135. Ibid., 60.

136. Murdoch, "Metaphysics and Ethics," 119–120.

137. Murdoch, *Sovereignty of Good*, 93.

138. Iris Murdoch, "Above the Gods: A Dialogue about Religion" in *Acastos: Two Platonic Dialogues* (New York: Viking Press, 1988), 100.

139. Murdoch, *Sovereignty of Good*, 42.

140. Sabina Lovibond, *Realism and Imagination in Ethics* (Minneapolis: University of Minnesota Press, 1983), 1.

141. Ibid.

142. Ibid., 22.

143. Ibid., 2.

144. Ibid.

145. Ibid.

146. Ibid., 3.

147. Murdoch, *Sovereignty of Good*, 58.

148. Ibid.

149. Ibid., 90.

150. Ibid., 93.

151. Ibid., 55

152. Murdoch, "Above the Gods," 100.

153. Murdoch, *Sovereignty of Good*, 92.

154. Ibid., 98.

155. Murdoch, "Above the Gods," 107–108.

156. Ibid., 110.

157. Iris Murdoch, *The Fire and the Sun: Why Plato Banished the Artists* (Oxford: Clarendon Press, 1977), 3.

158. Ibid., 4.

159. Murdoch, *Sovereignty of Good*, 70.

160. R. C. Cross and A. D. Woozley, *Plato's Republic: A Philosophical Commentary* (New York: St. Martin's Press, 1964), 202.

161. Ibid., 260.

162. Murdoch, "Above the Gods," 79.

163. Ibid., 99.

164. Ibid., 98.

165. Ibid., 104.

166. Ibid., 100.

167. Ibid.

168. Ibid., 108.

169. Ibid.

170. Ibid., 99.

171. Ibid., 87.

172. Murdoch, *Sovereignty of Good*, 70.

173. Ibid., 100.

174. Ibid., 98.

175. Ibid., my emphasis.

176. Murdoch, *Fire and the Sun*, 4.

177. Murdoch, "Above the Gods," 108.

178. Ibid.

179. Murdoch, *Sovereignty of Good*, 61.

180. Ibid., 63.

181. Ibid.

182. Ibid.

183. Ibid., 64.

184. Ibid., 74.

185. Ibid., 61–62.

186. Ibid., 62.

187. Ibid.

188. Ibid., 93.

189. Ibid., 88.

190. Ibid., 93.

191. Ibid.

192. Ibid., 62.

193. Iris Murdoch, "Art and Eros: A Dialogue about Art," in *Acastos: Two Platonic Dialogues* (New York: Viking Penguin Inc., 1986), 61.

194. Murdoch, *Sovereignty of Good*, 62.

195. Ibid., 89.

Chapter 3: The Critique of Consciousness in Existentialism and Linguistic Behaviorism

1. As defined by Charles Taylor, a moral ontology is a " 'background picture' lying behind our moral and spiritual intuitions." It "articulate[s] the claims implicit in our reactions" and represents "our mode of access to the world in which ontological claims are discernible and can be rationally argued about and sifted." See *Sources of the Self: The Making of the Modern Identity* (Cambridge: Harvard University Press, 1989), 8, and all of chap. 1.

2. Linguistic behaviorism is Murdoch's term for the branch of analytic linguistic philosophy influenced by the thought of Gilbert Ryle, Ludwig Wittgenstein, and others. These philosophers, in Murdoch's view, contributed to a "be-

haviorist" turn in philosophy by reducing private meaning to the public rules of language use, and denying the existence of introspectible contents of consciousness in favor of an emphasis on outward acts.

3. It is important to note that Murdoch's book on Sartre does not offer a systematic analysis of Sartre's philosophy. Rather, it is a synthetic attempt to analyze his phenomenology of consciousness in relation to both his fictional works and his practical and political philosophy. Accordingly, my exposition in this section does not follow the plan of Murdoch's book, but attempts to draw out the systematic elements of her critique of Sartre with help from other essays as well as Sartre's own works.

4. Iris Murdoch, *Sartre, Romantic Rationalist* (London: Bowes & Bowes, 1953), 50.

5. Ibid.

6. Ibid., 53.

7. Ibid.

8. Ibid., 58.

9. Jean-Paul Sartre, *Being and Nothingness*, trans. Hazel E. Barnes (New York: The Citadel Press, 1956), 61.

10. Ibid., 62.

11. Ibid., 65.

12. Murdoch, *Sartre*, 42.

13. Ibid., 42.

14. Ibid., 43.

15. Sartre, *Being and Nothingness*, 538.

16. Iris Murdoch, "The Existentialist Political Myth," *Socratic* 5 (1952): 56.

17. Ibid.

18. Murdoch, *Sartre*, 12.

19. Ibid., 16.

20. Murdoch, "The Existentialist Political Myth," 56.

21. Murdoch, *Sartre*, 15.

22. Ibid., 18.

23. Ibid.

24. Sartre, *Being and Nothingness*, 415.

25. Murdoch, *Sartre*, 42–43.

26. Ibid., 42.

27. Murdoch, "The Existentialist Political Myth," 57.

28. Murdoch, *Sartre*, 44.

29. Ibid., 45.

30. Murdoch, "The Existentialist Political Myth," 58.

31. Murdoch, *Sartre*, 44.

32. Ibid.

33. Murdoch, "The Existentialist Political Myth," 60.

34. Ibid., 58.

35. Ibid.

36. Murdoch, *Sartre*, 55.

37. Ibid., 44.

38. Ibid., 45.

39. It has since been published in both French and English. See Jean-Paul Sartre, *Cahiers pour une morale* (Paris: Editions Gallimard, 1983) and *Notebooks for an Ethics*, trans. David Pellauer (Chicago: University of Chicago Press, 1992).

40. Murdoch, "The Existentialist Political Myth," 58.

41. Murdoch, *Sartre*, 49.

42. For example, Sartre writes that freedom "is nothing else but the movement by which one perpetually uproots and liberates himself." See Jean-Paul Sartre, *What is Literature?* trans. Bernard Frechtman (New York: Harper & Row, 1965), 61.

43. Murdoch, *Sartre*, 48.

44. Sartre, *What is Literature?* 42.

45. Ibid., 40.

46. Ibid., 49.

47. Sartre, *What is Literature?* 43.

48. Ibid., 44.

49. Ibid.

50. Ibid., 49.

51. Ibid., 50.

52. Ibid., 56.

53. Murdoch, *Sartre*, 49.

54. Ibid., 48.

55. Jean-Paul Sartre, *Existentialism and Humanism*, trans. Philip Mairet (Brooklyn: Haskell House Publishers Ltd., 1977), 29.

56. Ibid.

57. Ibid., 29–30.

58. Ibid., 30.

59. Murdoch, *Sartre*, 49.

60. Murdoch, "The Existentialist Political Myth," 59. David Pellauer echoes Murdoch's observation in his introduction to Sartre's recently published *Notebooks for an Ethics*: "Somehow, 'man' here slides from the particular existing individual I am to humanity in general. Critics have seen this as a kind of unacknowledged Kantian element in Sartre's remarks on ethics that it is difficult to account for, especially on the basis of *Being and Nothingness*. Is there not an assumption at work here that ethics has to be universal?" See Sartre, *Notebooks for an Ethics*, xii.

61. See her introduction to the American edition, 9–10. Iris Murdoch, *Sartre, Romantic Rationalist*, first American edition, with a new introduction by the author. (New York: Viking Penguin, 1987).

62. Murdoch, *Sartre*, 54.

63. Murdoch, "The Existentialist Political Myth," 60.

64. Ibid., 61.

65. Murdoch, *Sartre*, 54.

66. Ibid., 54–55.

67. Ibid., 55.

68. Ibid.

69. Ibid.

70. Ibid.

71. Iris Murdoch, *The Sovereignty of Good* (London: Routledge & Kegan Paul), 10.

72. A note on terminology. Murdoch uses the term "the existentialist-behaviorist view" throughout *The Sovereignty of Good* especially to characterize Stuart Hampshire's position. In earlier essays, however, she uses both "behaviorism" (e.g., in the case of Ryle and Wittgenstein) and "linguistic behaviorism" to refer essentially to the same philosophical position. I use the term "existentialist-behaviorist" to reflect Murdoch's usage in the *Sovereignty of Good*,

where she is making the explicit point that the linguistic behaviorist view entails an existentialist assumption about the importance of the will. In all other cases, I use the term linguistic behaviorism throughout this chapter as the general term of which the existentialist-behaviorist view is an offshoot.

73. Ibid., 2.

74. Ibid.

75. Iris Murdoch, "Vision and Choice in Morality," *Aristotelian Society Supplementary Volume* 30 (1956): 34.

76. Ibid.

77. Ibid., 35.

78. Ibid.

79. Ibid., 43.

80. Iris Murdoch, "Metaphysics and Ethics," in *The Nature of Metaphysics*, ed. D. F. Pears (London: Macmillan & Co. Ltd., 1960), 102.

81. Ibid.

82. Murdoch, "Vision and Choice," 37.

83. Iris Murdoch, "Nostalgia for the Particular," *Proceedings of the Aristotelian Society* 52 (9 June 1952): 243.

84. Murdoch, *Sovereignty of Good*, 10.

85. Ibid.

86. Murdoch, "Nostalgia for the Particular," 243–244.

87. Ibid., 244.

88. Iris Murdoch, "Thinking and Language." Symposium with A. C. Lloyd and Gilbert Ryle. *Aristotelian Society Supplementary Volume* 25 (1951): 30.

89. Murdoch, *Sovereignty of Good*, 11.

90. Ibid.

91. Quoted by Murdoch, ibid., 12. Wittgenstein applied this argument to both mental and physical concepts. Murdoch holds that the argument works best when applied to physical concepts such as "red," whereas she believes that it runs into trouble when applied to complex mental operations such as "deciding," as we will see below.

92. Murdoch, "Nostalgia for the Particular," 244.

93. Murdoch, *Sovereignty of Good*, 11.

94. Ibid.

95. Murdoch, "Thinking and Language," 30.

96. Ibid.

97. Ibid., 31.

98. Ibid.

99. Ibid. This recalls the argument Murdoch advanced about metaphysical beliefs discussed in chapter 2. The importance of such beliefs lies is their "regulative" function as guides for consciousness on its pilgrimage towards reality, and is not dependent on whether they are "empirically verifiable" by philosophical or other arguments.

100. Ibid.

101. Murdoch, "Nostalgia for the Particular," 246.

102. Ibid., 246–247.

103. Murdoch, "Vision and Choice," 37–38.

104. Murdoch, *Sovereignty of Good*, 12.

105. Ibid.

106. Ibid., 24.

107. Ibid., 39.

108. Ibid., 38.

109. Ibid., 37. See also Ryle's contribution to the symposium "Thinking and Language," with Murdoch and A. C. Lloyd.

110. Ibid.

111. Hampshire's thought has evolved significantly in the years since he produced the works that Murdoch takes as paradigmatic of the existentialist-behaviorist view in *The Sovereignty of Good*. See for example his *Innocence and Experience* (Cambridge, Mass.: Harvard University Press, 1989).

112. Murdoch, *Sovereignty of Good*, 4–5.

113. Ibid., 7.

114. Ibid., 7–8.

115. Ibid., 8.

116. Ibid., 16.

117. Ibid., 10.

118. Ibid., 13.

119. Ibid.

120. Ibid., 15.

121. Ibid., 10.

122. Ibid., 9.

123. Ibid.

124. Murdoch, "Thinking and Language," 31.

125. Murdoch, "Vision and Choice," 40.

126. Ibid.

127. Iris Murdoch, *Metaphysics as a Guide to Morals* (New York: Allen Lane/ The Penguin Press, 1992), 153.

128. As I will demonstrate in the concluding chapter, Murdoch's critique of the behaviorist implications of the analytic turn to language as a threat to individual consciousness will return in her critique of the more recent turn to language in poststructuralism.

Chapter 4: Moral Agency, Consciousness, and the Concept of the Individual

1. Iris Murdoch, *Metaphysics as a Guide to Morals* (New York: Allen Lane/ The Penguin Press, 1992), 171.

2. Since Murdoch must defend the fundamental significance of consciousness before she can defend the idea of the individual, the order of my exposition in this chapter will be the reverse of Chapter 3. That is, I will treat Murdoch's constructive response to linguistic behaviorism first before turning to her reply to Sartre, where the concept of the individual and freedom come to the fore.

3. Iris Murdoch, *The Sovereignty of Good* (London: Routledge & Kegan Paul, 1970), 46.

4. Quoted in Peter Conradi, *Iris Murdoch: The Saint and the Artist* (St. Martin's Press, 1986), x.

5. Murdoch, *Metaphysics*, 153.

6. Ibid., 171.

7. Iris Murdoch, "Vision and Choice in Morality," *Aristotelian Society Supplementary Volume* 30 (1956): 38.

8. See Martha C. Nussbaum, *Love's Knowledge: Essays on Philosophy and Literature* (New York: Oxford University Press, 1990), 46.

9. Murdoch, *Sovereignty of Good*, 17.

10. Ibid.
11. Ibid.
12. Ibid.
13. Ibid., 17–18.
14. Ibid., 20.
15. Ibid.
16. Ibid., 21.
17. Ibid.
18. Ibid., 19–20.
19. Ibid., 22.
20. Ibid.
21. Ibid., 20.
22. Ibid., 22.
23. Ibid., 35.
24. Ibid.
25. Ibid., 28.
26. Ibid., 37.
27. Murdoch, *Metaphysics*, 110.
28. Murdoch, *Sovereignty of Good*, 18.
29. Ibid., 22.
30. Ibid., 8.
31. See Murdoch, *Metaphysics*, especially chap. 7.
32. Ibid., 32.
33. Murdoch, *Metaphysics*, 275.
34. Murdoch, *Sovereignty of Good*, 23.
35. Ibid.
36. Ibid.
37. Ibid., 32.
38. Ibid.
39. Ibid.
40. As I noted in the last chapter, Murdoch identifies certain beliefs (e.g., the idea of the private mental event, the idea of perfection, the idea of the individual) as ideal end-points or "regulative ideals" in the sense they act as implicit guides to moral perception. The idea of perfection is implicit in M's reflection on D.
41. Ibid., 29.
42. Ibid., 28.
43. Ibid., 29.
44. Ibid.
45. Ibid.
46. Ibid.
47. Ibid., 25.
48. Ibid., 29.
49. Ibid., 25.
50. Ibid.
51. Ibid., 26.
52. Ibid.
53. Ibid., 33.
54. Ibid.
55. Ibid., 34.
56. Ibid., 32.

57. Iris Murdoch, "The Darkness of Practical Reason," *Encounter* 27 (July 1966): 49.

58. Ibid., 28.

59. Ibid.

60. Murdoch, *Sovereignty of Good*, 25.

61. Ibid., 30.

62. Ibid., 28.

63. Ibid., 42.

64. Iris Murdoch, "Against Dryness: A Polemical Sketch," in *Revisions: Changing Perspectives in Moral Philosophy*, ed. Stanley Hauerwas and Alasdair MacIntyre (Notre Dame, Ind.: University of Notre Dame Press, 1983), 46.

65. Ibid.

66. Iris Murdoch, "The Sublime and the Good," *Chicago Review* 13 (Autumn 1959), 52.

67. Ibid.

68. Iris Murdoch, "The Sublime and the Beautiful Revisited," *Yale Review* 49 (December 1959), 254.

69. Ibid., 253.

70. Ibid., 254.

71. Ibid.

72. Ibid.

73. Ibid.

74. Ibid., 255.

75. Ibid.

76. Ibid.

77. The conceptual dyads of convention and neurosis, and Ordinary Language Man and Totalitarian Man will be addressed again in Chapter 6 in terms of their applicability to current thought.

78. Murdoch, "The Sublime and the Good," 52.

79. Murdoch, "The Sublime and the Beautiful Revisited," 250.

80. Ibid., 248.

81. Ibid.

82. Murdoch, "The Sublime and the Good," 51. It might be objected against Murdoch's reading that Kant does allow for respect for the existing person. But Kant is asking about the *origin* of respect and finds it in the universal reason that all agents share. Murdoch seems to want to block this "universalizing" move as a mitigation of respect for the radically contingent other. In contrast to Kant, she appears to hold that respect for the other is a self-evident first principle and requires no origin or justification.

83. Murdoch, "The Sublime and the Beautiful Revisited," 248.

84. Murdoch, "The Sublime and the Good," 52.

85. Murdoch, "The Sublime and the Beautiful Revisited," 268.

86. I have noted the significance of such end-points as guides to perception at several points.

87. Ibid., 250.

88. Ibid.

89. Ibid.

90. Iris Murdoch, "The Novelist as Metaphysician," *Listener* 43 (16 March 1950), 473.

91. Murdoch, "The Sublime and the Beautiful Revisited," 250.

92. Ibid.

93. Ibid.

94. Ibid., 250–251.

95. Ibid., 251.

96. Ibid.

97. Ibid.

98. Ibid., 252.

99. Ibid.

100. Ibid., 251.

101. Ibid.

102. Ibid., 267.

103. Although Murdoch does not cite her sources, her "non-hedonistic" reading of Mill in these passages seems indebted to the Mill of *On Liberty* rather than to the Mill of *Utilitarianism*. By neglecting to raise the issue of sentience in her interpretation of Mill, Murdoch avoids the problem she encountered in Kant's thought—her sense that respect for the radically contingent individual was being mitigated by the appeal to a universal value shared by all individuals.

104. Murdoch, "Against Dryness," 50.

105. Murdoch, "The Sublime and the Beautiful Revisited," 251–252.

106. Ibid., 252.

107. Ibid., 251.

108. Ibid., 249.

109. Ibid., 251.

110. Ibid., 269.

111. Murdoch, "The Sublime and the Good," 52.

112. Murdoch, "The Sublime and the Beautiful Revisited," 257.

113. Murdoch, "Against Dryness," 47.

114. Murdoch, "The Sublime and the Beautiful Revisited," 264.

115. Ibid., 265.

116. Ibid., 266.

117. Ibid., 264.

118. Ibid.

119. Ibid., 266.

120. Ibid., 265.

121. Ibid., 266.

122. Ibid., 265.

123. Ibid., 266.

124. Ibid., 265.

125. Ibid.

126. Iris Murdoch, "Existentialists and Mystics: A Note on the Novel in the New Utilitarian Age," in *Essays & Poems Presented to Lord David Cecil*, ed. W. W. Robson (London: Constable, 1970), 170.

127. Ibid., 169.

128. Murdoch, "The Sublime and the Beautiful Revisited," 266.

129. Ibid., 267.

130. Ibid.

131. Ibid., 257.

132. Ibid.

133. Murdoch, "Against Dryness," 47.

134. Murdoch, "The Sublime and the Beautiful Revisited," 257.

135. Ibid., 262.

136. Ibid., 257.

137. Ibid., 262.

138. Ibid., 257.

139. Ibid., 269.

140. Iris Murdoch, "Metaphysics and Ethics," in *The Nature of Metaphysics*, ed. D. F. Pears (London: Macmillan & Co. Ltd., 1960), 116.

141. Murdoch, "Against Dryness," 46.

142. Murdoch, "Metaphysics and Ethics," 117.

143. Ibid., 115.

144. Iris Murdoch, *Sartre, Romantic Rationalist* (London: Bowes & Bowes, 1953), 55.

145. "[D]eterminism as a total philosophical theory is not the enemy. Determinism as a philosophical theory is quite unproven." See *Sovereignty of Good*, 52.

Chapter 5: The Idea of the Good and the Transformation of Agency

1. The term is William Schweiker's. See his *Responsibility and Christian Ethics* (Cambridge: Cambridge University Press, 1995). For a condensed statement of this position see also Schweiker, "Radical Interpretation and Moral Responsibility" in *Power, Value, and Conviction: Theological Ethics in the Postmodern Age* (Cleveland: Pilgrim Press, 1998), 91–110.

2. Ibid., 3–4.

3. Iris Murdoch, "Metaphysics and Ethics," in *The Nature of Metaphysics*, ed. D. F. Pears (London: Macmillan & Co. Ltd., 1960), 100.

4. See for example Sabina Lovibond, *Realism and Imagination in Ethics* (Minneapolis: The University of Minnesota Press, 1993).

5. Ibid., 63.

6. For a discussion of the "first-person standpoint" in the history of thought, see Charles Taylor, *Sources of the Self* (Cambridge: Harvard University Press, 1989), 133.

7. Ibid., 510.

8. Murdoch characterizes her position as "a kind of inconclusive nondogmatic naturalism" in *The Sovereignty of Good*, 44.

9. This account is based on the article on "Naturalism" by Charles R. Pidgen in on *A Companion to Ethics*, ed. Peter Singer (Cambridge, Mass.: Basil Blackwell Ltd., 1991), 421–437.

10. Murdoch, "Metaphysics and Ethics," 100.

11. Iris Murdoch, *Metaphysics as a Guide to Morals* (New York: Allen Lane/The Penguin Press, 1992), 44.

12. G. E. Moore, *Principia Ethica* (London: Cambridge University Press, 1929), 9–10.

13. Ibid., 7–10.

14. Ibid., 9.

15. Murdoch, *Metaphysics*, 44.

16. Ibid., 44.

17. See Murdoch, "Metaphysics and Ethics," 120.

18. Murdoch, *Sovereignty of Good*, 26.

19. Quoted in Murdoch, *Metaphysics*, 44.

20. Murdoch, *Sovereignty of Good*, 29.

21. Ibid., 42.

22. Murdoch engages many aspects of the history of interpretation of the

proof in chapters 13 and 14 of *Metaphysics as a Guide to Morals*. It is worth noting that Murdoch is not alone in her use of the ontological proof in contemporary ethics, but her interpretation is nevertheless unique. See for example William Schweiker, *Responsibility and Christian Ethics*.

23. For a useful overview of the history of interpretation of the proof, see Arthur C. McGill, "Recent Discussion of Anselm's Argument," in *The Many-Faced Argument: Recent Studies on the Ontological Argument for the Existence of God*, ed. John Hick and Arthur C. McGill (New York: Macmillan Company, 1967), 33–110.

24. Taylor, *Sources of the Self*, 140.

25. Ibid.

26. Ibid., 141.

27. Other reflexive realists would identify a different subjective correlate to the idea of the good than self-consciousness. For example, Charles Taylor identifies human articulacy rather than consciousness, while William Schweiker identifies the power to act. These give rise to different interpretations of the ontological proof, though the reflexive structure of the proof is affirmed by each of these thinkers.

28. This line of interpretation has been pursued by Charles Hartshorne and Norman Malcolm. See McGill, *The Many-Faced Argument*.

29. Murdoch, *Metaphysics*, 395.

30. Ibid.

31. Ibid. Murdoch puts essentially the same argument in the mouth of the character Plato in "Above the Gods" in *Acastos: Two Platonic Dialogues* (New York: Viking Press, 1988).

32. Paul Tillich, *Systematic Theology*, vol. 1 (Chicago: University of Chicago Press, 1951), 207.

33. Ibid., 208.

34. Murdoch, *Metaphysics*, 395–396.

35. Ibid., 425.

36. Murdoch, *Sovereignty of Good*, 70.

37. "Anselm's Apologetic," in *Saint Anselm: Basic Writings*, trans. S. N. Deane, with an introduction by Charles Hartshorne (La Salle, Ill.: Open Court Publishing Co., 2nd ed., 1962), 167.

38. Murdoch, *Sovereignty of Good*, 61–62.

39. Murdoch, *Metaphysics*, 295.

40. Iris Murdoch, *The Fire and the Sun: Why Plato Banished the Artists* (Oxford: Clarendon Press, 1977), 81. I have explored Murdoch's account of moral change in an as yet unpublished essay, ""Moral Change and the Magnetism of the Good."

41. Murdoch, *Metaphysics*, 110.

42. Murdoch, *Sovereignty of Good*, 50.

43. Ibid., 48.

44. Ibid., 47.

45. Ibid., 43–44.

46. Ibid., 52.

47. Ibid.

48. Ibid., 51.

49. David J. Gordon, *Iris Murdoch's Fables of Unselfing* (Columbia: University of Missouri Press, 1995), 61.

50. Ibid., 68.
51. Murdoch, *Metaphysics*, 250.
52. Ibid.
53. Ibid., 148.
54. Ibid., 250.
55. Ibid., 177.
56. Ibid.
57. Gordon, *Fables of Unselfing*, 61.
58. Murdoch, *Sovereignty of Good*, 51.
59. Ibid.
60. Ibid.
61. Ibid.
62. Murdoch, *Metaphysics*, 24.
63. Ibid., 24–25.
64. Murdoch, *Metaphysics*, 24.
65. Murdoch, *Sovereignty of Good*, 84.
66. Ibid., 54.
67. Ibid., 51.
68. Ibid., 52.
69. Ibid., 67.
70. Ibid., 78–79.
71. Ibid., 68.
72. Ibid.
73. Ibid., 55.
74. Ibid., 31.
75. Ibid., 84. For an attempt to develop a Murdochian model of *askesis* in the context of contemporary ethics, see my "Contemporary Forms of *Askesis* and the Return of Spiritual Exercises in *The Annual of the Society of Christian Ethics*, vol. 18 (1998): 69–92.
76. Ibid.
77. Ibid., 70.
78. Ibid., 84.
79. Ibid., 67–68.
80. Ibid., 85.
81. Ibid., 84.
82. Ibid., 85.
83. Ibid., 88.
84. Ibid., 89.
85. Ibid.
86. Ibid.
87. Ibid., 90.
88. Ibid.
89. Ibid., 41.
90. Ibid., 85.
91. Ibid.
92. Ibid., 86.
93. Ibid., 87–88.
94. Ibid., 59.
95. Ibid., 64. This concern to approach the work of art objectively recalls Sartre's discussion of the "ethics" of reading in *What is Literature?* For

Sartre as for Murdoch, the work of art requires a moral discipline, a "purging" of selfish emotion on the part of the reader or spectator in order to disclose the objective value of the work itself. See my argument in Chapter 3.

96. Murdoch, *Sovereignty of Good*, 64.

97. Ibid., 65.

98. Ibid., 59.

99. Ibid., 65.

100. Ibid., 59.

101. Ibid., 65–66.

102. See Dipple, *Iris Murdoch: Work for the Spirit* (Chicago: University of Chicago Press, 1982), 30.

103. Ibid., 5.

104. Murdoch, *Sovereignty of Good*, 93.

105. Ibid., 87.

106. Ibid., 91.

107. Ibid., 37.

108. Ibid., 17.

109. Ibid., 34.

110. Ibid., 23.

111. Ibid., 18–19.

112. Ibid., 23.

113. Ibid., 90–91.

114. David Gordon, for example, argues that the highest form of unselfing in Murdoch's novels is that of the saint or mystic, which demands "nothing less than the death of the ego." See Gordon, *Fables of Unselfing*, 10.

115. Dipple, *Work for the Spirit*, 46.

116. Conradi, *The Saint and the Artist*, x.

117. Ibid., 64.

118. Ibid., 69.

119. Ibid., 70.

120. In this respect, my analysis of Murdoch as a reflexive thinker provides a coherent reading of her moral thought. It identifies the basic feature linking her philosophy and her fiction as the assumption that human beings are imaginative moral agents whose capacity for imagination may block the truth or provide access to it. I discuss Murdoch's concept of imagination later in this chapter. For a more detailed analysis of imagination in the context of her relation to Kant and Plato, see my essay "Imagining the Good: Iris Murdoch's Godless Theology" in *The Annual of the Society of Christian Ethics*, vol. 16 (1996): 223–242.

121. Murdoch, *Sovereignty of Good*, 103.

122. Murdoch, *Metaphysics as a Guide to Morals*, 344.

123. This identification of eros as the most basic dimension in the reflexive structure of human thought distinguishes Murdoch's position from that of other reflexive thinkers. For example, Descartes identified the pure thinking cogito as the primordial moment in his reflexive position; Kant identified the experience of self-legislating reason; for Charles Taylor, the primordial moment is human articulacy about value; for William Schweiker, it is the power to act. Each of these represents a different account of how objective reality is mediated through the structures of human subjectivity.

124. Murdoch, *Metaphysics as a Guide to Morals*, 241–242.

125. For a concise account of this distinction, see Schweiker, *Responsibility and Christian Ethics*, 142–148.

126. Ibid., 143.

127. Ibid., 146.

128. Ibid., 145.

129. Ibid., 146.

130. Ibid., 147.

131. Ibid. For the discussion of radical interpretation, see chap. 7, esp. 175–181.

132. Ibid., 146.

133. Ibid., 147.

134. Murdoch writes: "Freedom is not strictly the exercise of the will, but rather the experience of accurate vision which, when this becomes appropriate, occasions action." See *Sovereignty of Good*, 67.

135. Ibid.

136. Schweiker, *Responsibility and Christian Ethics*, 142.

137. Murdoch, *Metaphysics*, 293.

138. This typology is based on Taylor's discussion in *Sources of the Self*, 137–139.

139. This summary is based on the discussion of moral motivation in Singer, *A Companion to Ethics*. See the article on "Intuitionism," 411–420.

140. This assumption is based on Humean moral psychology, as noted in Singer, 414.

141. Murdoch, *Sovereignty of Good*, 66.

142. Ibid., 54.

143. Ibid., 37.

144. Ibid., 39.

145. Ibid.

146. Ibid., 39–40.

147. For a discussion of the Socratic position in this context, see Taylor, *Sources of the Self*, 138 and Singer, *Companion to Ethics*, 126.

148. Taylor, *Sources of the Self*, 139.

149. Murdoch, *Sovereignty of Good*, 40.

150. Ibid., 44.

151. Taylor, *Sources of the Self*, 138.

152. Ibid.

153. Ibid., 137.

154. Ibid., 138.

155. Ibid.

156. Ibid., 139.

157. The *locus classicus* of this problem in the Christian tradition is St. Paul's epistle to the Romans. For an incisive analysis of the problem of *akrasia* as a problem of the reflexivity of the will, see Hans Jonas, "The Abyss of the Will: Philosophical Meditation on the Seventh Chapter of Paul's Epistle to the Romans" in *Philosophical Essays: From Ancient Creed to Technological Man* (Englewood Cliffs, N.J.: Prentice-Hall, 1974).

158. Taylor, *Sources of the Self*, 136.

159. Ibid., 139.

160. Ibid., 138.

161. Ibid.

162. Murdoch, *Sovereignty of Good*, 40.

163. Ibid., 44.

164. Ibid., 40.

165. Taylor, *Sources of the Self*, 144.

166. Murdoch, *Sovereignty of Good*, 90.

167. Taylor, *Sources of the Self*, 138–39.

168. Iris Murdoch, "The Darkness of Practical Reason." *Encounter* 27 (July 1966): 49.

169. Ibid.

170. Murdoch, *Sovereignty of Good*, 37.

171. Ibid.

172. Murdoch, "Darkness of Practical Reason," 48.

173. Ibid., 49.

174. Ibid., 48.

175. Ibid.

176. Ibid., 49. This dimension of imagination indicates why Murdoch's position may be subject to the charge of "bad faith." Critics have generally neglected Murdoch's account of imagination in their exclusive focus on the role of vision in her thought.

177. For a particularity trenchant analysis of this circularity in the context of Pauline thought, see Jonas, "The Abyss of the Will," esp. 342–345.

178. Ibid., 49–50.

179. I.e., in the title of her article noted earlier.

180. Taylor, *Sources of the Self*, 139.

181. Ibid.

182. Ibid.

183. Murdoch, *Sovereignty of Good*, 40.

184. Ibid., 43.

185. Ibid.

186. Ibid.

187. Ibid.

188. Ibid.

189. Plato, for example, proposed such a division in the differing agendas of the *Republic* and the *Laws*. Seen in this light, Murdoch's attempt to articulate a public morality of rules and axioms is her response to the Plato of the *Laws*; but the question of the relation of this account to her general moral theory is precisely what is under investigation here.

190. Murdoch, *Metaphysics*, 356.

191. Ibid., 391.

192. Ibid., 349. This concern to integrate an account of the inner life of the moral agent into an account of public morality reaffirms Murdoch's placement as a critic of liberal procedural ethics. That is, she attempts to integrate an account of the self as concrete individual, and not merely as a subject of procedural rationality, into her theory of politics.

193. Iris Murdoch, "Art and Eros: A Dialogue about Art" in *Acastos: Two Platonic Dialogues* (New York: Viking Penguin Inc., 1986), 31.

194. Although it is risky to identify Murdoch with any of her fictional characters, Socrates' position on the role of the artist as "teller of secrets" is

close to some of Murdoch's own statements on the art of novel writing. Thus there is good reason to believe that his view represents her position on morality as well.

195. I owe this insight to William Schweiker. For a more extended analysis of the structure of this text, especially with respect to the relation between its form and its content, see Maria Antonaccio, "Form and Contingency in Murdoch's Ethics" and also David Tracy, "The Many Faces of Platonism," in *Iris Murdoch and the Search for Human Goodness*, ed. Maria Antonaccio and William Schweiker (Chicago: University of Chicago Press, 1996).

196. Murdoch, *Metaphysics*, 293.

197. Ibid., 367.

198. Ibid., 302.

199. Murdoch, *Sovereignty of Good*, 43.

200. Murdoch, *Metaphysics*, 303.

201. Ibid.

202. This was in fact Murdoch's critique of Sartre's voluntarist notion of freedom, i.e., that it represented moral choice as a leap without a background in consciousness as the unavoidable condition for moral choice.

203. Ibid., 304.

204. Ibid., 301.

205. Ibid., 294.

206. Ibid., 303.

207. Ibid., 302.

208. Ibid.

209. Ibid., 348.

210. Ibid., 300.

211. The Kantian aspects of this account of duty and the will are obvious. This whole discussion of the relation between duty and consciousness in fact testifies to Murdoch's conviction that the deepest aspects of Western moral philosophy lie in a dialogue between Kant and Plato. See *Metaphysics*, 57.

212. Ibid., 351.

213. Ibid., 366.

214. Ibid., 356.

215. Ibid.

216. Ibid., 381.

217. Ibid.

218. Ibid., 360.

219. Ibid., 356.

220. For Murdoch's discussion of the various types of individual, including the Hobbesian individual of classical liberal theory, the modern individual of capitalist society, the Romantic man, the authentic hero, the mystic, the demonic individual, and so forth, in the context of her theory of politics, see ibid., 350–355.

221. Ibid., 365.

222. Ibid., 364. This concern to preserve the value of the individual as "real impenetrable human person" is central to the type of liberalism Murdoch proposed from the beginning of her career. "That this person is substantial, impenetrable, individual, indefinable, and valuable is after all the fundamental tenet of Liberalism." See Iris Murdoch, "Against Dryness: A Polemical Sketch," in *Revisions: Changing Perspectives in Moral Philosophy*, ed. Stanley Hauerwas

and Alasdair MacIntyre (Notre Dame, Ind.: University of Notre Dame Press, 1983), 50.

223. Ibid.

224. Murdoch describes the axiomatic nature of this value as follows: "Human beings are valuable not because they are created by God or because they are rational beings or good citizens, but because they are human beings." See Ibid., 365.

225. Ibid., 386.

226. Ibid., 363.

227. Ibid., 381.

228. The following passage is illustrative: "It is an essential liberal idea that the Utopian concept of a perfect state, even as a distant vision, is radically misleading and damaging. Society, and so the state, *cannot* be perfected, although perfection is a proper ideal or magnet for the individual as moral agent. We set aside the idea of perfection in the one case, not in the other." See Ibid., 356.

229. Ibid., 350.

230. Ibid., 357.

231. Ibid.

232. Ibid., 390.

233. Ibid., 322. Murdoch's undeveloped suggestions about the role of imagination in the context of politics invite comparison with the effort of some feminist critics of liberalism, notably Seyla Benhabib, to revise liberal proceduralist ethics in order to account for the deliberation of moral agents as both "generalized" and "concrete others." See Benhabib, *Situating the Self: Gender, Community and Postmodernism in Contemporary Ethics*, chap. 5 (New York: Routledge, 1992).

234. Murdoch, *Metaphysics*, 322.

235. Ibid., 362.

Chapter 6: Prospects for Murdochian Ethnics

1. I have written on some of these topics elsewhere. See "Imagining the Good: Iris Murdoch's Godless Theology." *The Annual of the Society of Christian Ethics*, vol. 16 (1996): 223–242; and "Contemporary Forms of *Askesis* and the Return of Spiritual Exercises," *The Annual of the Society of Christian Ethics*, vol. 18 (1998): 69–92; and "The Consolations of Literature," *The Journal of Religion* (forthcoming).

2. See Iris Murdoch, *The Sovereignty of Good* (London: Routledge & Kegan Paul, 1970), 50, 56–57.

3. Iris Murdoch, *Metaphysics as a Guide to Morals* (New York: Allen Lane/The Penguin Press, 1992), 153.

4. This conception of validation is based on Charles Taylor's contention that a valid ethical position leads "from one's interlocutor's position to one's own via some error-reducing moves, such as the clearing up of a confusion, the resolving of a contradiction, or the frank acknowledgment of what really does impinge." See Charles Taylor, *Sources of the Self: The Making of the Modern Identity* (Cambridge: Harvard University Press, 1989), 505. For a more developed account of ethical justification that includes intersubjective demands on validation, see William Schweiker, *Responsibility and Christian Ethics* (Cambridge: Cambridge University Press, 1995), 217–222.

5. The terms of my analysis in these pages have been influenced by William Schweiker's typology of theories of responsibility in his *Responsibility and Christian Ethics*, esp. 78–94.

6. See, *Metaphysics* 356.

7. The ambiguity of Murdoch's position on the relation between morals and politics invites further analysis in the context of contemporary debates over the adequacy of liberal proceduralist ethics and question of the good and the right. Although I cannot engage these debates here, an important question for Murdoch's position is whether she is attempting to formulate a model of "political legitimacy" or one of "moral validity" or both at once. For this distinction as well as a useful discussion of contemporary debates in political theory on this point, see Seyla Benhabib, *Situating the Self: Gender, Community and Postmodernism in Contemporary Ethics* (New York: Routledge, 1992), esp. chap. 1.

8. See Stanley Hauerwas, "The Significance of Vision: Toward an Aesthetic Ethic" in *Vision and Virtue: Essays in Christian Ethical Reflection* (Notre Dame, Ind.: University of Notre Dame Press, 1981). For Hauerwas's most recent treatment of Murdoch's thought, in which he assumes a critical and ironic stance towards his earlier position, see his "Murdochian Muddles: Can We Get Through Them If God Does Not Exist?" in *Iris Murdoch and the Search for Human Goodness*, ed. Maria Antonaccio and William Schweiker (Chicago: University of Chicago Press, 1996).

9. This point recalls the claim of narrative ethicists that there can be no account of the moral self apart from the practices of the particular community that forms its identity. However, narrative ethicists such as Hauerwas tend to draw their assumptions from Wittgenstein's theory of language rather than from French poststructuralism. While Wittgenstein challenges the notion of the autonomous user of language by appealing to a social community of language users, poststructuralism denies the very notion of a subject of language in favor of the primacy of linguistic structure over subjectivity. For an analysis of these differences, see Benhabib, *Situating the Self*, 208–209.

10. Ibid., 208.

11. She criticizes these latter two philosophies in particular as advancing a form of linguistic monism, idealism, or determinism that effaces the reality of the individual in impersonal systems of language. See *Metaphysics*, 185.

12. Ibid., 194.

13. Murdoch, *Metaphysics*, 159.

14. Ibid., 193.

15. Ibid., 216.

16. Ibid., 268.

17. Ibid., 194.

18. Charles Taylor, "Language and Human Nature" in *Human Agency and Language: Philosophical Papers 1* (Cambridge: Cambridge University Press, 1985), 238.

19. Ibid., 246.

20. Charles E. Winquist, *Desiring Theology* (Chicago: University of Chicago Press, 1995), 10.

21. Ibid.

22. Ibid., 11.

23. Ibid., 10.

24. Ibid.

25. Ibid., 11.

26. Charles Taylor and William Schweiker have explored this terrain by tracing the development of different theories of language and correlating them with changing conceptions of subjectivity and the human good. See Taylor, "Language and Human Nature" in *Human Agency and Language: Philosophical Papers* vol. I, and Schweiker, "Consciousness and the Good: Schleiermacher and Contemporary Theological Ethics" in *Theology Today*, vol. 56, no. 2 (July, 1999): 180–186.

27. Schweiker, "Consciousness and the Good," 188.

28. Charles Taylor, "Introduction" in *Human Agency and Language*, 10.

29. Ibid.

30. Ibid.

31. Ibid., 8.

32. Taylor, "Language and Human Nature," 232.

33. Ibid., 231.

34. As Taylor puts it: "Language originally comes to us from others, from a community. But how much does it remain an activity essentially bound to a community?" Ibid., 237.

35. Ibid., my emphasis.

36. As Benhabib observes, the subject is replaced by "the community of selves whose identity extends as far as their horizon of interpretations (Gadamer) or it is a social community of actual language users (Wittgenstein)." See Benhabib, *Situating the Self*, 208–209.

37. Schweiker, "Consciousness and the Good," 184.

38. Taylor, "Introduction," 10.

39. Ibid.

40. Murdoch, *Metaphysics as a Guide to Morals*, 188.

41. Benhabib, *Situating the Subject*, 209.

42. Schweiker refers to this as the "inflation" of language. See "Consciousness and the Good," 184.

43. See Anthony Giddens, *Modernity and Self-Identity: Self and Society in the Late Modern Age* (Stanford: Stanford University Press, 1991).

44. Schweiker, "Consciousness and the Good," 194.

45. Giddens, 144.

46. Ibid.

47. Ibid.

48. Ibid., 8.

49. Ibid., 149.

50. For an attempt to articulate an account of freedom as rational dissent within a Wittgensteinian account of moral realism, see Sabina Lovibond, *Realism and Imagination in Ethics* (Minneapolis: University of Minnesota Press, 1983). Lovibond denies that grounding moral truth in the intellectual authority-relations within a language community necessarily prohibits the possibility of rational dissent from the community. See especially her critique of Bradley, 166–169.

51. Martha Nussbaum, "Love and Vision" in *Iris Murdoch and the Search for Human Goodness*, ed. Maria Antonaccio and William Schweiker (Chicago: University of Chicago Press, 1996), 36.

52. In this respect, Murdoch's positions bears some resemblance to the thought of Emmanuel Levinas. See especially *Totality and Infinity*, trans. Alphonso Lingis (Pittsburgh: Duquesne University Press, 1969). As Schweiker

notes, the Levinasian self comes to self-consciousness "in being encountered by the claim of an other on me." This encounter, "marked by the imperative 'thou shall not murder me,' is definitive of the ethical. . . . The self exists before the infinite, inescapable demand of the other. . . . Coming to self-awareness is always consciousness of being on trial, accused. Ethics . . . testifies to the event of the other's command." See Schweiker, "Consciousness and the Good," 186. Murdoch would reject the language of command, lordship, and accusation that pervade Levinas's account of the other's claim on the self, and she would likewise resist his constriction of the domain of ethics to the moral "ought." But the effort to reconstitute the ideas of consciousness and the good beyond the drive to totality is a point of resonance between the two thinkers.

53. As the M and D example demonstrates, M's change of heart about D is a process that takes place in consciousness and through language. But this activity is not wholly determined by public or shared uses of language; rather it is subject to M's own history and experience, and composed of reflections which are not in principle available to all members of the language community.

54. See *Metaphysics*, 185.

55. For example, her conception of metaphysics as a "picturing" activity; her critique of the fact-value distinction; her account of the shaping role of concepts in moral thinking; her insistence on the evaluative nature of language and consciousness—all of these indicate that Murdoch would grant the constitutive power of language.

56. Werhane makes this comment in a discussion of Wittgenstein in her essay "Levinas's Ethics: A Normative Perspective without Metaethical Constraints." See *Ethics as First Philosophy: The Significance of Emmanuel Levinas for Philosophy, Literature and Religion*, ed. Adriaan T. Peperzak (New York and London: Routledge, 1995), 61.

57. See Taylor, "Language and Human Nature," 238.

58. Ibid., 238.

59. Ibid.

60. Ibid., 247.

61. Ibid., 239.

62. Ibid.

63. Taylor, "Introduction," 11.

64. Giddens, 8.

65. Ibid., 8. "Such sequestration," Giddens notes, "is the condition of the establishing of large tracts of relative security in day-to-day life in conditions of modernity. Its effect . . . is to *repress a cluster of basic moral and existential components of human life* that are, as it were, squeezed to the sidelines." See 167.

66. Ibid., 8 and see also 167. "Wide areas of day-to-day life, ordered via abstract systems, are secure in Max Weber's sense of providing 'calculable' environment of action. Yet the very routines that provide such security mostly lack moral meaning and can either come to be experienced as 'empty' practices, or alternatively can seem to be overwhelming."

67. Ibid., 24–25.

68. Ibid., 27.

69. Ibid., 24.

70. Ibid., 17–20.

71. Ibid., 20.

72. Ibid., 23.

73. Ibid., 150.

74. See Mark C. Taylor, *Hiding* (Chicago: University of Chicago Press, 1997), 272–273.

75. See Taylor's provocative analysis of virtual reality in *Hiding*, chap. 6, "Interfacing."

76. Ibid., 325.

77. See Schweiker, "Consciousness and the Good," 182–183.

78. Giddens, *Modernity and Self-Identity*, 200.

79. Ibid., 202–203.

80. In addition to obvious fateful moments such as birth and death, Giddens notes that the return of the repressed can be detected in areas of culture as diverse as the contemporary preoccupation with sexuality, the treatment of the mentally ill, and the resurgence of religion. For example, "Sexuality has become separated from procreation and therefore from cosmic processes of life and death. But it still retains a moral charge and a generalisable significance which separates it from the egotistical concerns of the partners. . . . Sexuality both repudiates, and gives substantive form to the involvement of human life with morally transcendent conditions and experience." In the case of religion, he writes, "new forms of religion and spirituality represent in a most basic sense a return of the repressed, since they directly address issues of the moral meaning of existence which modern institutions so thoroughly tend to dissolve." See Ibid., 206–207.

81. Ibid., 208.

82. Ibid.

83. Murdoch, *Sovereignty of Good*, 30.

84. Ibid., 168.

85. Ibid., 167.

86. Ibid., 175.

87. Ibid.

88. Ibid., 175–176.

89. Giddens, *Modernity and Self-Identity*, 200.

90. Ibid., 199.

91. Giddens illustrates this point with evidence from the evolution in modes of family life in late modernity. See, for example, ibid., 177.

92. Giddens makes a similar point in a different context. See ibid., 209.

93. Murdoch, *Sovereignty of Good*, 99.

94. Murdoch, *Metaphysics*, 57.

95. Mark C. Taylor, *Hiding*, 314.

96. Murdoch, *Sovereignty of Good*, 59.

97. Murdoch, *Metaphysics*, 190.

98. Ibid., 165.

99. Murdoch, "Above the Gods: A Dialogue about Religion" in *Acastos* (New York: Viking Penguin, 1986), 88.

SELECTED BIBLIOGRAPHY

The following bibliography represents the major sources consulted for the research and writing of this book. For the most comprehensive bibliography on Iris Murdoch currently available, see John Fletcher and Cheryl Bove, *Iris Murdoch: A Descriptive Primary and Annotated Secondary Bibliography* (New York: Garland Publishing, 1994). Many of Murdoch's essays have now been collected in a single volume. See *Existentialists and Mystics: Writings on Philosophy and Literature*, ed. Peter Conradi (New York: Allen Lane/The Penguin Press, 1997).

I. Works by Iris Murdoch

A. Philosophy, Criticism, and Letters

Acastos: Two Platonic Dialogues. New York: Viking Penguin, 1986.
"Against Dryness: A Polemical Sketch." In *Revisions: Changing Perspectives in Moral Philosophy*, edited by Stanley Hauerwas and Alasdair MacIntyre, 43–50. Notre Dame, Ind.: University of Notre Dame Press, 1983.
"Art is the Imitation of Nature." *Cahiers du Centre de Recherches sur les pays du Nord et du Nord-Ouest* 1 (1978): 5–18.
"The Darkness of Practical Reason." Review of *The Freedom of the Individual*, by Stuart Hampshire. *Encounter* 27 (July 1966): 46–50.
"T. S. Eliot as a Moralist." In *T. S. Eliot: A Symposium for his Seventieth Birthday*, edited by Neville Braybrooke, 152–60. London: Rupert Hart-David, 1958.
"Existentialist Bite." Review of *Literature Considered as Philosophy*, by Everett Knight. *Spectator* (12 July 1957): 68–69.
"The Existentialist Hero." *Listener* (23 March 1950): 523–524.
"The Existentialist Political Myth." *Socratic* 5 (1952): 52–63.
"Existentialists and Mystics: A Note on the Novel in the New Utilitarian Age." In *Essays and Poems Presented to Lord David Cecil*, edited by W. W. Robson, 169–183. London: Constable, 1970.
The Fire and the Sun: Why Plato Banished the Artists. Oxford: Clarendon Press, 1977.

"Freedom and Knowledge." Symposium with S. N. Hampshire, P. L. Gardiner, and D. F. Pears. In *Freedom and the Will*, edited by D. F. Pears, 80–104. New York: St. Martin's Press, 1963.

"Hegel in Modern Dress." Review of *Being and Nothingness*, by Jean-Paul Sartre. *New Statesman* LIII (25 May 1957): 675–676.

"A House of Theory." *Partisan Review* 26, Winter 1959: 17–31.

"Important Things." Review of *The Mandarins*, by Simone de Beauvoir. In *Encore: The Sunday Times Book*, edited by Leonard Russell, 299–301. London: Michael Joseph, 1963.

"Knowing the Void." Review of *Notebooks*, by Simone Weil. *Spectator* (2 November 1956): 613–614.

"Let them Philosophise." Review of *Confessions of an Inquiring Spirit*, by S. T. Coleridge. *Spectator* (14 Dec. 1956): 873.

"Mass, Might, and Myth." Review of *Crowds and Power*, by Elias Canetti. *Spectator* CCIX (7 September 1962): 337–338.

"Metaphysics and Ethics." In *The Nature of Metaphysics*, edited by D. F. Pears, 99–123. London: Macmillan & Company, 1960.

Metaphysics as a Guide to Morals. New York: Allen Lane/The Penguin Press, 1992.

"Midnight Hour." *Adelphi* (January-March 1943): 60–61.

"The Moral Decision about Homosexuality." *Man and Society* VII (Summer 1964): 3–6.

"Negative Capability." *Adam International Review* 284–286 (1960): 172–173.

"Nostalgia for the Particular." *Proceedings of the Aristotelian Society* 52 (9 June 1952): 243–260.

"The Novelist as Metaphysician." *Listener* 43 (16 March 1950): 473–476.

"Philosophy and Beliefs." Symposium with Stuart Hampshire, Isaiah Berlin, and Anthony Quinton. *Twentieth Century* (June 1955): 495–521.

"Political Morality." *Listener* 78 (21 September 1967): 353–354.

"Rebirth of Christianity." *Adelphi* (July-Sep. 1943): 134–135.

"Salvation by Words." *New York Review of Books* 18 (15 June 1972): 3–8.

Sartre, Romantic Rationalist. London: Bowes & Bowes, 1953.

Sartre, Romantic Rationalist. With a new introduction by the author. New York: Viking Penguin, first American ed., 1987.

"Socialism and Selection." In *Black Paper 1975*, edited by C. B. Cox and Rhodes Boyson, 7–9. London: Dent, 1975.

The Sovereignty of Good. London: Routledge & Kegan Paul, 1970.

"The Sublime and the Beautiful Revisited." *Yale Review* 49, December 1959: 247–271.

"The Sublime and the Good." *Chicago Review* 13 (Autumn 1959) 42–55.

"Thinking and Language." Symposium with A. C. Lloyd and Gilbert Ryle. *Proceedings of the Aristotelian Society* suppl. vol. 25 (1951): 25–82.

Untitled review of *The Ethics of Ambiguity*, by Simone de Beauvoir. *Mind* LIX (April 1950): 127–128.

Untitled review of *The Emotions, Outline of a Theory*, by Jean-Paul Sartre. *Mind* LIX (April 1950): 268–271.

"Vision and Choice in Morality." *Proceedings of the Aristotelian Society* suppl. vol. 30 (1956): 32–58.

"Worship and Common Life." *Adelphi* (July-September 1944): 134–135.

B. Novels

Under the Net. London, 1954.
The Flight from the Enchanter. London, 1956.
The Sandcastle. London, 1957.
The Bell. London, 1958.
A Severed Head. London, 1961.
An Unofficial Rose. London, 1962.
The Unicorn. London, 1963.
The Italian Girl. London, 1964.
The Red and the Green. London, 1965.
The Time of the Angels. London, 1966.
The Nice and the Good. London, 1968.
Bruno's Dream. London, 1969.
A Fairly Honourable Defeat. London, 1970.
An Accidental Man. London, 1971.
The Black Prince. London, 1973.
The Sacred and Profane Love Machine. London, 1974.
A Word Child. London, 1975.
Henry and Cato. London, 1976.
The Sea, the Sea. London, 1978.
Nuns and Soldiers. London, 1980.
The Philosopher's Pupil. London, 1983.
The Good Apprentice. London, 1985.
The Book and the Brotherhood. London, 1987
The Message to the Planet. London, 1989.
The Green Knight. London, 1993.
Jackson's Dilemma. London, 1995.

II. Critical Commentary

A. Monographs and Edited Collections

Antonaccio, Maria, and William Schweiker, eds. *Iris Murdoch and the Search for Human Goodness.* Chicago: University of Chicago Press, 1996.

Baldanza, Frank. *Iris Murdoch.* New York: Twayne Publishers, 1974.

Bloom, Harold, ed. *Iris Murdoch.* Modern Critical Views. New York: Chelsea, 1986.

Bove, Cheryl. *Understanding Iris Murdoch.* Columbia, S. C.: University of South Carolina Press, 1993.

Byatt, A. S. *Degrees of Freedom: The Novels of Iris Murdoch.* London: Chatto & Windus and New York: Barnes & Noble, 1965.

————. *Iris Murdoch.* Writers and Their Work. London: Longman Group for the British Council, 1976.

Chevalier, Jean-Louis, ed. "Rencontres avec Iris Murdoch." *Centre de Recherches de Littérature et Linguistique des Pays de Langue Anglaise.* University de Caen, France, 1978.

Conradi, Peter J. *Iris Murdoch: The Saint and the Artist.* New York: St. Martin's Press, 1986.

————, ed. *Existentialists and Mystics: Writings on Philosophy and Literature.* New York: Allen Lane/The Penguin Press, 1997.

Dipple, Elizabeth. *Iris Murdoch: Work for the Spirit*. Chicago: University of Chicago Press, 1982.

Gerstenberger, Donna. *Iris Murdoch*. Irish Writers Series. Lewisburg, Pa.: Bucknell University Press and London: Associated University Presses, 1975.

Gordon, David J. *Iris Murdoch's Fables of Unselfing*. Columbia, Mo.: University of Missouri Press, 1995.

Johnson, Deborah. *Iris Murdoch*. Brighton: Harvester, 1987.

Rabinovitz, Rubin. *Iris Murdoch*. Essays on Modern Writers, No. 34. New York: Columbia University Press, 1968.

Ramanathan, Suguna. *Iris Murdoch: Figures of Good*. New York: St. Martin's Press, 1990.

Spear, Hilda D. *Iris Murdoch*. Modern Novelists. New York: St. Martin's Press, 1995.

Todd, Richard. *Iris Murdoch*. Contemporary Writers Series. New York: Methuen, 1984.

———. *Iris Murdoch: The Shakespearian Interest*. New York: Barnes & Noble, 1979.

Wolfe, Peter. *The Disciplined Heart: Iris Murdoch and Her Novels*. Columbia, Mo.: University of Missouri Press, 1966.

B. Reviews and Articles

Allen, Diogenes. Review of *Metaphysics as a Guide to Morals*. *Commonweal* 120 (April 23, 1993): 24.

———. "Two Experiences of Existence: Jean-Paul Sartre and Iris Murdoch." *International Philosophical Quarterly* XIV (June 1974): 181–187.

Antonaccio, Maria. "Contemporary Forms of *Askesis* and the Return of Spiritual Exercises." *The Annual of the Society of Christian Ethics*, vol. 18 (1998): 69–92.

———. "Imagining the Good: Iris Murdoch's Godless Theology." *The Annual of the Society of Christian Ethics*, vol. 16 (1996): 223–242.

———. Review of *Metaphysics as a Guide to Morals*. *Journal of Religion* 74 (April 1994): 278–280.

Baldanza, Frank. "Iris Murdoch and the Theory of Personality." *Criticism* VII (Spring 1965): 176–189.

Barrett, D. C. Review of *Metaphysics as a Guide to Morals*. *International Philosophical Quarterly*, XXXIV (March 1994): 111–114.

Blackburn, Simon. "The Good and the Great." Review of *Metaphysics as a Guide to Morals*. *Times Literary Supplement* (October 23, 1992): 3.

Blum, Lawrence A. "Iris Murdoch and the Domain of the Moral." *Philosophical Studies* 50 (1986): 343–367.

Eagleton, Terry. "The Good, the True, the Beautiful." Review of *Metaphysics as a Guide to Morals*. *Guardian* (December 5, 1993): 29.

Hacking, Ian. "Plato's Friend." Review of *Metaphysics as a Guide to Morals*. *London Review of Books* (December 17, 1992): 8–9.

Harrison, Bernard. Review of *Metaphysics as a Guide to Morals*. *Ethics* 103 (April 1995): 653–655.

Kenny, Anthony. "Luciferian Moralists." Review of *The Sovereignty of Good*. *Listener* 85 (7 January 1971): 23.

Lewis, Tess. Review of *Metaphysics as a Guide to Morals*. *American Scholar* 62 (Summer 1993): 466–470.

MacIntyre, Alasdair. "Good for Nothing." Article review of *Iris Murdoch: Work for the Spirit*, by Elizabeth Dipple. *London Review of Books* (3–16 June 1982): 15–16.

———. "Which World Do You See?" Review of *Metaphysics as a Guide to Morals*. *New York Times Book Review* (January 3, 1993): 9.

Majdiak, Daniel. "Romanticism in the Aesthetics of Iris Murdoch." *Texas Studies in Literature and Language* XIV (Summer 1972): 359–375.

O'Sullivan, Kevin. "Iris Murdoch and the Image of Liberal Man." *Yale Literary Magazine* 131 (December 1962): 27–36.

Pondrom, Cyrena N. "Iris Murdoch: An Existentialist?" *Comparative Literature Studies* 5 (December 1968): 403–419.

Quinton, Anthony. "Philosophy and Beliefs," *The Twentieth Century* clvii (June 1955): 495–496.

Rossi, Philip J. Review of *Metaphysics as a Guide to Morals*. *Theological Studies* 54 (December 1993): 762–763.

Sage, Lorna. "The Pursuit of Imperfection." *Critical Quarterly* 19 (Summer 1977): 61–68.

Vickery, John B. "The Dilemmas of Language: Sartre's *La Nausée* and Iris Murdoch's *Under the Net.*" *Journal of Narrative Technique* 1 (May 1971): 69–76.

Warnock, G. J. "The Moralists: Values and Choices." Review of *The Sovereignty of Good*. *Encounter* 36 (April 1971): 81–84.

C. Interviews

Bellamy, Michael. "An Interview with Iris Murdoch." In *Wisconsin Studies in Contemporary Literature* 18 (1977): 129–140.

Bigsby, Christopher. In *The Radical Imagination and the Liberal Tradition: Interviews with English and American Novelists*, edited by Heide Ziegler and Christopher Bigsby. London: Junction Books, 1982, 209–230.

Biles, Jack I. "An Interview with Iris Murdoch." *Studies in the Literary Imagination* XI (Fall 1978): 115–125.

Blow, Simon. "An Interview with Iris Murdoch." *Spectator* (25 September 1976): 24–25.

Bryden, R., with A. S. Byatt. "Talking to Iris Murdoch." *Listener* (4 April 1968): 433–434.

Haffenden, John. In *Novelists in Interview*, edited by John Haffenden. London: Methuen & Co., 1985, 191–209.

Heyd, Ruth. "An Interview with Iris Murdoch." *University of Windsor Review* (Spring 1965), 138–143.

Kermode, Frank. "The House of Fiction: Interviews with Seven English Novelists." *Partisan Review* 30 (Spring 1963): 61–82.

Magee, Bryan. "Philosophy and Literature: Dialogue with Iris Murdoch." In *Men of Ideas: Some Creators of Contemporary Philosophy*, edited by Brian Magee. New York: The Viking Press, 1978, 262–284.

Mehta, Ved. *Fly and the Fly Bottle: Encounters with British Intellectuals*. Boston and Toronto: Little, Brown & Co., 1962, 51–57.

Rose, W. K. "An Interview with Iris Murdoch." *Shenandoah* 19 (Winter 1968): 3–22.

Slaymaker, William. "An Interview with Iris Murdoch." *Papers on Language and Literature* 21 (Fall 1985), 425–32.

III. Other Works Consulted

Ayer, A. J. et al. *The Revolution in Philosophy*. With an introduction by Gilbert Ryle. London: Macmillan & Co., 1957.

Bayley, John. *Characters of Love: A Study in the Literature of Personality*. New York: Basic Books, 1960.

———. "Elegy for Iris." *The New Yorker*, July 27 (1998): 44–61.

———. *Elegy for Iris*. New York: St. Martin's Press, 1999.

Benhabib, Seyla. *Situating the Self: Gender, Community and Postmodernism in Contemporary Ethics*. New York: Routledge, 1992.

Berlin, Isaiah. *Two Concepts of Liberty*. Oxford: Oxford University Press, 1958.

Brink, David O. *Moral Realism and the Foundations of Ethics*. Cambridge: Cambridge University Press, 1989.

Caputo, John D. *Against Ethics*. Bloomington, Ind.: Indiana University Press, 1993.

Clarke, Stanley G., and Evan Simpson, eds. *Anti-Theory in Ethics and Moral Conservatism*. Albany, N.Y.: State University of New York Press, 1989.

Conradi, Peter, ed. *Existentialists and Mystics: Writings on Philosophy and Literature*. New York: Allen Lane/The Penguin Press, 1997.

Cross, R. C., and A. D. Woozley. *Plato's Republic: A Philosophical Commentary*. New York: St. Martin's Press, 1964.

Farley, Wendy. *Eros for the Other: Retaining Truth in a Pluralistic World*. University Park, Penn.: Pennsylvania State University Press, 1996.

Furrow, Dwight. *Against Theory: Contintental and Analytic Challenges in Moral Philosophy*. New York and London: Routledge, 1995.

Giddens, Anthony. *Modernity and Self-Identity: Self and Society in the Late Modern Age*. Stanford: Stanford University Press, 1991.

Hauerwas, Stanley. *Vision and Virtue: Essays in Christian Ethical Reflection*. Notre Dame, Ind.: University of Notre Dame Press, 1981.

Hick, John, and Arthur C. McGill, eds. *The Many-Faced Argument: Recent Studies on the Ontological Argument for the Existence of God*. New York: Macmillan Co., 1967.

Johnson, Paul. *Wittgenstein and Moral Philosophy*. London: Routledge, 1989.

Jonas, Hans. *Philosophical Essays: From Ancient Creed to Technological Man*. Englewood Cliffs, N.J.: Prentice-Hall, 1974.

Lovibond, Sabina. *Realism and Imagination in Ethics*. Minneapolis: University of Minnesota Press, 1983.

MacIntyre, Alasdair. *A Short History of Ethics*. New York: Collier Books, Macmillan Publishing Co., 1966

———. *After Virtue: A Study in Moral Theory*. Notre Dame, Ind.: University of Notre Dame Press, 2nd edition, 1984.

Moore, G. E. *Principia Ethica*. London: Cambridge University Press, 1929.

Nussbaum, Martha C. *The Fragility of Goodness*. Cambridge: Cambridge University Press, 1986.

———. *Love's Knowledge: Essays on Philosophy and Literature*. New York: Oxford University Press, 1990.

Pears, D. F., ed. *The Nature of Metaphysics*. London: Macmillan & Co., 1960.

Peperzak, Adriaan T., ed. *Ethics as First Philosophy: The Significance of Emmanuel Levinas for Philosophy, Literature and Religion*. New York and London: Routledge, 1995.

Platts, Mark de Bretton. *Ways of Meaning: A Introduction to a Philosophy of Language*. London: Routledge & Kegan Paul, 1979.

Putnam, Hilary. *Realism with a Human Face*. Cambridge, Mass.: Harvard University Press, 1990.

Rawls, John. *A Theory of Justice*. Cambridge: Harvard University Press, Belknap Press, 1971.

Sandel, Michael J. *Liberalism and the Limits of Justice*. Cambridge: Cambridge University Press, 1982.

———. "The Procedural Republic and the Unencumbered Self," *Political Theory* 12 (February 1984): 81–96.

Sartre, Jean-Paul. *Being and Nothingness*, trans. Hazel E. Barnes. New York: The Citadel Press, 1956.

———. *Existentialism and Humanism*, trans. Philip Mairet. Brooklyn: Haskel House Publishers, 1977.

———. *Nausea*, trans. Lloyd Alexander. With an introduction by Hayden Carruth. New York: New Directions Publishing Co., 1964.

———. *Notebooks for an Ethics*, trans. David Pellauer. Chicago: University of Chicago Press, 1992.

———. *What is Literature?* trans. Bernard Frechtman. New York: Harper & Row, 1965.

Schweiker, William. "Consciousness and the Good: Schleiermacher and Contemporary Theological Ethics. *Theology Today* vol. 56, no. 2 (July, 1999): 180–196.

———. "The Good and Moral Identity: A Theological Ethical Response to Charles Taylor's *Sources of the Self*." *The Journal of Religion* 72 (October 1992): 560–572.

———. "Matter and Medium in the Moral Life: A Critical Assessment of Charles Taylor's *Sources of the Self*." Unpublished paper presented to the Society of Christian Ethics, January 1994.

———. *Power, Value, and Conviction: Theological Ethics in the Postmodern Age*. Cleveland: Pilgrim Press, 1998.

———. *Responsibility and Christian Ethics*. Cambridge: Cambridge University Press, 1995.

Singer, Peter, ed. *A Companion to Ethics*. Cambridge, Mass.: Basil Blackwell, 1991.

Soper, Kate. *Humanism and Anti-Humanism*. La Salle, Ill.: Open Court, 1986.

Stout, Jeffrey. *The Flight from Authority: Religion, Morality, and the Quest for Autonomy*. Notre Dame, Ind.: University of Notre Dame Press, 1981.

Taylor, Charles. *Hegel*. Cambridge: Cambridge University Press, 1975.

———. *Human Agency and Language: Philosophical Papers*, vol. 1. Cambridge: Cambridge University Press, 1985.

———. *Sources of the Self: The Making of the Modern Identity*. Cambridge: Harvard University Press, 1989.

Taylor, Mark C. *Hiding*. Chicago: University of Chicago Press, 1997.

Tillich, Paul. *Systematic Theology*, vol. 1. Chicago: University of Chicago Press, 1951.

Tully, James, ed. *Philosophy in an Age of Pluralism: The Philosophy of Charles Taylor in Question*. Cambridge: Cambridge University Press, 1994.

Winquist, Charles E. *Desiring Theology*. Chicago: University of Chicago Press, 1995.

Wolf, Susan. *Freedom Within Reason*. New York: Oxford University Press, 1990.

Wyschogrod, Edith. *Saints and Postmodernism: Revisioning Moral Philosophy*. Chicago: University of Chicago Press, 1990.

INDEX

"Above the Gods" (in *Acastos*), 51–55
agnosticism, 104–107. *See also* tolerance
akrasia. See will, weakness of
Anselm
    proof for the existence of God, 123–129 (*see also* ontological proof)
    Proslogion, 55, 125
antihumanism, 3
antitheory in ethics, 11
Aquinas, 124. *See also* Thomism
art
    as analogue to ethics, 103, 107, 137–139
    as experience of unselfing, 137–138, 140, 215n. 95
    vs. fantasy, 137–138
    and perception of individuals, 110–111
    as route to the good, 58, 137–138
"Art and Eros" (in *Acastos*), 156
artist vs. saint, 141–142, 198n. 50, 200n. 66
ascesis (or *askesis*), 139, 141, 215n. 75
asceticism, 141, 142. *See also* unselfing
attention
    and direction of psychic energy, 133–134, 136
    and imagination, 149–151, 155
    and moral vision, 88, 123, 145

    as normative aspect of vision, 140–142
    to others, 48, 98
    as purification of desire, 140, 142, 147, 191
    and shattering of egoism, 134, 191, 194
    and Simone Weil, 140
    and the will, 149–151, 155
Augustine, 124
    on moral motivation, 147–153
    as reflexive thinker, 148–149
autonomy, 9, 28, 103, 113. *See also* freedom
axioms, 155, 156, 159, 170. *See also* duty
Ayer, A. J., 29, 30. *See also* verification principle

Baudrillard, Jean, 185
beauty
    in art, 57, 137
    as experience of unselfing, 135, 137–138
    in nature, 135–136
    as route to the good, 56
Beauvoir, Simone, de, 19, 108
Benhabib, Seyla
    on liberal ethics, 196n. 20, 220n. 233, 221n. 7
    on the turn to language, 3, 9, 172, 175, 178, 221n. 9
Berlin, Isaiah, 6–7, 29

99, 114, 210n. 40 (*see also* perfection)

identity. *See* subjectivity

imagination (*see also* attention)
  vs. fantasy, 137, 152–153
  and moral vision, 94, 136, 140, 165
  in politics, 162, 220n. 233
  as reflexive power, 174, 193, 216n. 120
  and the relation of public and private morality, 156–163
  and the will, 149–151, 155

individual, concept of (*see also* consciousness; self; subjectivity)
  as axiomatic political ideal, 161, 163
  as constituted by language, 177
  as creator of value, 62, 66
  as irreducible, 4, 61, 62, 73, 74, 91, 98, 112, 161–162, 169–170
  as limit to the drive of totalization, 190
  as locus of moral value, 98, 100, 106, 114, 129
  as paradigmatic of the real, 5, 98, 107, 129, 189
  as portrayed in the novel, 107–111
  poststructuralist critique of, 10, 172–175
  as rational agent, 104
  in relation to a metaphysical framework, 13–14, 45–48
  in relation to an ontology of value, 63, 85, 112, 170
  as subject and object of morality, 99–100, 163
  vs. totalizing systems of thought, 45, 161–162, 166, 189
  as unified, 162
  as unique particular, 12, 104–107, 121

information
  as replacing a notion of consciousness, 187, 193
  technology, 180, 184–185, 186–187
  as trope for reality, 186–187

inner life (*see also* consciousness)
  and Cartesian subjectivity, 176
  Murdoch's defense of, 87–95, 130, 167, 173
  vs. outward acts, 47, 75–84, 154, 155–163

intuitionism
  as "aestheticized" morality, 158–159
  in G. E. Moore's thought, 117, 122–123, 159
  in Murdoch's thought, 118, 122–123
  as threat to Murdoch's moral realism, 153–155, 158

Johnston, Paul, 31

justice
  as aspect of realistic vision, 140, 142
  proceduralist account of, 9, 11–12 (*see also* proceduralist ethics)

Kant, Immanuel
  on critique of metaphysics, 28, 33–35, 202n. 55
  and current debate in ethics, 6, 8, 167, 170
  on the experience of nature, 136
  vs. Hegel, 23, 103–107, 167, 171
  influence on modern British empiricism, 27
  vs. Kierkegaard, 105–106, 166
  and liberal theory, 103–107, 211n. 82
  vs. Mill, 23, 106
  and Plato, 166, 192, 216n. 120
  and post-Kantian ethics, 7, 85
  on proofs for God's existence, 33, 125
  as reflexive thinker, 216n. 123
  on regulative ideals, 28, 34
  on theoretical-practical distinction, 34–35, 202n. 55
  theory of the sublime, 104, 107

Kierkegaard, Soren
  vs. Kant, 105–106, 166
  and Kierkegaardian existentialists, 23, 105–106

language (see also moral language)
  expressivist theory of, 177–178,
    183
  inflation of, 178–180, 183, 185
  as medium of moral reflection, 20,
    171, 173–175, 178, 182, 183–
    184
  paradigm of, 3, 172, 184
  poststructuralist theory of, 10, 172–
    175
  primacy of 3, 90, 172–175
  as system, 3, 11, 185 (see also
    system)
  as technique of unselfing, 58, 136
  turn to, 4, 118, 165, 172, 176–
    180, 207n. 128
Levinas, Emmanuel, 222n. 52, 223n.
  56
Liberal view
  and linguistic behaviorism, 77
  vs. Natural Law view, 23, 24, 46–
    47, 61, 104, 111–112, 168,
    171
  vs. Romanticism, 103–107
  as "type" of morality, 14, 197n.
    34
liberalism
  contemporary critique of, 5, 9, 11,
    61, 166, 167–168, 218n.
    192
  and current debates over self, 8–
    12, 167–175
  legacy of, 4, 105–107
  and moral change, 192
  Murdoch's theory of, 100–107,
    219n. 222
  and Murdoch's theory of
    literature, 107–111
  and public morality, 14, 161–162
linguistic analysis (see also linguistic
    behaviorism)
  and constriction of morality, 42
  and critique of metaphysics, 13,
    33–35, 168
  and critique of naturalism, 32–41
  influence on Murdoch, 17–18,
    198n. 46
  on logical neutrality of ethics, 32,
    41
linguistic behaviorism (see also
    linguistic analysis)

defined, 62, 205n. 2
and denial of inner life and
  private mental event, 75–84,
  88, 167, 172
and "existentialist-behaviorist"
  view, 75, 207n. 72
moral consequences of, 80–84
as surrender to convention, 102
literature (see also the novel;
    Nussbaum, Martha)
  and current debates in ethics, 5,
    18–20, 166, 198n. 51
  as moral education, 20, 171
  and Murdoch's theory of
    liberalism, 107–111
  Sartre's theory of, 70–72
Locke, John, 106
logical positivism, 29 (see also Ayer,
    A. J.; verification principle)
love (see also eros)
  Christian notion of, 152–153
  as ideal end-point of moral vision,
    97, 99, 114, 129, 182, 189
  as knowledge of the individual,
    110–111, 129, 189
  as moral concept, 92–93
  as purified eros (compassion), 145,
    182
  in relation to neurosis and
    convention, 103
  as technique of unselfing, 139–
    140
  as tolerance for others, 107–111,
    129
Lovibond, Sabina, 49–50, 222n. 50
Lukacs, George, 73

M and D example, 22, 24, 87–95,
    98, 121, 123, 129, 140, 170,
    223n. 53
MacIntyre, Alasdair, 9, 12, 201n. 29,
    202n. 55
Magee, Bryan, 19, 199n. 56
Marxism, 14, 40, 46, 111
maxims, 158 (see also duty)
McGill, Arthur, 124
metaethics, 48–60, 116–123
metaphysical framework, 12, 13, 14,
    24–25, 40, 45, 61
  as locus of morality, 46–47, 168,
    170, 171

in relation to the idea of the individual, 68, 74, 111–112, 181

metaphysical realism, 11–14, 45, 58 (*see also* moral realism)

metaphysics
  as conceptual exploration, 22, 33–34
  and the debate over naturalism, 33–35
  elimination from ethics, 12, 13, 25–31, 118
  figurative dimension of, 13, 20, 22
  and metaphysical beliefs, 29, 34, 208n. 99
  and metaphysical ethics, 11, 12, 25, 30, 116, 165, 171
  and Murdoch's philosophical method, 11, 42–43, 44, 200n. 4 (*see also* picturing the human)

Metaphysics as a Guide to Morals, 6, 10, 17, 21, 26, 51, 86, 166, 172
  and defense of inner life, 84, 89, 90
  on obligation 155–163, 170
  on ontological proof, 55, 56
  on problem of totality, 166 (*see also* system; totalization)
  structure of, 157, 219n. 195

Mill, J. S., 23, 106–107, 110, 212n. 103 (*see also* tolerance)

modernity, 6, 185–186 (*see also* Giddens, Anthony; reflexive modernization),

Moore, G. E.
  and the elimination of metaphysics from ethics, 49, 117
  on the epistemology of moral properties, 120–123, 128, 154
  on the good, 43, 116–123, 128
  on indefinability of the good, 117, 120
  Principia Ethica, 119–120

moral change, 91, 93, 115, 116, 129–134, 136, 142, 144, 147, 152, 165, 192–194 (*see also* moral progress; transformation of agency)

moral freedom. *See* freedom

moral language (*see also* language)
  as conceptual exploration, 32, 33, 93, 122
  as function of individual perception, 87–95, 173–175
  as mediating the relation of fact and value, 121, 172, 182
  and the metaethics of the good, 116–223
  and moral choice, 37, 87
  and moral differences, 37–38, 43, 121
  and moral vision, 37–38, 42–44, 87–95, 121, 182, 183
  and Murdoch's philosophical method, 42–43, 170 (*see also* metaphysics)
  and ordinary language philosophy, 90, 92
  private vs. public meaning, 75–84, 86, 172–173
  and the refocusing of psychic energy, 140, 182
  in relation to moral facts, 37–38, 87, 121
  and secondary moral words, 38, 44, 90, 140

moral motivation (*see also* the will)
  Christian vs. Socratic models of, 146–153
  circular vs. linear theories of, 147–153
  and internalism vs. externalism, 146–147
  reciprocal theory of, 149–153

moral ontology, 25, 61, 85, 95, 170, 171, 181, 205n. 1

moral perception, 13, 92, 94. *See also* moral vision

moral pilgrimage, 35, 51, 128, 132

moral progress, 41 (*see also* moral change; transformation of agency)
  as function of moral language, 91, 93, 99
  and purification of desire, 139, 182
  as quality of moral perception, 86, 91, 99, 169

and portrayal of character, 107–
108
twentieth-century, 107–111
Nussbaum, Martha, 13, 19–20,
198n. 56, 198n. 58, 87, 180

obligation, 153–155, 163 (*see also*
duty)
ontological proof (*see also* Anselm;
the good)
history of interpretation, 124–125,
214nn. 22–23
logical aspect of the argument,
124–129, 145
metaphysical or perfectionist
aspect of the argument, 56–
58, 123–129, 145
and reflexive realism, 15, 169
reflexive structure of, 86, 124,
135, 165, 173
and the transcendental good, 51–
52, 55–56, 123–129
Ordinary Language Man,
vs. Totalitarian Man, 23, 102–103
and Wittgenstein, 181
other, the
and the idea of tolerance, 103–
107
as object of moral consciousness,
95–100
as paradigmatic of the real, 85,
95, 97, 103, 107, 170, 171,
174, 189, 191
and problem of subjective
dominance, 176, 177, 180

particularity, 5, 11, 170
and the idea of the individual, 99,
105–107
and moral perception, 90, 94, 99
perception. *See* moral perception
perfection, 48, 55, 68, 92, 94, 142
(*see also* the good)
as ideal end-point of moral
knowledge, 34, 93, 113, 174,
189
as imperative of Murdoch's ethics,
194
as norm of realistic vision, 115,
119, 128
in Sartre, 96–97, 100

personality, 4, 101. *See also*
consciousness, the individual
"Philosophy and Beliefs," 29
picturing the human
and M and D example, 22, 88
and the method of the book, 17,
192 (*see also* conceptual
hermeneutic)
as task of Murdoch's metaphysics,
13, 24, 32, 42, 44, 170–171,
194
pilgrimage. *See* moral pilgrimage
Plato
and cave allegory, 22, 127, 131,
149
as character in *Acastos*, 53–55
as cognitivist, 131–135, 136
on the idea of the Good, 33, 50,
52, 53, 126, 166
and metaphor of the sun, 22, 126
as metaphysical ethicist, 13, 26,
31, 54, 118
on moral motivation, 147–153
Republic, 52, 53, 54, 127, 218n.
189
Platonic ethics, 5, 166
political morality (*see also* liberalism)
and Murdoch's theory of
obligation, 155–163
and public-private distinction,
155
rights claims in, 160–161
role of axioms in, 159–161
postmodernism, 3, 4 (*see also*
modernity; poststructuralism)
poststructuralism
and current debate over
subjectivity, 10–11, 167–172,
175, 185
and erasure of the subject, 178,
183
primacy of language in, 90, 172–
175, 177–178, 183
and problem of moral change, 193
and problem of totality, 186–187
proceduralist ethics, 12, 162, 170,
218n. 192. *See also* justice;
liberalism
psyche. *See* consciousness; Freud;
moral psychology
psychic energy. *See* eros; fantasy

psychoanalysis, 134
Putnam, Hilary, 13, 201n. 39

Quinton, Anthony, 29–31

Rawls, John, 9
realism (*see also* reflexive realism)
  and aesthetic perception, 92, 94,
    137–139
  moral realism, 5, 25, 48, 107,
    168, 175, 198n. 50, 200n. 1
  in Murdoch's novels, 138–139
  "naive," 183
  and objectivity, 93, 138–139
  varieties of, 119, 122
reality, 11, 25, 99, 104, 188
reflexive modernization. *See* Giddens,
  Anthony
reflexive realism, 15, 124, 128, 130,
  135, 139, 197n. 35, 216n.
  120
  and importance of language, 117,
    173–175
  and Murdoch's contribution to
    current ethics, 165, 167–175,
    177, 187–194
  and the norm of Murdoch's ethics,
    130, 133, 135, 139
  and the ontological proof, 124–
    128, 214n. 27
  in relation to metaethics of G. E.
    Moore, 116–123
  (*see also* moral realism; realism)
reflexivity, 51, 96, 149–153, 172,
  174, 189
religion, 5, 51, 53–54, 77, 131–133,
  141. *See also* God
religious ethics, 8, 9, 167, 170, 177.
  See also Christian ethics
Romanticism
  and expressivist theory of
    language, 177, 183
  and Hegel, 101, 103–107, 108,
    181
  legacy of, 4, 105–106, 136
  vs. liberalism, 103–107
  and the novel, 103–107, 109
rules, 160–161. *See also* duty
Russell, Bertrand, 92
Ryle, Gilbert, 76, 77, 80, 86

saint. *See* artist; Conradi, Peter
Sandel, Michael, 9
Sartre, Jean-Paul 9, 10, 13 (*see also*
  existentialism; voluntarism)
  on bad faith (*mauvaise foi*), 65, 66,
    67, 72, 96, 100, 112–114,
    145
  Being and Nothingness, 63, 69, 70,
    71, 72
  on consciousness, 63–75, 95–100,
    170
  on contingency, 64, 65
  on the defense of the individual,
    62, 64, 111–114, 170
  Existentialism is a Humanism, 70–
    72
  on freedom, 65–75, 95–100, 111–
    114
  influence on Murdoch, 17–18, 73–
    75, 101, 112
  on insincerity, 66, 73
  and Kant, 71
  and Kierkegaard, 106
  Marxist critique of, 73–75
  Nausea, 64–65
  Notebooks for an Ethics, 207n. 60
  as novelist, 108
  politics of, 69, 72, 161–162
  and problem of determinism, 74,
    113, 213n. 145
  on the pursuit of perfection, 96–
    97, 100
  as "romantic rationalist," 101
  on self-deception, 65–66
  on self-transcendence, 66, 73
  What is Literature?, 70–71, 207n.
    42, 215n. 95
Sartre, Romantic Rationalist, 16, 21,
  61, 206n. 3
Schweiker, William (*see also* reflexive
  realism)
  on moral freedom, 143–145
  on radical interpretation, 144
  on reflexive modernization, 178–
    179
  as reflexive thinker, 197n. 35,
    216n. 123
  on the turn to language, 176–177
  on validating an ethical position,
    220n. 4

self, 3, 4, 9, 10, 14, 61 (*see also* consciousness; individual, subjectivity)
   as "discursive effect" of language, 10, 84, 173
   in relation to the good, 4, 7, 8, 10, 25, 58, 59
   as "unencumbered" or "radically situated," 7, 8, 45, 61, 169–172, 176–177, 179
selfishness. *See* egoism
sequestration of experience. *See* Giddens, Anthony
sittlichkeit, 185, 186
solipsism, 50, 72, 74, 95, 106
   in neurosis and convention, 101–102, 171, 176, 180
The Sovereignty of Good, 5, 20, 21, 51, 86, 104, 106, 117, 155, 166
   on egoism, 130–135
   on the "existentialist-behaviorist" view, 75–76, 81, 86, 89
   on the limits of moral vision, 153–155, 158
   on moral motivation, 149–150
   and Natural Law view of morality, 105, 111
   on the ontological proof, 55, 127
   (*see also* M and D example)
Stout, Jeffrey, 6
subjective dominance, 166, 175–184, 185
subjectivism, 16, 48, 50, 115, 128, 130, 153–155, 168, 183
subjectivity (*see also* self)
   critique of, 3, 4, 165, 175–180, 194
   current debates over, 8–10, 165, 167–175
   and "erasing" strategy, 178, 179, 180, 183, 193, 194
   and "reconstituting" strategy of, 180–184
   and "situating" strategy, 45, 61, 100, 176–177, 179, 180, 181, 185, 193, 194
"The Sublime and the Beautiful Revisited," 103–107
Symbolist movement, 5, 108, 109

system(s), 5, 187
   abstract, 165, 166, 178–179, 188, 190, 223n. 66
   critique of, 17, 21, 161–162, 166, 200n. 63
   impersonality of, 3, 167, 183, 187
   linguistic, 3, 11, 173, 175, 178, 179, 183, 185
   and loss of individuals, 45, 161, 162, 166, 173, 187
   totalizing nature of, 45, 166 (*see also* totality; totalization; whole)

Taylor, Charles, 195n. 3, 205n. 1, 220n. 4
   and contemporary ethics, 4, 7, 9
   on "inescapable frameworks," 15, 45
   on moral motivation, 147–153
   on "moral ontology," 61
   on ontological proof, 124–125
   as reflexive thinker, 119, 124–125, 214n. 27
   on theories of language, 175, 177, 183
Taylor, Mark C., 186–187, 193, 224n. 75
"Thinking and Language," 76
Thomism, 14, 40, 46, 111 (*see also* Natural Law view)
Tillich, Paul, 9, 126
tolerance, 108–111 (*see also* love; Mill J. S.)
Totalitarian Man
   in Hegel and Romanticism, 181
   vs. Ordinary Language Man, 23, 102–103
totalitarianism, 5, 161
totality, 104, 106 (*see also* totalization; whole)
   and irreducibility of the individual, 73, 74, 100, 161, 166
totalization
   as cultural dynamic, 184–194
   as effect of systems, 45, 178 (*see also* system)
   of ego in neurosis, 180, 182